SINCE THEN

SINCE THEN

How I Survived *Everything* and Lived to Tell About It

DAVID CROSBY

and CARL GOTTLIEB

G. P. Putnam's Sons

New York

G. P. PUTNAM'S SONS
Publishers Since 1838
Published by the Penguin Group
Penguin Group (USA) Inc., 375 Hudson Street, New York, New York 10014, USA • Penguin
Group (Canada), 90 Eglinton Avenue East, Suite 700, Toronto, Ontario M4P 2Y3, Canada
(a division of Pearson Penguin Canada Inc.) • Penguin Books Ltd, 80 Strand, London WC2R 0RL,
England • Penguin Ireland, 25 St Stephen's Green, Dublin 2, Ireland (a division of Penguin
Books Ltd) • Penguin Group (Australia), 250 Camberwell Road, Camberwell, Victoria 3124,
Australia (a division of Pearson Australia Group Pty Ltd) • Penguin Books India Pvt Ltd,
11 Community Centre, Panchsheel Park, New Delhi–110 017, India • Penguin Group (NZ),
Cnr Airborne and Rosedale Roads, Albany, Auckland 1310, New Zealand (a division
of Pearson New Zealand Ltd) • Penguin Books (South Africa) (Pty) Ltd,
24 Sturdee Avenue, Rosebank, Johannesburg 2196, South Africa

Penguin Books Ltd, Registered Offices:
80 Strand, London WC2R 0RL, England

ISBN 0-399-15381-0

Printed in the United States of America
1   3   5   7   9   10   8   6   4   2

Book design by Meighan Cavanaugh

While the authors have made every effort to provide accurate telephone numbers and
Internet addresses at the time of publication, neither the publisher nor the authors assume
any responsibility for errors, or for changes that occur after publication. Further, the publisher does not have any control over and does not assume any responsibility for author or
third-party websites and their content.

My dad at the wheel of a schooner, 1928. *(David Crosby personal collection)*

Floyd Crosby and Betty Cormack Crosby, my father and stepmother, a blissful couple. *(David Crosby personal collection)*

Floyd and Aliph, my father and mother, filming in Brazil. *(David Crosby personal collection)*

My brother, Ethan, who taught me to play guitar. *(David Crosby personal collection)*

Early Byrds (and special guest): from left to right, me on guitar; Gene Clark, our songwriter, on vocals; Bob Dylan playing the harp; Michael Clarke on drums; and Roger (then Jim) McGuinn with a twelve-string guitar. *(Courtesy Michael Ochs Archives)*

Croz in a Russian hat. This and the Borsalino were distinguishing headgear for the sixties Byrd. Note the new mustache. *(Courtesy Everett Collection)*

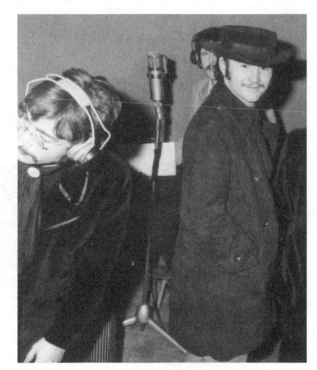

vo Beatles, one Byrd: ın Lennon, Paul McCartney ırtly hidden), and David osby, in London, circa 1968. *David Crosby personal collection)*

Me, Neil, Stephen, and Graham, the *Déjà vu* look—also appropriate gear for "Cowboy Movie." *(Photo cour Tom Gundelfinger O'Neal)*

The sixties in the Canyon: Joni Mitchell, me, and Eric Clapton, who's fiercely contemplating the music. *(Photo courtesy Henry Diltz)*

More mustache, trademark Borsalino hat: Buffalo Springfield.
(Photo courtesy Henry Diltz)

I'm not sure when or where this was taken; I do know that it looks as if I'm a ventriloquist, working Sly Stone's head. *(David Crosby personal collection)*

Dudes in shades: Jerry Garcia trying to hitch a ride on my bird.
(David Crosby personal collection)

Looking aft from the bowsprit of the *Mayan*—a constant in good times and bad. *(Photo by Dana Africa)*

INTRODUCTION

A short time after publishing *Long Time Gone: The Autobiography of David Crosby* in 1988, we started making jokes about having written it too soon. The first book covered my early years, the folk music scene, forming the Byrds, being thrown out of that band, forming Crosby, Stills, and Nash, and linking up with Neil Young; the lives and deaths of loved ones; adventures in sailing; a midnight gunfight, escalating excessive lifestyle choices, drug abuse, arrest, detention, detox; Texas prison, release, recovery, and redemption.

This new book tells the story of what's happened since then (hence the title). But it isn't a catch-up collection of details laid out in chronological order—it's a subjective narrative, cutting across time and place as ideas unfold. With its impressionistic approach and thematic (rather than strictly chronological) organization, *Since Then* employs some of the structures and conventions of a screenplay, complete with camera directions for the reader.

If you've flipped through the pages before coming to this beginning, you've noticed a variety of typographical styles. Since memory is an imperfect journal of experience, we've added to my recollections the memories of others, together with recordings and transcriptions of a public life. That's why this book speaks with multiple voices, printed in three type styles. First, there's me (no surprises there). This body of text is how I describe my life the way I think I lived it, correcting the record, or creating a record where none existed before. That makes for the first-person narrative common to autobiographies, which should be reassuring to the reader. There are also passages representing voices other than mine. By way of example, I offer this flattering note from a writer who's a friend and a fan, Spider Robinson. He's talking about a song I wrote a long time ago, when I was in the Byrds.

SPIDER ROBINSON:

I don't think a month of my life has gone by since the summer of 1967 that I have not taken out my guitar and taken a crack at "Everybody's Been Burned" at least once. What could be better than a haunting, heartbreaking story—with a happy ending? I know of no character more fascinating and admirable than the man who has been badly hurt and still refuses to quit hoping, still gambles on loving.

Thank you, Spider. Finally, slightly indented and in italic text, you'll see the more or less objective words of my coauthor, writing in a presumably omniscient voice, because we agree that a third-person narrative would be appropriate for presenting credentials, explaining sources, setting the stage, supplying background information, and introducing characters who add alternative views of what happened. As he does here:

> *There are a number of other voices and comments from third parties, some of them not friends of David, many recorded in transcriptions of interviews and conversations, both in person and on the phone. The authors have included alternative versions of some events to correct any imbalance that might've crept into Crosby's otherwise perfect account of a compli-*

cated life, imperfectly documented in its time. Only in the last decade have the Crosbys kept a master date book and a coordinated calendar. Nonetheless, true to his show-business roots, David's never missed a gig unless he was hospitalized, under arrest, in jail, or recovering from one of the above. When arrested in New York City in 2004, he was released (after spending a night in jail) in the afternoon and played that night's gig in Glenside, Pennsylvania.

Back in the mid-eighties, when Carl and I published the story of my life up to that point, our primary resources were pen and paper, the prevailing (and primitive) computer word-processing technology of the day, analog tape recorders, patience, and the kindness of friends and strangers.* In the modern world, our horizons have been stretched toward the infinite. The Internet and the World Wide Web connect us all: friends and enemies, fans and fanatics. Nothing can duplicate the collective ongoing energy of the fans and their devotion to facts, details, conjecture, and rumor, not to mention the actual recordings of performances, whether or not they were ever intended to be preserved. Never have we few owed so much to so many. As Graham Nash has said (and his quote is reproduced on the opening page of a website somewhere in cyberspace): "They know more about us than we do."

Because my father was a cinematographer and I grew up in Hollywood, I do sometimes think of my life as a film script. A long time ago, I even wrote a song—"Cowboy Movie"—drawing on my rather chaotic life of the moment, and populating the story with my friends and partners, giving them what I thought were clever disguises. They all saw right through it. In my father's time, films were usually organized in a

---

*This is the first and last footnote. Additional details will be supplied in the endnotes, organized by chapter, thus: "Introduction: 'When Carl and I published the story of my life . . .' refers to *Long Time Gone: The Autobiography of David Crosby,* David Crosby and Carl Gottlieb (New York: Doubleday, 1988).

straightforward chronology. They began, the plot moved the story forward (perhaps with a few flashbacks to explain what happened earlier), and they ended, usually happily. The good guy gets the girl, the villain is punished, virtue triumphs, order is restored. If only!

Modern movies play tricks with narrative time, and this book does the same. The introduction is followed by a prologue, and subsequent chapters occur in thematic, not chronological, sequence.

> *If David Crosby's a star of any magnitude in the music of our popular culture, his story lends itself to a cinematic narrative. After all, the audiovisual arts of music, film, and television are how we memorialize our heroes. I'm a screenwriter (*Jaws *and* The Jerk*), and as much David's tied to music, I'm bound to movies. That may lead us to a skewed perspective, but it certainly makes it easier to sing and tell Crosby's story.*

Which brings us to what I do for a living, and what I must do, to live. As they say in screenplays, when one sequence merges into another . . .

DISSOLVE TO:

Prologue

A FAMILY REUNION

alk about matters of life and death—I'd been rescued very recently from end-stage hepatic failure, thanks to the miracle of a successful liver transplant, and now was recovering with my wife, Jan, at our home in Santa Ynez, California. Jan, too, was in the midst of a miraculous physical transformation: after suffering through infertility treatments for years, she was at long last pregnant. In four more months, our son Django would be born.

But Django, as it turns out, wouldn't be the first male child to carry my particular genetic wiring. I'd recently learned that I had another son, a young man named James Raymond, who had been given up for adoption by his birth mother in 1961. We had never met, hadn't even spoken. A few weeks earlier, while I was at the UCLA Medical Center, he'd reached out to me; now, from the safety of home, I finally called him on the telephone.

To say the call was "awkward" is simplifying one of the most complex and emotional phone conversations I've ever had. The voice on the other end was normal—a little restrained, but as sincere as everything else about the entire process of reconnecting us. I was scheduled to go back to the hospital for a follow-up appointment, postop and postdischarge, so we agreed to meet in the cafeteria at UCLA Medical Center. I sat waiting for him, and if ever there was an emotionally loaded moment, that was it. He walked through the door, and I knew it was him. I remember thinking, "Jesus, he's good-looking." He was a really handsome man, and not fake handsome. James had unconscious grace and unforced good looks, he was great-looking and didn't appear to care, wasn't preening, just wore himself comfortably. I leaped to my feet, and went over to shake his hand. I was also on the edge of tears. I suggested we go outside, and we sat at a little table. I can show you which one it is—I go back and visit it sometimes.

> *There's something about hospital cafeterias that goes way beyond simple nourishment. They are not "destination dining"; staff eat there because they must, and because they get a discount, while hospital visitors are there because they will eventually want more than snacks and soft drinks from vending machines in a corridor. Cafeterias are a place to go while patients can't have visitors, or in anticipation of a conference with medical staff about diagnosis, condition, or prognosis. With the exception of visitors to the maternity ward who are celebrating life, most folks are waiting for bad news, or have just received some. UCLA runs a large public cafeteria, no worse and actually slightly better than similar institutions. In addition to the fluorescent-lit Formica tables and plastic chairs, there's an outside patio area, with some struggling trees and shrubbery fighting for the light. It includes benches, and it's quiet.*

We sat on the benches outside, and got to know each other. I must say, it felt right from the beginning, although I imagine we were both eyeing each other pretty carefully, trying to assess the situation. Normally, when kids are adopted out and they meet their parents later on in life, it doesn't work. More often than not, the person you've been imagining to be wonderful turns out to be some drunk in a trailer, or a kid that you wouldn't really want to know. The child given up for adoption, very often and sometimes quite rightly, brings along a lot of resentment. "Why did you leave me and Mom? How could you do that?" There's the potential for sadness and anger and resentment to an astounding degree, and disappointment often ensues when people meet. The chemistry's not there; it's just that you've never met each other. Preconceptions and expectations are what really usually sink that ship.

James, completely contrary to all that, came with absolutely no baggage at all. He was willing to give me a clean slate. I was trying to find a way to say "I'm sorry that I wasn't there for you," but James read me like a book, and started first. "There are some things you need to know," he said. "I've never been hurt, never been hungry, nobody ever beat me up." I will be grateful to him until the day I die because he was so kind. He knew my heart, knew what I was thinking and what my fears were. He knew that I wanted him to love me, and that I loved him and that I felt terrible for not being there and raising him, and he eased me through it. He took me by the hand emotionally and led me through it and came out the other side and became a big part of my life. He's a helluva lot smarter than I am, and more grown-up too, and very centered, comfortable in his own skin, very confident, and very human. I can't think of a single thing about him that I don't think is wonderful. He's talented beyond belief, and he's four times the musician I am.

Toward the end of our meeting, Jan, five months pregnant with our own son, joined us. There we were, sitting on the cafeteria benches at the UCLA hospital, all three of us teary and emotional, "we are family," and all that. Then James dropped a quiet bombshell: he told us in matter-of-fact terms that we were about to be grandparents. On that particular day, his wife, Stacia, was in labor at Cedars-Sinai Hospital, just down the road in West Hollywood. It was a double hospital day for James. First, he came to Westwood to meet his birth father. Whatever came of that, win or lose, the inescapable fact was that he was about to become a father himself. Stacia was having a baby, practically as we spoke. He waited to drop that bit of information on me as we were finishing our conversation; incredible timing. Grace Raymond was born that night. Clearly, I suddenly had reasons to live, a reason for being, and a pressing need to provide for everyone, somehow.

I first met James early in 1995. The previous year was marked by financial disaster. It was a year in which my life almost ended before Christmas, only to be redirected in directions unpredictable at the time, and still astonishing in retrospect.

CUT TO:

One

SHAKEN, NOT STIRRED

I woke out of a sound sleep feeling like a rat shaken by a terrier. I don't know if there is a description for the huge, low-frequency grinding noise that filled our house, but it came at us with the intensity of locomotives colliding in a tunnel. This growling, rumbling, terrifying sound woke my wife, Jan, and me. We realized our whole house was moving, a foot one way and then a foot the other. Our old frame house was riding the shock waves of a major earthquake, swaying like a ship at sea. The only rigid structure was the chimney, which couldn't sway—it just came down, blowing the contents of the fireplace out into our bedroom.

The Northridge Quake took place at 4:30 a.m. on January 17, 1994. It registered 6.7 on the Richter scale, and shook the Los Angeles Basin from the San Gabriel to the Santa Monica mountains, toppling structures, dropping elevated concrete freeways into the dirt, severing gas and water mains, and opening cracks that lifted pavement and jarred houses off their foundations. The Southern California Earthquake Data Center puts it this way:

The Northridge Earthquake . . . occurred on a blind thrust fault [one that doesn't break the surface], and produced the strongest ground motions ever instrumentally recorded in an urban setting in North America. Damage was widespread, sections of major freeways collapsed, parking structures and office buildings collapsed, and numerous apartment buildings suffered irreparable damage. Damage to wood-frame apartment houses was very widespread in the San Fernando Valley and Santa Monica area, especially to structures with "soft" first-floor or lower-level parking garages. The high accelerations, both vertical and horizontal, lifted structures off of their foundations and/or shifted walls laterally.

We were absolutely terrified. I grew up in California; I knew what this was. It seemed certain the roof would come down at any moment. The windows had already broken, our lamps were on the floor, and it was so dark we couldn't see, though we could feel something falling on our skin. We couldn't know it at the time, but it was soot and ashes, plaster, and concrete dust. Jan's first rational thought was to find our animals, while I was groping for a flashlight and my most precious guitar. We couldn't stand up. No one could have. I crawled off the bed to where I knew there was a big square nine-volt battery lantern, grabbed it, and turned it on. My first thought was *It mustn't be working* because I couldn't see a damn thing through the floating dust and the ash. But that's just how black the air was. I crawled back, got Jan, took my guitar off the wall, and the three of us—Jan, the guitar, and me—somehow got ourselves downstairs.

There was nothing in that house that wasn't on the floor. The furniture, every painting, every piece of decoration, every window, every glass, every dish, *everything* was down, scattered, broken, or wrecked. There was glass underfoot everywhere. The monster's growl finally stopped, the floor quit heaving, and the house swayed to a halt, unsteady on its shaken foundations. There was an aching silence that lasted only a moment— and then every alarm in the valley went off, all at the same time. Burglar alarms, fire alarms, car alarms, bells ringing, automobiles whooping and shrieking. The bells and whistles of disaster. We made our way out of the house, and when Jan and I saw each other we added hysterical laughter to the cacophony around us. We were covered in dust and plaster, circus clowns in whiteface, bewildered by the unpredictable and catastrophic collapse of the Big Top.

My old-style 1920s wood-frame apartment house in West Hollywood has a low-level parking garage, but when it was built in 1928, concrete was cheap, and the building is solidly anchored. Nevertheless, furniture moved, ceiling beams shifted and dropped, shelves emptied onto the floor, windows cracked, and the structure swayed disturbingly. In West Hollywood— twenty miles farther from the epicenter than the Crosby's house in Encino—we were lucky. No gas lines broke, and electricity was restored within hours. Through my bedroom window it looked as if a giant audience stretching to the horizon was snapping its flash cameras; the night landscape was filled with thousands of popping points of light as transformers on power poles across the city failed and blew up in a shower of electric arcs and sparks. The San Fernando Valley probably looked the same to anyone watching from the hills, except for the addition of towers of flame where gas mains ruptured.

JAN CROSBY:

We woke up because the house was shaking so badly I thought a Boeing 747 was coming through the window. That's the sound I heard. And at the same time that I heard that sound, I reached over and grabbed David's arm and I said, "What is it?" And he said, "Stay calm, it's an earthquake." He was profoundly cool. He was really amazingly cool. This went far beyond anything I experienced in LA. I'd probably been through twenty or twenty-five little tremors, I'd guess you'd call them, like riding a surfboard for a few seconds on dry land. No big deal. Well, at that point I finally realized what the words "earth" and "quake" meant, and this wasn't anything I knew anything about. It was a different kind of shaking. We were four miles from the epicenter, I came to find out later, but my memory of it at that moment was that I was asleep one second and the next minute I was reaching for David. I was terrified. With capital letters. I've had guns held to my head, I have had my ribs broken by people, I have had true fear coursing through my body, and it didn't touch the kind of fear we felt that morning, while we were riding the second story of an old house.

It sounded like a demolition ball had hit the house. The chimney was collapsing and everything in the house was crashing: the china cabinets were throwing dishes, the pantry was throwing bottles and cans, everything that was in the house was falling and crashing. And the bed, which we still sleep in, is so heavy it takes four men to help move it. It was like "being in the mouth of a dog with a little shaky toy," as David put it.

The Crosbys lived south of the Boulevard—real-estate code for the expensive part of Encino below Ventura Boulevard, with big lots, large new houses, and purely residential zoning. Ventura is the main east-west commercial street, a wide thoroughfare lined with shops and supermarkets and mid-rise office buildings. North of it, a standard street grid overlies the land all the way to the San Gabriel Mountains, which surround the suburban geological formation known as the LA Basin, a natural sink that collects hydrocarbons, vapor, dust, and automobile exhaust. Population pressure after World War II transformed the San Fernando Valley into a huge suburban sprawl of bedroom communities. Encino, once a ranch and farming community with wooden sidewalks and hitching posts, became a mini-city within a city, complete with a civic center, bail bondsmen, furniture outlets, and a large, ethnically diverse community in the small houses that run for miles in the flat former fields and orchards. The upper-middle and wealthy classes settled (as usual) on the high ground, trying to get above the smog and have a view, while rainwater, mud, and their disposable income flowed downhill. The Crosby's house was on flatter, lower ground, not far from Ventura Boulevard, and close to where Graham Nash and his family lived for more than twenty years. The Nashes have incorporated a crack in the wall into a decorative element that remains in their house to this day.

GRAHAM NASH:

My wife, Susan, had it redecorated to look as if we'd uncovered a mosaic from ancient Rome or Etruscan Italy, as a memorial to that day.

When we finally got outside, we were worried about our neighbors and friends, the Nashes in particular. When it was daylight again, we drove around to see if they were okay, and they were. We went over to see if Kirstie Alley was okay, she was fine, and so was Dr. Gary Gitnick, who took care of me then as well as he does now, which is saying quite a lot, because he's saved my life more than once.

KIRSTIE ALLEY:

We were in the yard, the power lines were flashing and arcing, it was all dusty and hideously surreal, and out of the darkness, like a benevolent Loch Ness monster, comes David, calling out, "Is everybody all right in there?" Like he was making his rounds of the neighborhood, to make sure everyone was safe. I couldn't see him but I could hear his voice. Unmistakable. Most people were surveying their own property, taking care of their own families, and I thought it was really cool that David had hit the streets [to see if] everyone in his neighborhood was okay. Later, we went to their place, which was a mess, with the chimney on the ground. . . . That day I was so freaked out because I had a new baby. We left town and went to a ranch we owned in Oregon. Ironically, the next day in Oregon, there was an earthquake out of the clear blue sky.

The Pacific Rim is called the Ring of Fire, because of the instability of the tectonic plates intersecting, so the Northridge Quake sent shivers north to Alaska and south to Mexico. The fun in Encino wasn't over right away. What isn't widely known outside of earthquake country is that quakes don't stop with the first one. There are aftershocks as the earth tries to restore equilibrium and the ruptured fault lines grind to a slow halt after the major slippage that caused the quake in the first place.

Each time an aftershock starts, your body thinks it's the Big One *again,* and dumps about a quart of adrenaline into your system and you lie there gyrating for another two or three hours until you recover. Then there's another aftershock. And another. The fortieth time that happens, you're just a puddle of Jell-O, not at all together. The aftershocks were hard for us to handle. We couldn't go back to bed; we couldn't bring ourselves to go back upstairs. We laid a mattress down on the floor in the kitchen someplace, and slept there because we were too scared to sleep upstairs and go through that rocking, swaying motion on the second floor and then try to get downstairs in the middle of it. We were so nervous we slept on the floor downstairs for weeks.

Across the valley, my daughter Donovan was in college, living on the campus at Cal Arts (California Institute for the Arts), which is in Valencia, just north of the quake's epicenter. As soon as we could, we called her. Donovan was raised by her mother, and I wasn't the best father when she was growing up, seeing as how I was addicted, estranged from her mom, and eventually jailed. But by 1994, Donovan and I were happily reconciled. I was proud of her, and now I was fearful for her safety. Nothing much was moving, and the freeway that ran from our house to Cal Arts was too damaged for travel. Like many resourceful people, she coped with the situation until her mother could make it through the damaged road system. Donovan stayed out of school for a few weeks, and resumed classes when the campus moved to temporary, less damaged facilities.

DONOVAN CROSBY:

I was a freshman at college, alone in my dorm room, and when the ground stopped shaking I had a fish tank left, with no fish. I had fallen out of my bed, dreaming that people were throwing things at me, but it was the quake I was feeling. I wandered out, soaking wet, with all my other schoolmates. I was up in Valencia for two days before some of my family came to collect me, so we went to Sav-On, got some baby wipes so we could clean up, bought some food, and circled the wagons [our cars] in an empty lot away from power lines and whatnot. It was an interesting time. We were pretty much on our own. A group of friends and I didn't want to be on campus, so we left and took care of ourselves. We were thinking it was a very communal experience—people were coming together and helping each other, we thought—but as soon as we started expounding on that idea, we saw people beating each other up on the street in the traffic for no reason.

The day after the quake, Jackson Browne and Shawn Colvin and a few other people showed up to see if we were okay. They were as shaken as we were, but like the great good friend he is, Jackson was reaching out to friends and neighbors once the car alarms shut off and the screaming died down. This was the sort of thing everyone in Los Angeles was doing, extending a helping hand wherever they could. There wasn't much anyone could do: lights and power were off and on, most stores were closed, and the whole city was digging out from under and trying to assess the damage. We were jittery as cats, and our cat was even more jittery than that— she had disappeared inside the walls of the house someplace, meowing and refusing to come out.

The Crosbys have always had companion animals. At present, they host a pair of rambunctious dogs and some cats, birds, and horses. Their son Django's room is home to odder, smaller creatures appropriate to an inquisitive eleven-year-old: an aquarium filled with miniature hermit crabs and a hamster habitat. Jamaica, an elegant, beautifully tawny Abyssinian, lived to a happy old age, an old lady cat most comfortable perched on a shelf behind some warm stereo equipment, from which she ventured only when it was time to feed and when the Crosby dogs were busy elsewhere. Jamaica passed on in 2006. Back in 1994, she was a nervous adolescent.

JAN:

I couldn't find one of my cats. I found Smokey and I put him in a cage and I even stopped to have a conversation with him. I told him that I wasn't going to freak him out or hurt him. "I'm coming back for you. I can't let you free because I don't know what's going to happen." Nobody knew what would happen next. I checked on Isaac and Gus [the dogs] because they were crying. The dogs were freaking out. We couldn't find Jamaica, and I wasn't leaving the building until I found her. David was a little mad at me because he didn't want to stay in that building anymore, but we stayed there for the next three days waiting for my cat. And there were so many aftershocks, all so frightening because once it would start, no matter how short it was, the adrenaline would make you seriously ill, just going through your body.

Harper Dance is Jan Crosby's mother, a diminutive Southern woman from Tuscumbia, Alabama. Twice married, she raised five children (including Jan), and when they were old enough to take care of themselves, she dropped out, went to live in a commune on a boat in Miami in the sixties, a forty-one-year-old self-actualized, self-defined hippie. Talkative, hospitable, a doting grandmother, she lives near the Crosbys and has a personal history as interesting as that of anyone in David's life. Whatever their differences (and there are many), David and Harper adore each

other. Harper came to California working for Stephen Stills, and has her
own work history with Stills that predates her daughter's involvement
with David Crosby. But this isn't about that.

HARPER DANCE:

David grew up here in California and probably had gone through
some other earthquakes. He was the one who would turn almost green
when we would have an aftershock, you know. The first time we had
one after they had brought me over to their house, he jumped up and
said, "Come on, Jan, let's go." He's starting to go out the door, and I
said, "David, where do you think you're going? In the first place, what
are you going to do? Run off and leave all of the animals here, while
your poor mother-in-law has to sit and take care of them while the
building collapses around her? Where are you going?" And he stopped
and said, "You're right. I can't go anyplace. I don't know where to go."
Then I said we should just stay put, and I think my level head helped
him in a way. It sort of provoked him, because he's always pooh-
poohed things that I say, and then he'll turn around and he'll say to
me, "I just hate it when you're right."

And then there are times when I'm right and Harper's wrong, but
she's my mother-in-law, and they don't tell mother-in-law jokes for nothing. The animals were freaking out, but at least they were where we could
see them and hold them, but Jamaica was simply gone. We could hear
her buried in or under the house, but couldn't see her. Jan wouldn't leave
the house until the cat was recovered, so there we stayed.

Eventually, Jackson and Shawn visited. They heard the anguish in
Jan's voice, and agreed that the cat should be found immediately, so they
pitched in and we finally figured it out. We found the cat's escape route
in our shattered bedroom, where some electrical and antenna wiring went
through a hole in the wall that hadn't been exposed till the quake caused
the sixty-pound TV set to jump out of its niche. Shawn Colvin finally

crawled into the walls and she and Jan lured Jamaica out, herding the cat with kind words and sardines. It was a mess, but happily resolved.

The larger mess was trying to find a place to live. Our house was broken and we needed a place to stay. If the earthquake had hit a few weeks before, we'd have felt blessed in some way, because at least we thought we had some money then. Money solves a lot of problems in situations like this. But all of a sudden, as quick as an earthquake can destroy your house down to its foundations, Jan and I had found out we didn't have any money. Here's how that happened.

FLASHBACK:

Two

DEFICIT FINANCING YOUR LIFE

EXTERIOR — CROSBY HOUSE ON RANCHO DRIVE,
ENCINO — DAY — 1993

As the 1993 Christmas season took over the valley, the lady who showed up unannounced at the door of our Encino home might have been collecting for charity or trying to involve us in some sort of community project to celebrate the holidays. She might also have been one of Santa's helpers—if elves wore business suits and took things away instead of bringing them. Instead, she was a field collection agent of the Internal Revenue Service and she wanted an inventory of everything we owned—the house, my guitars, Jan's horses, the cars, boat, clothes, carpets, furniture, and the piano. Why? To sell it to recover what we owed in unpaid taxes, interest, and penalties, which at that point was approaching a million dollars. Not something Santa would do, in my opinion.

Eventually we would discover, the hardest way possible, that our former business manager and accountant had been juggling sums, cooking the books, and neglecting crucial details. I wasn't just in a pickle, I was in a whole barrel. To understand how I could marinate myself in that much sour brine, it helps to understand the system. There are two styles of business management and accounting in show business. One is, "Here's how much you make, here's how much you spend, here's what you're worth, here's what you could do, here's what you should do, here are your options, you make the choices, you sign the checks, this is my advice." This is good management, for adults. Unfortunately, I was in the other camp, the place where the kindly counselor patted me on the head and said, "You want the lollipop? Sure. You want a Ferrari? You deserve a Ferrari." I infantilized myself and let myself be treated like a child. I wanted to be reassured I could have my toys. It's an embarrassing confession, but I was in my fifties before I started signing my own checks.

California professional licensing records show that David's finances were in the hands of someone whose CPA license was revoked during the period in question, and there are some criminal case records of an individual with the same name and middle initial to be found in the online search engines that track these things for a fee. We're calling him "Ed Blue."

I made the classic false assumptions of a short-term high earner. In that respect, rock musicians are like ballplayers, boxers, and bozos with winning lottery tickets: we've got a ton of money now; we think we'll have tons of money years from now. After going to jail, marrying Jan, and getting sober, I developed a more realistic attitude about income, but not enough. When I first signed with Ed, it was because he had a long history with my manager, Bill Siddons, going back to the days when they both worked for the Doors in the 1970s. I was warned that Ed had a problem once, but I was forgiving. I knew better than anyone how a personal problem could derail a life, and how recovery depended in some part on forbearance and understanding. So I signed with him. So did Bill.

Time passed. Periodically, at Jan's urging, I'd insist on an accounting.

I thought I was being a grown-up. David Crosby, appearing in the role of grown-up. "No problem," Ed would say, promising a monthly statement. Months later I'd ask, "Where's the accounting?" and Ed would answer, "New girl in the office; she's a little behind on the paperwork." Jan and I weren't that worried. We recalled seeing large checks made out to the Internal Revenue Service for tax bills.

Bill Siddons was managing Crosby and Nash at the time, and he brought them together with Ed Blue. Siddons started as a road manager with Jim Morrison and the Doors, and he's even a character (played by Josh Evans) in Oliver Stone's feverish Doors *movie, which starred Val Kilmer. Bill rose through the ranks, and was working for another management team when he left to become the principal adviser to Crosby, Stills, and Nash. A woman named Debbie Meister ran his office, a small operation housed in a Craftsman bungalow on Larchmont Avenue in central Hollywood. There's almost always tension between clients and managers in show business; it's simultaneously a symbiotic and adversarial relationship. Managers need clients, clients rely on managers, the standard commission of 15 percent plus certain expenses becomes a source of constant friction when high earnings are involved. Even after their peak years in the seventies and eighties, Crosby, Stills, and Nash were still good earners by any measure.*

BILL SIDDONS:

Ed went though a similar scene sometime around 1974, when he lent money from one of his clients to another of his clients, but never had it documented. He was left holding the bag for about $400,000, and was out of business for a few years. I told Crosby about this when he got involved. Ed had two problems: one, he really wanted his clients to like him, and two, he was addicted to investing other people's money. . . . I never had any idea that he was actually taking money out of people's accounts again until I had a conversation with Graham's accountant after a Crosby-Nash tour, and she said, "How come Graham can't get paid? . . . Your accountant did the tour books, and you've been paid." I said, "No, I haven't," and she said, "Yes, you have." And I yelled, "Debbie! Did the Crosby-Nash tour pay us yet?" and Debbie says, "Not a penny."

When recalling the adventure, Debbie sighs; the IRS went after her for tax fraud, for the unpaid withholding taxes "deducted" from clients and employee checks. Her only salvation was that she had never signed a document and was not in any way an officer or an agent of the sham enterprises. Blue, in turn, never spent money on himself; he lived modestly in the valley in a small house appropriate to a mid-level accountant, and never bought himself or anyone else fancy cars or expensive jewelry. Nothing in his lifestyle would suggest he was spending beyond his means.

Every time a client's funds disappeared into one scheme or another, Ed would raid another client's account to make up the balance. A lot of it was done for me—I had new cars, I rebuilt my schooner, Jan had her horses. Ed, meanwhile, had the degenerate gambler's hope that one big score would enable him to reimburse everyone and keep a little for himself. It wasn't to be. Bill Siddons told Graham's accountant we hadn't received any money either, and that sent the whole house of cards tumbling like dominos, to mix a couple of apt metaphors.

DEBBIE MEISTER:

Ed didn't use any of the money personally. He may have invested one client's money in something and needed more money to make a house payment for someone else. Bill and I were seeing statements and checks, but who would have believed Ed was simply not mailing them! Of course, that led to state and federal authorities trying to get me and Bill for the payroll taxes which were never paid. Unbelievable. At that point we knew he had to be stopped, one way or the other, so we went to the North Hollywood police and turned him in.

It is the inevitable conclusion of all Ponzi schemes, when the apparently reliable fiscal entity is revealed to have been robbing Peter to pay Paul. Siddons confronted Blue with the facts, filed a complaint with the district attorney's office, then spent weeks documenting every discrepancy, every shortfall, every diversion and conversion of client funds.

Clearly, it was time to switch accountants. I'd trusted Ed, and my attitude toward money could be summed up as, "Oh, gee, I'm so glad to be out of jail. Gosh, this is fun. I'm really having a grand time, and look—I have a brand-new BMW!" As I said, I was behaving like a child, and I'll take as much blame for it as I lay on Ed. I let him do it. And I credit Jan with having the good sense to say to me, one day, "Y'know, this is all kind of weird because you supposedly made like a million and a half last year and we don't have any money." It was a slap in the face. Ed didn't pay the taxes and he told me that he had, and that's when it started to seriously stink. The IRS showed up and eventually they said, "You owe us a million point two," and the state Franchise Tax Board wanted four or five hundred thousand dollars. Thanks to Ed, I didn't have any of it. A high-profile actor friend had an accountant that he knew and trusted, with a firm that had experience with guys like me, and who might advise me and do something to help.

I went to them, after the messy job of getting my records and statements and accounts together. That was a bad joke. I had boxes of papers and stacks of statements that didn't relate to each other, most of which were pure invention. The dreaded punch line would come when the expert I was hiring to help me saw that I couldn't afford to pay him. Nevertheless, this man stepped up in ways that astonished me, and he saved my life.

The life-saving accountancy firm will also appear here with an assumed name: let's call them Goodstein, Smartstein, and Straightstein, with offices somewhere in the Los Angeles area. The accountant who helped David would discuss his file only if I guaranteed his anonymity. The firm appreciates David's endorsement and gratitude, but one of the things that makes them good, smart, and straight is their absolute refusal to discuss any client's affairs publicly. Discretion is the accountant's stock in trade, as it is for priests and doctors. It happened that the accountant in the firm who first examined David's accounts is a fan of the music and he respects the man who made it. He's also a principal and partner.

ANONYMOUS ACCOUNTANT:

I got a phone call saying, "David Crosby's going to be in your office tomorrow at nine o'clock in the morning." . . . He said he was referred by a friend, and showed me an IRS collection officer's business card. They'd been at his door the day before. When you get that card, you're way down the road. It's not just the early stages in a process that can be deferred over time. . . . The card might as well read, "This is trouble." If David told me a moving truck had been there with them, I wouldn't have been surprised.

BILL SIDDONS:

Ed had other clients, not in show business, who had also suffered. It was beyond bad. There was one that made me almost retch in court. A fucking eighty-pound black paraplegic in a wheelchair, whose insurance settlement was supposed to be administered by Ed Blue, who lost it all. I went to Ed's sentencing to plead for maximum sentence. . . . The damage that he did to me [is] minor compared to what he did to everyone else. He took over a million dollars out of his brother-in-law's retirement fund. He took a hundred and a quarter from his wife, money she inherited from her parents. . . . Everybody within ten feet of Ed Blue had been fleeced, and guess where the money went? Crosby.

This is probably where David and I have very different recollections, but I watched Ed continually do anything possible to make David happy. I never knew how he was getting away with it or how he was doing it, and it didn't register with me that he told me he was borrowing it from clients. . . . He had me and Crosby sign loan papers a couple of times, so I'd at least seen that the process was something that looked like the right way to do it. I always marveled: "Where the fuck are you coming up with all this money for Crosby's personal needs? The guy doesn't have any credit."

Which is true, but Ed didn't need credit—he just ripped people off and told me everything was fine. The creep even stole a small trust account I had scraped together for my daughter Donovan, and hung all kinds of mortgages on the Encino house. He'd put papers in front of me, explain they were formalities necessary for funding. I'd sign, some toys would show up, we had a nice house. Then there was no more money to steal.

BILL SIDDONS:

Everything Ed did, in essence, was to make David happy so Ed Blue could say he represented David Crosby; that just came right back to bite him in the ass.

ANONYMOUS ACCOUNTANT:

I don't like clients who will spend on the credit cards. . . . The credit card bill gets paid because they bought what was there, and then they complain that they don't have any money. Well, I say, "You were the person at the point of purchase. I wasn't there. It wasn't me who laid out the credit card to buy the jewelry, the car, whatever." By the time

I hear about it, it's too late, you've already driven off in the asset, whatever it is. But as for David, when we took over books and records that David had with his prior accountant, that was an interesting set of books. . . . We had a meeting with Ed Blue, and I had a lot of questions that couldn't be answered . . . [the only possible response] was, "Let's just start from here. We don't need to worry about yesterday because it's a mess and probably not recoverable." My initial goal was to get the IRS off the doorstep and see where we'd go from there, because we still had David Crosby, somebody who I thought could have a career, ability to earn income, and could solve his way out of the whole situation.

An attorney with tax experience hooked up with the new accountants and got the IRS to withdraw to a safer distance. A different attorney was, at the same time, concluding a settlement negotiation with a Japanese motorcycle-parts manufacturer, the people responsible for an accident in 1991, when I dumped my Harley (or my Harley dumped me) on a street near my house in Encino. How did *that* happen?

CUT TO:

Three

A MOTORCYCLE'S NEVER HEAVY WHEN IT'S MOVING

EXTERIOR — ENCINO STREET — DAY
SOUND EFX — MOTORCYCLE ENGINE AT HIGH REV

I've always loved motorcycles, and owned a variety of Harley-Davidsons for years. One day in 1991, I was coming home, riding solo, and I came into a turn, downshifting at high rev. When I popped it back into gear, the engine stayed revved. I let go of it and nothing happened. In the middle of a turn, you'd rather be winding down than winding up. Accelerating out of control, the bike lurched ahead and put me ass-over-teakettle, and that's all I remember before waking up in the hospital the next morning.

JAN CROSBY:

I get a phone call and I hear a woman's voice say, "I'm your neighbor. Your husband's lying in the street, you better come now. I think he's still alive." That's all she said and she hung up. I ran out the door and got into my car, looking for this accident in the road. About half a mile down my street, there was Dave, lying in the road, the motorcycle on its side. When I got up to him, I looked in his eyes and I could see the pain, as well as some relief when he saw it was me. He said, "I think I hurt myself really bad this time." His leg was going one way and his foot was going the other, but he didn't know it. He just knew something was wrong. So I pretended everything was fine and I looked him in the eye and said, "It's okay, we're just going to take your shoe off and put you on a stretcher. You just hold on to me."

I was told later that I objected to having my shoes cut off my feet. They were custom-made boots from some famous Texas bootmaker, and it wasn't until Jan and the paramedic explained my foot was pointed in the wrong direction and probably broken that I finally consented. They took me to a local hospital that had no idea how to handle a trauma case like this. They X-rayed me, and said it looked like a bad break. Judging from the direction of my foot and the pain in my hip and shoulder and ribs, I thought that was a reasonable diagnosis, if an incomplete one. I asked for something for the pain about seventeen times, Jan remembers. She called Buddha and Bobalou [Bob Benavides] and they simply took me to out of there without treatment and trucked me in another ambulance to the emergency room at Cedars-Sinai.

JAN:

> I rode in the ambulance with him and I was very scared, because I didn't know how serious a break it was, or what else was broken. But I also was afraid because it was going to be the first time he had to be on serious medication since our sobriety.

"Buddha" wasn't the deity; he was Donald Miller, one of those people buried deep in rock and roll who have astonishing capabilities. Buddha was a biker, a roadie, Jackson Browne's full-time manager; in his free time he could be found doing prep work for Alice Waters at the world-class Chez

Panisse in Berkeley. He currently manages both Jackson and Graham Nash, and cooks a gourmet lunch for his staff every day. A longtime Harley and Indian rider, he was the first to answer Jan's calls for help. Earlier, he connected Jan and David with another overqualified biker/roadie, Bob Benavides, known as "Bobalou." They were charter members of the Ugly Motorcycle Club, a loose association of nonoutlaw bikers who hung out at the Glendale Harley shop. Bobalou had helped renovate David's house on Rancho Drive and crewed on David's boat, the schooner Mayan. *He lived in the Crosby's guest room adjacent to the garage. At Cedars-Sinai, David was installed on the celebrity floor, in a room large enough to accommodate Jan. She stayed at the hospital with him for two weeks while he recovered from surgery, and Bobalou helped take care of David during his long convalescence. At the hospital, the Ugly Motorcycle Club provided security against the tabloid press. It was reassuring and charmingly bizarre to see huge men in beards, bandannas, and leather biker gear sitting respectful watch outside the Crosby suite. There's been nothing like it at Cedars before or since.*

I had broken my ankle in five places and my shoulder in three. The shoulder was completely dislocated, as was my ankle. A very fine orthopedic surgeon named Gene Harris did an excellent job putting my broken bones together and getting things to work right again, but it took months of recovery. The postoperative time at the hospital was the most difficult part of the experience, because I required serious medication for the pain. For someone like me, who was trying to be sober, that's a tricky business. I had a history of opiate abuse, I had a residual high tolerance for drugs like morphine and Demerol, and I did *not* want to be strung out again, ever. But even Alcoholics and Narcotics Anonymous recognize that medication for pain is not in itself a relapse into addiction—although the possibility is always there, and one has to be extremely watchful, and supervised. A meddlesome jerk from the program, who used to be a friend and colleague, was outside my room at Cedars, trying to instruct my nursing staff to discontinue my morphine. The meddlesome jerk left the music business and now makes a living as a drug and rehabilitation counselor, which is a cautionary note of some sort.

BUDDHA (DONALD MILLER):
CSN had a literal road case with them when they toured [a box specially built to transport equipment by truck, much like a cargo container on a ship; in this instance, a case that held three motorcycles securely] and they would all go riding. That's a little later on, when motorcycling became very, very popular. It was a status symbol. I guess enough people have fallen down now that it's kind of weeding itself out. Nowadays, when someone says to me, "I really want to get a motorcycle, what do you think?" I say, "You know you're gonna fall down, right?" They look at me, I say it again: "No, I'm telling you, you know you're gonna fall down. Long as you know you're gonna fall down, you're ready for a motorcycle, but don't kid yourself. 'Cause you're going to fall down." And they just look at me, like "Oh man, you're ruining my day." And I tell them, "You could be ruining your life."

JAN:
The bone breaks on the left side of his body were so severe that he had a morphine drip for the pain. I think we spent eleven days there before he was released, and on one of the nights when David was transferring from morphine to the next level down I was asleep next to him. He cried out at three o'clock in the morning, woke up, thought he was in a closet. Didn't know he had been hurt. Didn't know he was in a hospital bed, connected up to all these support systems, traction, tubes, drains, and things. He woke up out of a stupor and was terrified. Later, he told me he thought he was in a meat locker, with corpses hanging on hooks.

That's morphine for you: awful hallucinations. And at one time I used to think morphine was the Queen of Drugs! Queen of the Damned is more like it.

Eventually, the haze cleared and I was discharged and sent home, where I lived downstairs for months on a hospital bed in our living room. That was tough on Jannie and Bobalou, who was a wonderful friend. He stayed and worked with us and for us, and was invaluable in helping me move around. I had a shoulder cast that suspended my arm out in front of me and plaster all over my ankle. I was the mummy's bride. Bobalou got a van and made sure I got to my AA meetings and my follow-up appointments at the hospital.

The van had a chair lift with tie-downs, and an extra accessory only Bobalou could think of: a rubber arm that he rigged on the rear door to look as if the door had been slammed on someone inside. At Cedars, a doctor chased us down and pulled us over, saying, "I'm a doctor. There's an arm sticking out of your truck." We acted totally surprised: "There is?" It was funny, and the situation required humor. At that point I was dependent on Jan and my friends for every awkward detail of my life, including the messy jobs of fetching and emptying bedpans and changing dressings.

BOBALOU:

At the hospital, I knew who needed to get through to him, so I was able to ride herd on all the goodwill wishers that really didn't need to be bugging him. When we moved him home I became his nurse. Even took him to the ceremonies in New York when he and the Byrds were inducted into the Rock and Roll Hall of Fame. That was a trip. They had ramps up behind the stacks, going up to the stage, and I told Croz I wanted to get some black tennis shoes for traction, because I had to wear a tuxedo. He wouldn't let me get them, so when it came time to roll his wheelchair up the ramp, I couldn't get traction. I had

to get the stagehands to put a foot behind my foot, block it for traction each step, so I could get up Croz up the ramp. That made me
laugh. Wouldn't let me have tennis shoes, man, and I had to wear them
slippery damn formal shoes.

And to top it off, five minutes before the ceremonies started, [the
U.S.] started bombing the Middle East. There were big TV screens at
the Waldorf-Astoria for the show, and instead of the musical acts,
they're putting up the live video feed, with George [Bush] Senior saying, "Well, we've started bombing . . ." That put a weird twist on the
evening's festivities.

*The ceremony marked the last time the original Byrds would ever be or
play together. Gene Clark died later that year, and Michael Clarke the
year after. The evening itself was memorable. But for now . . .*

FLASH FORWARD:

Four

HAPPY CANYON

FADE IN:

EXTERIOR — SANTA YNEZ VALLEY — DAY

Somewhere between Lake Cachuma and Ballard, in the Santa Ynez Valley, there's a place called Happy Canyon Road. The idea that there could be such a place as "Happy Canyon" was intriguing to us. After the quake, our house in Encino was totaled. It was uninhabitable—just wood and plaster and chimney bricks on broken grounds by a cracked pool. It certainly wasn't what we once loved. Thanks to Ed Blue and the IRS, we were sure we'd be losing it anyway. We had looked everywhere within fifty miles for an alternative place to live, but rentals were out of the question. Housing was suddenly a hot and overpriced commodity and price gouging was unrestrained. I finally said to Jan, "Look, if we're going to look as far as this, let's go up to Santa Barbara." That's my old stomping grounds, and I knew there was good stuff to be had.

As happens so rarely in my life, I was completely wrong. We looked

in Carpinteria, in Montecito, in Hope Ranch, and all around Santa
Barbara and Ventura County. Finally, we heard about a house in Santa
Ynez, and came up to look at it.

*David and Jan first saw the Santa Ynez house in an advanced state of
disrepair. It was badly fenced and was equipped with only two bedrooms
and two baths. It wasn't for sale, it was for rent, but the price was right.
It stood on five acres of gently rolling pasture, and it could be mightily
improved under the terms of the lease. It was a small, rambling, single-
story ranch house with adobe walls, on a few acres in the cozy, insular
Santa Ynez Valley, thirty miles above Santa Barbara. The valley is home
to large horse ranches, farms, and thousand-acre parcels of undeveloped
land. The towns of Santa Ynez, Ballard, and Los Olivos are quaint, with
few traffic lights, quiet streets of wood-fronted Victorian stores, and more
upscale restaurants with long wine lists than you'd expect, until you realize what property values are these days. The schools are good, and in
1994 there was more affordable housing than there is today.*

The house looked terrible because nobody had been doing any gar-
dening or watering, but Jan had a vision for it. She knew that we could
make something out of it. It belonged to an old doctor, who loved books
and had a library, a feature we loved. He had died, and his heirs were renting the place until they could find a buyer, which eventually turned out
to be us, as soon as we could afford it. Making the house whole again took
years of effort: we built a barn, added a pool, put in a garden, did land-
scaping, planted redwoods and fruit trees. As I write this, we have twenty-
five-foot trees out front that we planted when the tops were eye level. As
unsettling as the earthquake was, it got us out of Los Angeles, which I'm
convinced is no place to live. It's my firm belief that when any area can
no longer support animals, wild or domesticated, it's no longer any good
for human beings. By way of contrast, there are a couple of hawks that
have nested on our property in Santa Ynez for years, raising their chicks

in the trees that shade our house, deer and bobcats roam the hills, and there are horse and cattle and ostrich ranches all around us.

We packed up and moved to Santa Ynez, and I went back into the studio with Graham and Stephen to record an album with producer Glyn Johns [*After the Storm*, released in August 1994]. I started to tour again, because I owed the tax man.

CUT TO:

Five

LIFE ON THE ROAD

Elevated, you're elated,
'Cause I waited a year for you,
If you're thinkin' what I'm thinkin',
Then I'm gonna make my love to you,
Don't run, the time approaches,
Hotels and midnight coaches,
Be sure to hide the roaches . . .

"Pre-Road Downs"
MUSIC AND LYRICS BY GRAHAM NASH

L ife on the road is everything you can imagine it to be—better and
worse than anything you can think of, whatever Willie Nelson says.
When you tour, there's no opportunity to eat right, or sleep right, or live

on any kind of schedule except to get to the venue, do a sound check, do the show, get back on the bus, and ride to the next city. At 11:30 at night, as the show is ending, you're excited, the audience is excited, the lights are up, the music's loud, and when you play the last encore you're surfing a wave of joy shared with the audience and your fellow musicians. It's about as high as you can get without taking drugs, and the truth is that you're higher than most people ever get *on* drugs, certainly higher than I've ever gotten on drugs.

You come offstage, you congratulate each other on what a good show it was, and ask, "Did you see the babe?" (There's always at least one spectacular, augmented, skimpily dressed woman in the front row. Usually the stage crew spots her first and gives us a "cleavage alert" before we go on. Maybe there's a secret agreement between concert promoters to provide eye candy for the acts; girl bands probably have their own version. The visuals are even more dramatic at casino venues where there's gambling.) More often than not, we're also complimenting the audience: "Wow, they really *got* it . . ." We walk out of the building, thanking the crew as we go, and the security team walks us to the bus. A portion of the crowd is standing out back, cheering us again, and thanking us for the show as we walk to the bus. Then the door slams, the air-conditioning kicks in, and we're "home," which is what the bus is when you're on the road.

So now you're on the bus, and you're happy. You've done your job, you feel that you've done it well; you've just spent a whole lot of energy, so you're hungry. Unfortunately, there's nothing open in the hours after the show, except for maybe a pizza joint or someplace called "Jade Empress/Palace/Pavilion" (pick one), featuring awful Chinese food. We won't even discuss fast food, which may be fast, but rarely resembles food or provides any actual nourishment. So you're limited to whatever you can find, or what you have stashed on the bus. "Stay hungry" may be a good slogan for weight lifters, but it doesn't cut it for me.

It was Napoleon who said, "an army marches on its stomach." He was talking about provisioning and supply, and from the Royal Navy's hardtack and tinned beef to the modern army's MRE (Meals Ready to Eat) with their own heat source, a traveling troupe has always looked forward to satisfying its appetite. Whether it's a circus with its own cook tent or a movie company that brings a catering truck on location, the purpose is always the same: to keep the cast and crew happy and productive. David was an undiagnosed diabetic before he went to jail in 1985. The prison diet in the Huntsville, Texas, penitentiary didn't help. As David recalls it, "I kept putting on weight, because all they feed you is five kinds of starch a day. They feed you cereal, bread, rice, beans, and potatoes. If there's meat, it's some form of pork—that's the only animal protein. No eggs, even though there was a farm attached to the prison. I never found out what they did with the chickens; maybe the guards ate them. Under any circumstances, the pork served in prison is always the lowest, worst cut of hog. It's jail meat."

Released from prison, by 1987 David was diagnosed with a serious case of type 2 diabetes and began his unending involvement with diet and nutritional issues, which leads us back to the problem of finding a decent meal on the road.

When the bus starts to roll, you have between a four- and ten-hour ride to the next town. Getting to sleep takes a while, because your system's still coming down from the rush of doing the show. So you read a book for a little while, make your eyes tired, go to sleep. On a smooth main highway, when you get in your bunk and snuggle down, you go to sleep easily. But then the bus hits a bump . . . and you wake up. The road smooths out, you go back to sleep. A little while later, the bus hits another bump, and the result is you never really get a full night's sleep, ever.

Most often, you get to the hotel in the next city before dawn, or at sunrise or during the morning rush hour. Even if you're lucky enough to have been able to get to sleep in the predawn hours when traffic's light and the going is smooth, the change in the bus's rhythm as it gets off the interstate and enters the new city will wake you up. The turns, the brakes, the sounds of traffic are your unwelcome alarm clock. Paradoxically, if it's a motel with a parking lot, you're in good shape—you stay in your bunk and get some *real* sleep, because the bus is no longer moving. But more often, you're booked into a hotel downtown, and they don't have valet parking for buses. So the bus has to park somewhere else and you have to get up, get semi-dressed, get a substantial portion of your gear together (meds, books, cell phones, computers, chargers, etc.), and shuffle, half asleep, into the hotel and try once again, at long last, to go back to sleep, praying that Housekeeping will honor the "Do not disturb" sign on your door.

When you wake up, either in the bus or in the hotel, guess what? They've stopped serving breakfast. You call your road manager. He calls the hotel manager, he has a fight with the chef, and after considerable back-and-forth—"We're renting thirty-five rooms in the stinking hotel, you *will* get him breakfast"—the tray comes, but typically it's a shitty breakfast, reluctantly thrown together from stale materials, cooked with resentment, and served cold. You get it down, one way or another, because you're hungry.

When I travel with my family, I don't just go back to bed after the meal. We get up, get out, and try to do something outside the confines of the hotel, where people are scratching at the door, saying what sounds like "housecreeping." At the very least we try to take a walk, and if we're lucky, there'll be a park or a bookstore near the hotel. We never walk past a bookstore without going in and stocking up for the road ahead. If there's a theme park or a fair, Jandy and Josh—our road manager, Josh Vanderslice—will take Django on the rides. (I don't do roller coasters.) Museums and art galleries are our other favorite off-the-bus, out-of-the-hotel destinations.

Then we try to find lunch. By about three or four o'clock, you have to be repacked and you need to complete a "dummy check" of the room, particularly for phone chargers, phones, toothbrushes, reading glasses, and fragments of vegetable matter. You get back on the bus. Now there's a relatively short drive to the venue, where, if all has gone well with the crew, they're ready for a sound check. Sound checks can be fun—they can also be a nightmare, if the technical gremlins have got you again, or if one or more of the principals shows up hung over, pissed off, hungry, angry, lonely, or tired.

Then comes the big moment of the day . . . dinner! The thing to understand about dinner is that concert promoters have to provide a hot meal for performers and crew between setup and show time. Since it's an inevitable expense, it inevitably follows that promoters hire the caterer who puts in the lowest bid. So you're guaranteed an interesting nutritional experience. We musicians have written songs about cat food sandwiches and mystery meat. If the tour is big enough—i.e., if Neil Young is on board—you can have your own caterer on the tour, who will provide a much higher grade of food, cooked to your specifications.

On the road, the man with the responsibility for everything is the tour manager. The job description requires a hybrid hands-on, detail-oriented, results-based authoritarian workaholic who can function for weeks on very little sleep. Outside of touring with rock and rollers, the only people with similar jobs are the first assistant director and unit managers of film companies; sergeants major, master gunnery sergeants, and chief petty officers in the military; and the first mate of a ship at sea. A half dozen or so gifted individuals have shepherded the band over the last three decades, among them production manager John Vanderslice, a compact, energetic man with a handlebar mustache who answers to the name of "Slice."

JOHN VANDERSLICE:

The tour manager is basically responsible for the tour to the management company from the business side. The production manager's job is to oversee everything that doesn't have to do with performing: that would be crew travel, catering, security, stagehands at the venue, advance with the promoter, load in and load out of the day. The tour manager is responsible for the band and anything that has to do with artist relations. With artists like Crosby, Stills, Nash, and Young, each of those guys has an individual road manager, who attends to their personal needs, makes sure they make their daily press contacts, gets them to and from their bus, blah, blah, blah. We're all paid by the management company, but you have to answer to the artist as well as the management company. That's what always makes it a fun dance. You have a foot in each boat. You have artists that want to spend more money than they're making, and you have a management company that wants you to make sure you don't spend that money. Unless you keep the artist happy, you don't keep your job, but if you don't watch the money, you also don't keep your job.

Slice also runs production for the Jimmy Buffett extravaganza Margaritaville, which is an elaborate stage presentation. Touring musicians who do stadium stage shows like the Dixie Chicks and the Rolling Stones can carry something like eleven crew buses and seventeen trucks full of equipment. On the other hand, Paul Simon can tour with a single guitar case and a carry-on bag of clothing, if he wants to. In between those extremes, there's CSNY, which is a relatively light production touring package.

JOHN VANDERSLICE:

Sometimes we carry our own caterer. Most of the tours use a venue-provided caterer—it depends upon how badly you want your own food. Luckily, there are caterers who understand what we want done, the presentation and quality of the product. I mean, you can put in the catering rider [an addendum to the contract between act and promoter] "We want a cheese and cracker tray." Now, a box of Ritz crackers and a block of cheese from the grocery store, in a court of law, that's a cheese and cracker tray, but the guys we use get four or five kinds of nice specialty cheeses and a variety of crackers. That's what it's all about—it's not just blindly picking the first tomato off the shelf. You get the nice ones. You don't get the oldest bananas, and some caterers have learned how to do that.

Josh Vanderslice is a second-generation music guy who started as a kid roadie with Carole King's tour in 1989 and toured with Keb' Mo' and a host of other acts. Since 2003 he's been David's personal road manager, and has a lot of stories to tell. At this point, we're just talking about food. The present is a lot more comfortable than the past that Croz is recalling.

JOSH VANDERSLICE:

If he needs something to eat, he needs something to eat. You've got to figure out where to get what he needs. We're trying to keep his blood sugar right, working on Atkins diet stuff, so we keep some deli meats and I try to get him to do roll-ups instead of sandwiches and keep him on the right track. Most of the time we can find Boar's Head flat meat anywhere. I brought out a little grill for the summer. I love to grill, and Dave and Jan were both into it. At least once a week I'd be able to break out the grill, make them something nice, and I had a little steamer so we were able to steam up veggies that he wanted. Jan would make the salad that he likes, so it was practically a home-cooked meal right there.

Now we've eaten and we're back on the bus, waiting to do the show. I usually stay on the bus until showtime, because all too often the dressing rooms are locker rooms redolent with *essence de sweat sock* and *eau de jock*. When eight o'clock rolls around, we're loosening up our voices in the corridor backstage, focusing ourselves. Finally, the hall goes dark, the electricity of expectancy ramps up to a sizzle, and you walk onstage. It's the only reason you're there, three hours of doing what you were put on the earth to do. It is a joy. But when you finish, you still have nowhere to go but down. Jackson Browne said it best of all:

THE LOAD-OUT

Now the seats are all empty, let the roadies take the stage.
Pack it up and tear it down—
They're the first to come and last to leave, working for that
minimum wage. . . .
Now roll them cases out and lift them amps
Haul them trusses down, and get 'em up them ramps. . . .

Tonight the people were so fine
They waited there in line
And when they got up on their feet they made the show
And that was sweet—
But I can hear the sound
Of slamming doors and folding chairs
And that's a sound they'll never know

But the band's on the bus, and they're waiting to go
We've got to drive all night and do a show in Chicago
Or Detroit, I don't know, we do so many shows in a row.
And these towns all look the same
We just pass the time in our hotel rooms, and wander 'round backstage
Till those lights come up and we hear that crowd
And we remember why we came . . .

In the bad old days, after the show was when I would do the most drugs, simply because I didn't want to come down from the performing high. It hurt too much. Now, I have my family, we can climb back on the bus together, and roll on down the road. Although Donovan had been out with me for a few weeks one summer when she was still in high school, usually it was just me and Jan on the bus, and the usual suspects in the crew, who never tired of the game they called "Get Croz." In one memorable case, it became the episode known as "Dances with Boxes."

QUICK CUT TO:

INTERIOR — STAGE — NIGHT, AUSTRALIA, 1991
CROSBY IS CENTER STAGE

JOHN VANDERSLICE:
With all the artists I have know, there's some you joke with on the stage and some you leave alone. Dave always had this target on his back; he enjoyed the gags and was great onstage with it, once he figured it out. He just digs that kind of attention, I don't know why. When we went to Australia, David wasn't walking easily, because of the bike accident. When he came to his solo part, where he'd usually be standing up playing acoustic guitar, he had to sit in a chair. Nash would introduce him, as he always does, "Here's my friend David Crosby," and we'd sit him in his chair, put the guitar on him, and get the mike down while he rested the guitar. He had to have his foot propped up, so I found a metal box at some theater and we used it all the time.

MUSIC CUE — "A THOUSAND ROADS"

If you will recall the great Andrés Segovia, and other classical guitar soloists, you will get the mental picture of the artist center stage, one foot on a small cushion or footstool to provide an elevated leg on which to rest the body of the guitar. This was David on the 1991 Australian tour in his solo spotlight, alone onstage, foot on a small dark metal box, sharing his art with a rapt audience. Until one night.

JOHN VANDERSLICE:

Some gags, I'll just pull the trigger myself, but some of them, like this one, I had to make sure I wasn't overstepping it, so I got Graham's blessing before I did it. I glued David's foot to the box. Totally stuck it on there, by coating the top with super glue. As we settled him center stage for his solo set, I grabbed his foot and put it down real hard on the box, smiled, and walked off. He starts "A Thousand Roads," and when he goes to tap his foot, the whole box comes up with his foot. Me and the guitar tech are offstage, just dying, hiding. He finally gets it, and makes some remarks to the audience: "You know the kind of people I pay to work for me? These are the kind of friends I have— they glued my foot to my box." After that, Graham started introducing him as "My friend David, who dances with boxes," and that became his nickname: "Dances with Boxes."

There were other gags, once at Graham's expense, when the crew constructed a perfect miniature replica of the famous Stonehenge set piece memorialized in *This Is Spinal Tap,* and lowered it onto Graham's grand piano during the very solemn opening chords of "Cathedral." That's a song with a lot of mood lighting, it's a song Nash takes very seriously, and he performs the hell out of it. Until the night this funny little set piece comes dropping down from the rafters and settles there, mocking the moment. He kept the model in his home for years, always good for a chuckle.

Grace Slick of the Jefferson Airplane shares a recollection of life on the road with a fun-loving Crosby in a concert in San Diego during the early seventies.

GRACE SLICK:

The Airplane was playing down here somewhere. It was Crosby's idea to buy I don't know how many pies—they were just stacked up all over the place just offstage. I know it wasn't Nash, because he's not quite like that. He'll get into it, because he did, and Stephen and Neil, it wouldn't be their idea, so let's put responsibility on Dave. We were saying "Thank you very much," it was the end of our set, when all of a sudden a pie came onto the stage and hit one of us. I forget who it was. It was me or Paul [Kantner] probably, and the pie fight just started. I mean, it was just pies all over the place, on the crew, on our band, on their band, just pies all over the place. That's one of the things I like about David—he can be absolutely silly, like a little kid, but after he starts that stuff you realize you're enjoying it. You think, "What a great idea! Let's hammer everybody with pies!"

John Gonzalez, "Gonzo" for short, was David's guitar tech for more than a dozen years on the road. He was responsible for watching out for David onstage and off, tuning and maintaining the instruments, and taking guitars offstage and bringing them on, in the order in which they're used in the sets. Musicians of David's caliber have instruments that can be worth tens of thousands of dollars each, and in the case of historic fretted instruments made by great luthiers, they are literally irreplaceable.

JOHN "GONZO" GONZALEZ:

A couple of years ago in Denver we were at Fiddler's Green, an outdoor amphitheater, playing to a crowd of about eight thousand people. John Vanderslice was in on this. We went out in the afternoon and bought a real inexpensive acoustic guitar, and then we took a half saw to the neck and cut about three-quarters of the way through it, through the truss rod and everything so it would break real easy. During the show, before a song when Crosby needed an acoustic guitar, I came over to my little tuning station and Slice pretended to be distracting me so that we could stall. Of course, David, he's Mr. Patience, right? He waited, like, "Where's my guitar," you know. I acted like I'm all flustered; "Oh, jeez!" I grab this rigged guitar and go running out and trip and shove the guitar into the stage and of course the neck gets smashed, breaks clean, shattered, like it's one of David's precious D45's, you know, that he bought in 1970 or whatever.

There was a collective gasp from the audience, Graham and Stephen were startled—it could just as well have been one of their precious instruments hanging in pieces from its strings. David reacted, but was the first to realize it was a hoax, and a good one.

GONZO:

The whole audience went, "Ooh, that guy's going to get fired," but Croz, I don't think we fooled him for more than about five seconds. We didn't fool David for long, but he enjoys it, he loves it when somebody pulls a gag on him. He gets a big kick out of it whenever we try and wind him up.

CUE MUSIC OUT:

DISSOLVE TO:

Six

SICK, SICKER, SICKEST

In 1994 there weren't a lot of laughs. I had been feeling bad for months. I always felt as if I had eaten a basketball—a poisonous basketball. I couldn't figure it out, because I was trying to be good. Before we left Encino, I was going to a gym, trying to eat right, and, most of all, being absolutely straight. I had been sober nine years, and was hoping my physical condition would reflect that fact. I should have been feeling well, and things ought to have been going well. They weren't. I'd go to the studio and wind up collapsed on the couch, feeling shitty. Every time. That's not a good way to make a record.

It only got worse when we went on the road for the summer. I was getting progressively more and more tired. Worse than tired—debilitated, beat down. By the time midsummer came around, I knew I was very sick, but I was afraid to admit it to myself. Jan was concerned, but I don't think I shared my deepest fears with her then. We were under the constant scrutiny of the IRS, my finances were still a mess, the album wasn't yet released, and only the joy of making music kept me going.

Screenwriter Jim Hart and his wife, Judy, became acquainted with Crosby in 1991 during the making of Hook, *a Steven Spielberg film that starred Dustin Hoffman and Robin Williams. David played one of the pirates. The Hart's children, Jake and Julia, were all on the set, and the family bonded with David and Jan. They were true fans who followed the band to see shows in dozens of different venues, and enjoy a close relationship with the Crosby's to this day.*

JIM HART:

They were touring and timed it so they could hit Woodstock in that July-August. We were groupies. We had an incredible time at Saratoga, and were following the bus to Lake George at two in the morning. David's hungry, so the bus pulls into a Safeway in some little mountain town, and Jan has to buy him stuff. They're staying in a hotel, but she likes to have the bus loaded, and I'll never forget this, all the checkout people recognized him, and started calling their friends to come over and see David Crosby. I'll always remember him standing in the aisle with two boxes of doughnuts. He had powdered sugar all over his face, and when he saw me looking at him, he said, "I'm not eating them, I'm just holding them."

JUDY HART:

I turned to Jan. She had been so on him about being careful, and she was so worried about what he ate, I expected her to be really upset, but she said, "See how happy he looks . . ."

JIM HART:

The next day was a day off and David says, "I've got to talk to you." And I had been concerned because there was something going on. The numbers were bad on his diabetes, he was heavy, and he ate constantly. He told me about all the financial trouble they were in. We went outside for a walk, beautiful day, and we sat down on a bench at a Lake George hotel and he told me the story of his liver. He told me hepatitis C was killing his liver and there was nothing to do about it. He was taking certain medications, they weren't very hopeful about anything being arrested, or any kind of remission, and it was only a matter of time before the liver had to come out or he would die. We must have sat on that bench for about an hour. I didn't say much. I just listened.

It was as strange a gig as any we've done, returning to Woodstock twenty-five years after the original festival in 1969, which had been an event that made history. It's been filmed, documented, analyzed, and all the old stories about it have been published so often, there's no point in repeating any of them here, except to note that it was only the second time Crosby, Stills, Nash, and Young had performed in public. All our peers, friends, and competitors were watching us, and between our filmed performance and Joni Mitchell's song of the same title, our place in musical history was secure. The only other bands at the twenty-fifth anniversary concert who had been there originally were the Band, Santana, Joe Cocker, Country Joe McDonald, and John Sebastian, who sat in during our set.

Some of the commercial rules that govern filmmaking are truisms in the music business as well. The example that comes to mind is called the Iron Law of Sequels: Only the Last One Loses Money. In that respect, the Twenty-fifth Anniversary Woodstock Festival was no different from Jaws II, or Police Academy VI. It was for the money, and the event had already been memorialized on its tenth and twentieth anniversaries, and would be again in 1999. As in 1969, it rained at the 1994 concert, and there was mud everywhere. But despite the obvious commercialism, there was still a nostalgic twinge to be felt by anyone who identified with the original event. Once onstage, David perked up, and Jan felt better.

Woodstock II was scary: huge, crowded, and no room for the buses to move. Once we were in, we were stuck until the crowds left, or until a helicopter could lift me out if I got into serious trouble. We went on, and in addition to the thrill of performing, an added bonus was a welcome counterbalance to my illness. Our old friend Kirstie Alley showed up in Woodstock with her babies.

KIRSTIE ALLEY:

We had fun. I'd been in Maine, so it was like trains, planes, and automobiles [to get there]. We took the car to the boat, the boat, then a car to a plane, another car to a helicopter, flew into Woodstock in a helicopter, landed in the middle of all the tents, went up on the stage, and listened to him play and do his thing. The crowd went berserk. I had two little babies, it was raining, it was like solid mud and everyone was throwing everyone around in what was a giant muddy mosh pit.

JAN CROSBY:

At that point we're getting close to the twenty-fifth anniversary of Woodstock [August 12–14, 1994]. David was having a very hard time just getting his job done, to sing every night. Often he'd be too ill to stand there, so some of us would stand offstage in the wings to look after him. They redesigned the set so there'd be a spot for David to rest between songs, while Graham or Stephen did a solo.

Finally, when it took two guys to help me offstage and back on the bus when we played Washington, DC, I said, "This has gone too far," and we took the bus the next day to Johns Hopkins in Baltimore. I will never know why they put a hospital that good in a neighborhood that bad. They were as good as everybody says they are. The upshot was that I found myself sitting with a woman doctor, whose name I can't remember. What I do remember is that she told me: "You have hepatitis C, and your liver is very bad." I can't recall her exact next words, but the information was clear: "Your liver is shot. You're dying—soon."

JAN CROSBY:

When they diagnosed him at Johns Hopkins, they gave him medication for ascites, which was what was happening in his abdomen. His liver was leaking and filling up his abdominal cavity. The fluid was pressing on all the other organs. He had the worst reactions to the ascites medication and it was hard to see him. On top of that, he was having moments of encephalopathy, which is when the ammonia in your body poisons your brain. He had nightmares attached to that . . . I was witnessing my husband's end-stage liver disease.

Being told you're dying is a sobering experience, to put it mildly. I thanked the doctor and walked back out to the bus, wondering how I was going to tell Jan what I knew. We're all dying; life is a terminal illness, and we all expect to go, sooner or later, but at some date in the indefinite and unknowable future. I had just learned I was going to die soon. Like, right away. Maybe not on the bus, but before the year was out, for sure. They can treat ascites with a hollow needle, by sticking a big syringe into you and draining the fluid. It was nothing I wanted to do while I was still working almost every night, and to be frank, it's nothing I would want to do ever, except as a life-saving procedure. But soon enough, I wasn't working; we did as many dates as I could manage, and we finished the tour.

Ascites is a medical condition that plagues people with serious internal diseases. Fluid accumulates in the abdomen, distending the stomach and putting invasive pressure on all the internal organs. It accompanies heart disease, liver failure, and pancreatic cancer, among other grim companions. It's the result of the body's accumulation of fluid, as overtaxed or-

gans fail to maintain the system's delicate balance. It's not uncommon to drain many liters of fluid, weighing many pounds, as a temporary measure to reduce the discomfort. The procedure is uncomfortable and frightening: a hollow needle is inserted into the abdomen to allow the fluid to escape, like tapping a foul keg.

Meanwhile, Jan was shuttling back and forth, splitting her time between being with me on the road and going back to LA. My liver was giving out but Jan and I were continuing to try to have a baby of our own. For a couple of years, we'd been working with fertility expert Dr. Richard Marrs. We were seeing a lot of Dr. Marrs—he came to Woodstock for the anniversary concert too.

JAN CROSBY:

Every month, I would go up two weeks with David, two weeks up a hill of hope to conceive. You peak at that two-week break, you find out in a three-day window if you're pregnant or not, emotionally you're anxious, and when you find out that you're not pregnant, you both come sliding down that hill of hope and you crash into a sea of despair.

Dr. Richard Marrs is a youthful-looking reproductive endocrinologist and director of the Center for Reproductive Medicine at Santa Monica–UCLA Medical Center. He's on the boards of numerous medical and scientific organizations, is well known for his research and work in infertility, and specializes in difficult cases like the Crosby's. Unlike most doctors, who work at preserving and extending and saving life, the basis of his practice is the creation of life. In 1982, barely through with his fellowship at USC and at age thirty-four, he was responsible for just the second live birth of an in vitro baby in the United States. He's been helping couples make babies ever since.

DR. RICHARD MARRS:

Eighty percent of the couples that I see are pretty much at the end of the line when they stagger through the door. They've been beaten on and hammered and prodded and poked—I always tell them I treat the terminally infertile. I see couples that are having a lot of issues about their fertility. They have issues about their marriage. They have issues about each other. But when David and Jan came in [in 1992], it was obvious they had a spiritual connection. They were two people who accepted who and where they were, and just wanted to know how they could have a child. It wasn't a big-pressure deal, they weren't stressed, they simply said, "We just want to have a baby and what do we need to do to do it?" Then they did it.

JAN CROSBY:

We tried everything, First, injections and pills to bring the hormonal balance up to specs, followed by lovemaking. That didn't work, so we went to the next stage, injections of hormonal drugs to help boost your ability to be receptive to conception, and implantation of collected sperm through your navel, not the old-fashioned way. It's a surgery, and it's painful. They test to see if your tubes are clear by shooting dye though all the avenues that can make you pregnant, and if they're clear, then they give the go ahead for the implantation. David seemed to be having as much fun as he could. There's a point where the quest to conceive takes precedence over simple good times in bed. There are facilities where you put your sperm in a cup, or have your eggs collected. One of the times we went to a lab to leave sperm, there was a "collection room," where the man can watch some porn tapes by himself and produce a specimen. David thought it was a little odd to be alone, so I went with him to help. Why not? Four hands are better than two. Inside, we discover a television set, a pornographic movie in the video player, a light switch on the wall and a couch, and behind the couch a counter with a huge box of Kleenex and a basket of sperm collection cups. The light switch had a little sign above it that said "Mood lighting." Yeah, that would do it.

The "mood lighting" switch made us laugh so hard that we had difficulty getting through what was usually a simple and fun task. To this day, all either of us has to do to make the other laugh is say "mood lighting." Nevertheless, that day we did what we had to, and Jan struggled through the same difficult cycle of kicking her hormones up for two weeks, undergoing egg harvesting, waiting for the fertilization to take place, failing, and repeating. Imagine years of that. In May, before I left for the tour, we had collected some sperm and a fertile egg, and Richard did his magic. A live embryo was created in the lab, and frozen until it could be implanted in Jan's system. Right after the Woodstock concert, on August 31, 1994, the single cell that was to become our son was thawed in a delicate computer-controlled environment, allowed to grow in the lab for three days to make sure it was viable, and then transferred to Jan, who went in for blood tests and lab work again a few weeks later to get the results. The pregnancy was confirmed on September 14, a few days before Jan's birthday. I was home from the road, not feeling particularly well, when I heard Jan screaming from another room. A good scream. A resounding "Yippee! Yippee! David!"

JAN:

Here's what happened. I got my usual phone call from Dr. Marrs, on schedule. He says, "It's Richard. Are you sitting down?" I said, "Yeah." He says, "Good, because I want to tell you that you're pregnant." I jumped up and spun around and jumped some more and said, "Yippee!" about four times at the top of my lungs, then I calmed down for long enough to say, "Are you sure?" and he said, "I'm completely sure. Congratulations, you're on your way." After everything we went through, that was that.

On September 30, ultrasound confirmed the embryo was in place and developing normally. I was elated, overjoyed, incredulous, and then elated again. Unfortunately, the emotional elation was trumped by my physical distress. I was exhausted, ill, and generally feeling like crap. I went to see my old Encino neighbor and friend, Dr. Gary Gitnick, at UCLA.

Dr. Gitnick is professor of medicine and chief of the Division of Digestive Diseases at the UCLA School of Medicine, which means he's in charge of the largest gastroenterology division in the world. He was chief of staff of the UCLA Medical Center, was medical director of the UCLA Health Care Programs, and is president of the Medical Board of California. This is a man who knows what he's talking about. Dr. Gitnick had one thing to say: "At my first evaluation it was clear that David Crosby had end-stage liver disease."

He repeated all the tests, and told me gently but firmly that unless I had a transplant to replace my diseased liver, I didn't have long to live. I was a candidate for a transplant, and a colleague of Gary Gitnick's at UCLA was the guy to do the job.

Dr. Ronald Busuttil is chief, Liver and Pancreas Transplantation Division, and Chairman, UCLA Department of Surgery. A pioneer in the field, he had been doing the operation for ten years by 1994, and recalls that by the time he saw David, he had done more than a thousand liver transplants.

RONALD BUSUTTIL:

The people who get on the transplant list have been so overwhelmed by the disease . . . so overwhelmed by their inability to function, so overwhelmed by the fact they know they could die at any moment, [because] the liver transplant is the biggest operation a human being could ever undergo. [It's] more technically demanding, more strenuous on the body, than any other operation. There's no question about that.

The heart is nothing but a pump; it has only one function. The liver is a central repository, storage facility, filter, and manufacturer. It's a much more complicated organ, with more delicate connections and interactions with other organs. The heart has two pipes in, two pipes out, and a blood supply, that's it. That's why even a heart transplant is not as challenging as a liver transplant, in my opinion.

RONALD BUSUTTIL:

People awaiting transplantation have been through so much that you don't have to do a lot of convincing that they need it. They just realize that they have to undergo it if they really want a chance . . . they don't have a chance without it. We don't do liver transplants on people for quality of life. We do liver transplants on people because if [we don't] . . . they're dead.

The process was accelerating; my liver was less and less functional. So I came to terms, as much as one can, with the knowledge I might be dead before much longer. My only chance was to get a replacement, like swapping out an engine in a car. Except you can't just order a new liver like a new engine; you never know if there's going to be one for you. The uncertainty of it is awful. It doesn't matter how much money you have, or who you are, you're at the mercy of a wonderful organization, the National Organ Donor Registry. They'll find a matching donor if they can, and if they don't get a match for you in the time you've got left, you die. Meanwhile, what happens to you is that one thing goes wrong, and then another, and that causes three more things to go wrong. It's like a house of cards.

The liver does ninety percent of the chemical functioning in your body. It's connected to multiple organ systems, and when this domino falls, it's "game over." Being diabetic complicates matters, because the sugar in your blood is messing with your other organs. I was fast approaching the end stage, and I was becoming really scared. Fear became the overriding emotion. The clock's ticking, and all you can think about is, "Will they find a match?" That drove me to the point where I made a profound choice about what I had to do.

I decided to go sailing and get in a few last dives.

CUT TO:

Seven

AHOY, BELAY, STAND BY
TO COME ABOUT

EXTERIOR — SANTA BARBARA MARINA — DAY

A LARGE SCHOONER (THE *MAYAN*) ROCKS AT HER MOORINGS

> *David's schooner, the* Mayan, *has been a constant in his life. Ahmet Ertegun, a legendary founder of Atlantic Records, said, "The one thing I remember he loved was the boat. . . . Being out at sea . . . would give him a kind of serenity that he probably missed in those hectic tours and all that. The boat was his escape, a last resort." That observation has been echoed by anyone who's ever stood on a deck with him at any time in his life. David's daughter Donovan puts it this way:*

DONOVAN CROSBY:

I think the most spirit and heart and content I've ever gotten from David and the most, the deepest bond of interaction he and I have ever had is when he's completely removed from society. He's on the boat and he's away from the world and he's in his element, so to speak . . . That's where I see him come to life the most. And I think that the most that we've ever connected is at five o'clock in the morning over a cup of coffee, when he taught me how to steer the boat and we were looking at the phosphorescence in the water and the stars in the sky and not really talking much, actually, just being there.

I honestly thought it might be the last shot I had at being on the *Mayan,* and that means the world to me. The boat has always been a touchstone. She's something that elevates my being, takes me out of my problems, and focuses my thinking like nothing else. The relationship between a boat and the ocean leaves no room for ego or attitude. The ocean doesn't care who or what you are; wind and weather are the same for everyone. A perfect storm can sink a perfect sailor, but catch a perfect wave and you'll want to surf and sail for the rest of your life.

JAN:
It was frustrating, because I heard the doctor say, "David, this is a dangerous time for you. You need to be inside the hospital for us to help you," and then I watched David say, "Okay, I got that message. Let's go sailing." I was afraid we'd lose him on the sail, but I thought that if he was at the end of his life, he should have what he wants.

Bought for a song, refitted, neglected, rebuilt, sailed thousands of miles across open ocean from the Caribbean to the South Seas and back, the Mayan *has been rebuilt yet again, a place of rebirth and renewal. In the autumn of 1994, Milan and Georgeanne Melvin were living aboard, taking care of the boat. I had introduced Milan and David years earlier; they all had a long history together. The regular skipper of the* Mayan *was Jeff Parrish, who was living ashore in Santa Barbara.*

Milan and Georgeanne were going through a rough patch; they had been through a boom-and-bust cycle, and needed a place to stay. Their ranch in Oregon was being sold, and they had roots in Santa Barbara.

They knew their way around boats. Milan was also a certified dive master. He'd sailed the South China Sea from Bangkok in a boat he rebuilt himself, and on which, by the way, he'd delivered his son when his previous wife went into labor while they were at sea.

Also on hand for the festivities was Dana Africa, an old friend from Sausalito days, another highly experienced sailor who leads dive tours all over the world. She came down from her home in the Pacific Northwest, and my pal Jim Hart flew out from New York.

JIM HART:

I wasn't sure what I was walking into. They wanted him in the hospital, and he wanted to go diving and he wanted to go on the *Mayan,* thinking maybe for the last time. . . . My wife, Judy, said, "I think you need to be on that boat," so I said, "Okay, I'm going." I met them in Catalina. Georgeanne and Milan were on the boat, on the same run, and Dana Africa. It was like Joseph Conrad.

Dana has salt water in her veins; she's spent years at sea. As a kid she sailed around the world with Sterling Hayden on his yacht, Wanderer, *on which her father, "Spike" Africa, was first mate. She's been a nurse, a dive master, and now, in her forties, she's working for her able bodied seaman's papers and getting ready to go out on big ships. Her brother's a licensed captain, and her twenty-four-year-old daughter is a graduate of the California Merchant Marine Academy and has her third mate's license. Dana first stepped aboard the* Mayan *when she was eighteen, and has been a blue-water sailor with David on many of the schooner's voyages. On this occasion, she was unaware of the gravity of his condition.*

DANA:

David was obese and poisoned, and the gear was not what I'd call up to snuff—and he wanted to go diving. His wet suit was too small for him . . . so ungainly. I'm a dive master and I've dived with a lot of beginning divers and compromised divers, and this one was really scary. But the love is so intense you didn't want anything to happen to this man. You realize that you've got to take him under and watch him like a hawk. This was when I realized that since I need bifocals to see my gauges and this guy's ten years older than me, he cannot read his gauges. . . . [But] he was determined to do it, and I'm glad he went.

I was feeling pretty crappy. I wasn't in good shape. I was having terrible cramps in my legs as well as the ascites, the fluid buildup in my abdomen. I also had encephalopathy, which meant that I was getting ammonia poisoning in my brain, and that wasn't good either. But I wanted to go diving a couple of times. They told me I couldn't go very deep. I laughed at them and did it anyway.

DANA:

More than anything I noticed his mentation was so off. I haven't practiced nursing for over twenty years but yeah, I'm an RN, so I have a medical background. I was afraid that he had gotten bent [a case of the "bends," a diving hazard involving undissolved nitrogen in the blood]. I was afraid that he had embolized something, afraid that he had thrown a clot. I just had no idea what was going on and of course he's so resistant to anything . . . I would have put him on oxygen, just because he was acting so strange. What I didn't know was that he was in liver failure.

JIM HART:

David had to go into town to get some supplies, but he looked good and looked outwardly happy. We set sail that night, sailed the rest of that day out to San Clemente Island, and anchored there for the night. We were going to go diving the next morning. . . . That night on the boat, David went to his stateroom to lie down. He said "I have to lie down." And Jan was doing anything . . . to be busy, to not deal with what was really going on. She's pregnant, he's dying. He's about to bring a kid into the world they've been trying to have for ten years. They're on the *Mayan*. The tour is in jeopardy. The IRS is after them. They're [living on] money from a shoe box. And he's not sure if he's going to be around this time next year . . . I can't write this stuff.

That night, Jan said, "Just go in there and sit with him." So we sat there and he was scared and I just held his hand. The ammonia had really gone to work and so I talked to him about the ammonia, and he said the liver's not working, so I said, "Let's change your diet. Let's put less ammonia in the air," but he was still eating meat. Everything you're not supposed to do, he was doing. [My feeling was] David was thinking, "If I'm not going to be here, if they can't do anything for me, I'm going to have a good time on the way out."

At this point, if David were a child, you'd spank him, grab his chubby little fist and march him into hospital, with or without his consent. Medical literature supports this course of action: "Hepatocerebral degeneration and the neurological syndrome it causes may occur in any case of acquired liver failure including hepatitis. [It's] a brain disorder caused by liver damage. It is usually a chronic condition and may lead to irreversible neurological symptoms," says the online MedlinePlus Encyclopedia, *which obviously no one was consulting that week. Which prompts this song, from the Crosby, Stills, and Nash album* Daylight Again *(1982) written by old friends Craig Doerge and Judy Henske:*

MUSIC CUE:

MIGHT AS WELL HAVE A GOOD TIME

There are windows on the water
Lighting up the silver strand

Shining on the sea, shining on the sea
And the ocean's just a player
On an old piano
Who repeats one melody, who repeats one melody
I belong on the shore
Hustlin' nickels and dimes
'Cause it ain't long, before it's gone
You might as well have a good time . . .

DANA:

I remember David's wild mood changes and lapses in judgment, which were unlike him. . . . He was always a whiz at dropping anchor or snagging a buoy. He drives the *Mayan* like a Toyota with a turning radius of a dime, when actually he's got seventy-two feet of boat in front of him. I was always impressed with his ability to do that. But that particular trip he was really scary. . . . Jeff and I would look at each other like, "What? What was that?" Mooring at Catalina, he misjudges where the boat was supposed to be. And then he'd get very angry at one of us for not having anticipated that the buoy was where it was. Where is this coming from? And ten minutes later he'd be back to his old self. We were just unaware that he was so sick. Had no idea this guy is . . . being poisoned by ammonia or something in his blood from the failing liver. How scary is that?

JIM HART:

Dawn comes and we go scuba diving. [During the night] I had talked to Jan a little bit: "You know, he really needs to be off this boat, in the hospital." And he was not going. He was going to go scuba diving, and to be honest with you, if he had died under water, I think he'd have been just happy, with a big grouper in his face. . . . Milan dove with David. I figured out that Milan's job was to make sure David was okay. When we all came up, back on the boat, David was thrilled. "God, you should have seen this grouper with the big lips, grouper came up, gave me a big kiss." He was ebullient, effervescent. . . . Putting him in the wet suit was like dressing a walrus. It's the funniest thing I've ever seen. I drew a picture of him, a gigantic pear with appendages. And he flipped me the bird in full scuba gear, gave me the famous Crosby finger. We sailed that night, back to the other side of Catalina, which was where it really got bad. He ate tacos and taco meat and all I can see is a little ammonia gas in his head, rotting his brain. He was hurting. We wanted to take one more dive in the morning off the bird shit mountain where the wrecks are, down in all of the kelp. A fantastic dive, but it was hairy. Jan and I had a long talk on the boat that morning when I came back and they were still out, and she was scared. And that night, when we got back to Catalina, after dinner we got back on the boat and Milan and I spoke and we all agreed. "You have to go to the hospital and you got to start doing something about this if you want to live."

Georgeanne Melvin:

There was no telling that boy no. We had some great, happy, wonderful moments, a lot of laughing, a lot of singing; you'd never know anything was wrong. He went diving a few times and he really looked like a walrus, and it was always good to see him pop up again. But then he'd start having pain and cramping every night, and we'd be up with him, massaging him and talking to him while he was flat-out frozen, in horrific pain. We took turns but nobody could really sleep because inside a boat is very close quarters. . . . We just felt horrible. . . . After a couple of days of continuing pain, it got to be too much, so all of a sudden we pulled up anchor. Nobody was in a panic. We did what we could. The hospital was called, everything was done in advance, so when we got to Long Beach, he walked off and he was gone.

By all accounts, the guests and crew hammered at David. Jim Hart said "I don't want to be the guy on the boat that had you out at sea when you should have been in the hospital." Milan and Georgeanne chimed in, "You cannot expect all of us to be responsible. You've got to be here for this kid. You have to live to be this kid's father." David, in pain and addled by his liver failure, finally agreed, and they crammed on sail for the run back to the mainland, where he continued his willful behavior. Luckily, it didn't kill him early. The MedlinePlus Encyclopedia *again: "Thorough neurological examination may reveal signs of dementia, involuntary movements, and gait instability. Laboratory studies may show an elevated ammonia level and abnormal liver function tests." Duh!*

JIM HART:

We hauled ass. Jeff had all the topsails up. This thing looked like the *Cutty Sark.* We pulled in there in the afternoon. David loved to come into a port under full sail, hated motoring in, so we came into the channel under canvas, Ski-Doos going by, past other boats who all know the *Mayan.* David's shooting his finger to all the guys on their Jet Skis. All of us felt very good that he had taken this step, put in at Long Beach, and was headed for the hospital.

Not quite. The Crosbys were good friends with Whoopi Goldberg, one of those friendships that began professionally when David was a guest on her talk show. Later, she and Jan had looked for a house in Santa Ynez, and they frequently saw each other socially, enjoying each other's company. As luck would have it, Whoopi was getting married at exactly the same time as the Mayan *sailed into Long Beach Marina.*

JAN:

When we finally got back to land, I was under the impression that we would go right to the hospital, but we saw a two-day window to honor a friend of ours—Whoopi Goldberg—who we both loved dearly, and in retrospect, I'm really glad that we did. I didn't have strong fears because there was life inside me, and that balanced out my own ability to make myself scared to death. The wedding was in Los Angeles, in Pacific Palisades, and it was one of those events where reporters in helicopters were flying over the ceremony. We went from Whoopi's party to the hospital.

Whoopi was getting married to a guy named Lyle Trachtenberg, at her home in Pacific Palisades. We went. I finally admitted to the fact that I was safer in the hospital than I was walking around. Even carrying a beeper wasn't a solution; living in Santa Ynez or touring, I was too far from the transplant center at UCLA to make it in time if, by some miracle, a donor organ suddenly became available. I was admitted to the UCLA Medical Center Transplant Unit the first week of October 1994, dying a little too quickly to be walking around unsupervised.

DISSOLVE TO:

Eight

HOSPITAL DAYS AND NIGHTS

I went through the admissions procedure, lost my street clothes, and had baseline vital functions recorded, plus the first of several thousand blood draws. When they finally rolled me into a room and I could "relax," I finally understood how sick I was. You might say I'd been practicing a profound form of denial—let's call it "terminal avoidance." I knew two things at the core of my being: first, I didn't want to be there, and second, I might die if I stayed. On the other hand, I'd certainly die if I left or delayed treatment further. I was terrified and trying not to show it. I was polite to the nurses and interns, I was nice to the administrative clerks who processed my admission and insurance paperwork, I was polite and made a major effort to make everyone like me. Of course I wanted people on my side, but I needed help to resolve the conflicts and anxieties that were frightening me.

Then there was the small matter of money: I had none. Our short sailing adventure had exhausted whatever cash we still had, and although we had things to sell, like my house and car, we weren't ready to do that yet, even though the tax people would've loved it. Whatever we made touring had gone to pay bills and doctors, keep our house, and stave off the vultures from the IRS, who were attaching everything in sight, examining tour receipts and bank accounts, looking for assets. They'd snatched my Woodstock money before we left the stage.

We, in turn, were doing what we could to protect the things we loved, everything from guitars to the schooner. At the time I was admitted, we had eight hundred dollars to our name. Mercifully, I had AFTRA and SAG health insurance. AFTRA laid out over a quarter of a million dollars; they stood up and did what they said they were going to do, and God bless them for it. You will never see me let my union membership health coverage lapse, if I can help it.

The American Federation of Television and Radio Actors (AFTRA) and the Screen Actors Guild (SAG) are the unions to which working members of the profession belong. Any dues-paying member who earns a modest annual minimum from covered employment gets his or her health insurance free through the union. Although these talent unions are currently struggling with the same escalating health-care costs that affect the national economy, in 1994 all the plans were solvent, and members who qualified for coverage, like David, enjoyed a high standard of care. His earnings as an actor were infrequent, and not significant as a percentage of his overall income from his music, but the inherent health benefits turned out to be immeasurable. Priceless, in fact, considering the cost of organ transplantation and the ensuing complications.

For political and business reasons, and because a free-market ideology pervades a Republican-controlled Congress and executive branch, we don't enjoy a national single-payer health-insurance plan that covers everyone. Canada and most European nations have it, and there are some inclusive statewide plans in Hawaii and Oregon. But here in the United States it's a very cold deal. If you don't have the money or adequate insurance, you will not get an organ transplant. A heart, a liver, kidneys, lungs—any one of them costs at least a quarter of a million dollars, and that's if there are no complications. You have to live on costly immuno-suppressant drugs for the rest of your life. You will also not get a new liver if you're not a candidate for transplant. People with liver cancer are not eligible. Recovering alcoholics and drug addicts with a verifiable history of uninterrupted years of sobriety (like me) are eligible. Noncandidates who've damaged their livers aren't eligible for a replacement organ, even if they can pay for one, unless they travel to someplace like Switzerland, which is one of the few places in the world where free-market "if the price is right" economics is an ideology even more pervasive than in the United States, with the added bonus that for four hundred years no Swiss bank has ever failed and stranded its depositors without recourse.

Of course, there's a dark side to free-market economics, places in the world where the sale of an in vitro organ like a kidney is the only solu-tion for the desperate and impoverished. India, the Philippines, and Malaysia come to mind, as well as persistent rumors that there are places in the Third World where you can say, "I'll pay a million euros or a bil-lion yen or yuan for a liver, no questions asked, get it by any means necessary." Maybe it's an urban legend—like the one about the guy who goes to Rio or Mardi Gras or Central Park, gets mugged, and wakes up in a bathtub of ice with a kidney missing—but the rumors persist that someone will kill to get a viable, salable organ. We also know there are countries where an organ-harvesting team waits just behind the executioner—an unintended but logical consequence of frequent capital punishment in an authoritarian regime. In the USA, we're a lot more transparent, organized, and impartial, as I learned.

The Organ Procurement and Transplantation Network (OPTN) is the unified transplant network established by the United States Congress in 1984 and administered by the United Network for Organ Sharing (UNOS). It's the neutral agency that tracks the whereabouts of available viable organs and all candidates for transplant, matching one with the other in a grim game of catch-up; candidates fail to survive and new names are constantly being added to the eligibility list. A complicated proprietary equation calculates the tissue-matching criteria, the candidate's critical status, the geographic proximity of donor and available organ, and the inexorable constraints of time; a harvested liver can last only a short time outside its original host before it's no longer viable for transplant. UNOS exists both as a clearinghouse and as a neutral arbiter, balancing need against availability and making a final choice, beyond appeal, that essentially determines who lives and who dies. Patients, doctors, and the survivors, heirs, and autopsy sources who supply the organs all agree to the system, otherwise it wouldn't work. Despite that fact, cynical speculation still exists that David Crosby got a liver because he was a star and a popular public figure, as if the system were run by groupies and fans instead of dedicated physicians and ethicists.

I've heard it myself, that a star gets special treatment, that a transplant organ was somehow manipulated for me, to my benefit. That's absolutely and categorically untrue. I waited in line, same as everyone else. I qualified for a transplant in every possible way. I was dying and I had been sober for a long time. There was no secret favoritism. I track the donor scene closely—I have a vested interest in keeping it honest. There's only one impropriety of which I'm aware: baseball star Mickey Mantle. He got a liver when he shouldn't have, because of who he was. That's the only exception to the rule that I've ever heard about. Because he had liver cancer, he shouldn't have been a candidate. When you smash the immune system flat to make it accept a donor organ with the wrong DNA, the cancer recurs, almost always. That's its nature. The Mick, Number Seven, shouldn't have been eligible, but he was loved, he was famous, he was a legend, he was in Texas, he was born again, and in June 1995, six months after me, he was transplanted in Dallas, at Baylor University Medical

Center. He died of his metastasized cancer less than three months later, leaving the Mickey Mantle Foundation to raise awareness of organ and tissue donation.

Surprisingly, the biggest controlling factors affecting organ donors and transplant candidates are helmet laws. Doctors refer to motorcycles as "donorcycles," because where there are no helmet laws, there are plenty of organs to transplant. Young, healthy people stack themselves onto concrete abutments with head injuries and there you are, healthy organs looking for new homes. It happens all the time: if you have a helmet law, there are very few organs; if you don't have a helmet law, there are plenty of organs. If you're on the list in a region where it takes two years to find an available match, you might as well pack up and move someplace where they don't have helmet laws, and get on that regional list. It will be a hell of a lot shorter wait. I know people who've done it.

Nowadays, the world has gotten much more used to transplants, and everyone's aware of the regulations and the protocols. Which is not to say the tabloids and shit-sheets don't keep trying to find scandal. There's no suppressing the yellow journalist's gut-level instinct to dig for dirt wherever there's misfortune.

SOUND — HELICOPTER IN FLIGHT

CUT TO:
INTERIOR — DR. GARY GITNICK'S HOME — DAY

Dr. Gary Gitnick was watching television news while walking on a treadmill, and saw an image of me in bed in my hospital room, which seemed highly suspicious to him. He hadn't been asked if I could have a film crew in my hospital room. He watches the shot more carefully, because he knows there's no possible vantage point at the UCLA Medical Center where a cameraman could stand and get a picture of me in my bed in my room at the hospital. Sure enough, it's a sky cam on *Chopper Six—Live News* or whatever. Still on his treadmill, Gary calls the nurse's station, tells them to draw the blinds, and sure enough, on *Live at Five,* you can see a nurse drawing a curtain, blocking me from further media exposure.

FLASH FORWARD:

EXTERIOR — CROSBY HOME IN SANTA YNEZ — DAY
NEWS VANS ARE PARKED IN THE DRIVEWAY

When I left the hospital, the news creeps tried to catch me on the way out, but we knew they were lying in wait, so we snuck out a different way and they missed us. By the time we got home, they were already sitting in our driveway. I'd like to know how they knew the location and what route they took to beat me there, because that's a long drive and I used the shortcut. Maybe they radioed to Santa Barbara and got a local news van. In any event, there was a guy in my driveway talking to my mother-in-law, Harper, who was watching the house. She was baffled by the interviewer; she was asking him, "What are you doing here?" and the guy was pressing her with those inane "How do you feel about . . ." questions when I drove in and said, "Get the fuck off my property."

In the conversation that followed, I used "fuck" every other word so they'd have to bleep everything I said and not get footage they could air. I knew I couldn't hit them, as much as I wanted to. I was just out of the hospital, I still had tubes and bags and all kinds of crap connected to me, I was sick as a dog, and I'd nearly died. I did what I could, which was what managers and players do to umpires in baseball: I kicked dirt on him. Thanks, Mick! Since we have a gravel driveway, I kicked a lot of gravel at the newsman. He was (a) on my property without permission; (b) trying to hustle dear old Harper into making some kind of sensational revelation; and (c) coming after me.

Besides Mickey Mantle, some other very public people had survived organ transplantation that same year, including Larry Hagman, the star of Dallas. The ethics issue made transplants natural fodder for news shows of every stripe. What wasn't discussed was that David was subject to something known as MELD (Model of End-Stage Liver Disease), a test score based on the lab values that objectively indicate the degree of illness of the patient suffering liver impairment.

That was the highest score I'd ever got on a test. Yes, it got me a chance at life—but also a chance to be a moving target for sensationalist journalism.

FLASH FORWARD AGAIN:

INTERIOR — CROSBY HOME — DAY
NBC *DATELINE* CREW IS SET UP FOR AN INTERVIEW

They had called, of course, and explained that they wanted to talk about organ transplants. I agreed. It was a favorite topic, still is, and I still do all I can to encourage people to be donors. They implied that because they were a big old established network, I should trust them to do some in-depth reporting, not like the upstart new guys like Fox and the cable channels. So far, so good—we invited then out to the house. I welcomed them into my home, everything started out on the up-and-up, then halfway through, the guy looks at his producer, as if to say, "Here it comes," and says something to this effect: "Don't you feel bad about the idea that you get a liver and probably deprived some other innocent person of getting that organ? You're a person who did this to yourself with drugs and alcohol."

I replied that I also had hepatitis C, which they conveniently forgot.

It was a genuine qualifying factor for organ replacement. I said that if they wanted a confrontational interview, I was more than ready to do it. Then I responded to the original question, about whether I felt bad about getting the liver, and I said, simply enough, "No, I don't." Following that little moment, I got more expressive, and my anger at being tricked came out. "Now that I think about it, you guys have kind of fucked me, so fuck you, get out of my house," I said. Then I threw them out. When the segment was edited, it was obvious what they had done: they found a kid who had cystic fibrosis, played guitar, and was waiting for a lung transplant. They cut between him and me, asking if I ever drank and used drugs. I was being honest—it's certainly never been a secret—so I said "Sure I did, lots of them." Cut back to the kid, asking him: "How do you feel about this guy, Crosby, getting a transplant?"

Naturally, he feels bad about it and he cries on camera about how stars can get transplants and he can't. Sadly, tragically, the kid didn't have insurance, and they don't do transplants for free. And they never aired anything about hepatitis C, or the Donor Network, they just cut between me and the doomed kid and bang, they had their piece. As cheap a shot as anyone could possibly take. Will I ever talk to *Dateline* again? No, not under any circumstances. And there are worse, much worse, out there.

DISSOLVE BACK TO:

INTERIOR — UCLA MEDICAL CENTER, CROSBY'S ROOM — DAY

While the tabloids were circling like vultures, I felt as if I had also fallen into the hands of benevolent and kindly vampires—the nurses and technicians who were drawing blood from me at what seemed like fifteen-minute intervals. They were just doing their job, and I love them for it, but for someone who doesn't like pain and needles, it was a constant reminder of my precarious condition. I was scared to go to sleep because I wasn't sure I was going to wake up. I was scared when I woke up because I wasn't sure I'd last until I went to sleep. I spent very long days waiting.

I was living with fear. My mind would wander and wonder, while up on the wall was a big clock ticking away my life, which was measurable in days and weeks, not years. Would they find a match? Jan was there every day. She'd come to the hospital in the morning like Little Red Riding Hood, with a cape and a hood, carrying a small basket with a muffin or some other little treat to supplement the usual lukewarm tray of bad, bland hospital food. Sometimes she'd bring breakfast from the hotel, and every day she'd stay until nightfall. Thanks to Ed Blue and the IRS, we were dependent on the kindness of friends for our fiscal survival. Phil Collins's wife Jill paid for the nearby hotel room where Jan stayed for the duration of my hospital stay. Other friends, many of whom appear in this book and a few who don't, lent us cash—in envelopes, like you see on *The Sopranos* or in the wedding scene in *The Godfather,* and for the same reason: the IRS. Jan kept the money in a shoe box, and used it for expenses. It was all we had.

The relationships among ex-Byrds Crosby, Chris Hillman, and Roger McGuinn have always been extremely complex—one might even say loaded—yet the nature of Chris's generosity at this particular time was typical, and characteristic of the community of friends that Jan and David had acquired over the years. The illness to which he refers was a liver problem, similar to David's.

CHRIS HILLMAN:

Jan and David had no money; my wife, Connie, and I got some cash together, put it in an envelope, and slipped it to Jan. I said, "Here, don't worry about it," and left. David survived, and when he got back on his feet he made sure he called me. He says I want to give you this money back that you loaned me . . . I met him down at his boat and he paid me the money back, and he was just very grateful that I thought of him. When I got sick, a year later, all of a sudden, it was hell on earth. Crosby got me a phone call with the head guy at UCLA, who was very difficult to get hold of, very hard . . . I survived it, completely cured, but David went through a lot of trouble to make sure I had the very best care and whatever I needed. But that's how you measure who your friends are, right?

Dustin Hoffman paid me a visit at the hospital and slipped in completely unnoticed, using what magicians call "misdirection," sending the eye away from the trick. Dustin brought a large furry teddy bear as a get-well gift. The plush stuffed toy, as big as he was, was the object of all the attention; everyone's eyes were on the bear and nobody paid attention to the man carrying it. We enjoyed our visit, and the bear later went to a good home.

Jan Crosby:

Jackson Browne came one night with books, novels, literature, and sat beside the bed where David lay and he read to both of us. I fell asleep to the sound of his voice reading us a story, and I'll never forget that as long as I live.

Finally, word came that a liver was available, so they immediately prepped me for transplantation. In some ways, that was worse than the operation. For surgery, you're unconscious. Preparing for surgery, you're wide awake, getting your system cleaned and purged, quickly and completely, emptying bowels and bladder and stomach with a suddenness that made me cry (and shit). At the same time, they were pumping me full of massive doses of antibiotics, cyclosporine, mega-cyclosporine, a variety of awful stuff that my system would need to survive the shock. Then, after all the shots and drips and purges, when I felt like total dog poop, the transplant team came into my room with embarrassed, worried looks on their faces. They told me the liver they planned to use had tumors in it and couldn't be used.

DR. RON BUSUTTIL:

In many cases we prep patients that we call in for liver transplants but don't actually take them down to the operating room until we visualize the liver and see what's going on with it. It's not routine, but it's not at all out of the ordinary.

Jan shouted *"Damn,"* and literally banged her head on the wall. I wept. Beyond the physical rigors of being prepped, there was a severe psychological letdown. We were beyond the point of no return. My systems were failing. I was collapsing from within. I couldn't pee or shit or breathe or eat or perform any normal human function without pain. I had tubes coming out of places where I don't even have places. That false alarm was the lowest point in the whole experience. In blessed retrospect, of course, I was lucky to have any chance of life at all. The odds against me were changing like the tote board at a sports book, 30 to 1, 40 to 1, 100 to 1 . . . In any other country in the world, at any other time in medical history, they would have just made me comfortable, called my friends and family, summoned a priest, lit some candles, tidied me up, and said good-bye.

Then a second liver appeared. I know something about the donor, even though I'm not supposed to have that information. I know he was a thirty-four-year-old black man, and I know that he saved four people's lives that night. He gave his heart, lungs, kidneys, and liver. He was a healthy young guy and, God bless him, he had signed a donor card. They harvested his organs, checked the lists and the matches, and cases and numbers came up; no names, just the information that there was an eligible recipient nearby.

Graham Nash was one of the last people I saw before I went into surgery. At my bedside, he said all of the things you'd say to your best friend, a brother, someone like me, going into an operating room for an operation I might not survive. It was incredibly touching. As he was leaving, he said something he knew I'd appreciate. It was from the heart, and it sure as hell lifted my spirits and added to my will to live.

GRAHAM NASH:

I got a call at four-fifteen in the morning from Gary Gitnick, who happens to be a neighbor of mine in Encino. He said that they'd found a liver for David and they were going to do it this morning, did I want to go? So he picked me up at my house at about twenty to five and we drove to UCLA, and spent some time with David, cracking jokes and trying to make light of it as much as possible, given the severity of the situation. At five-thirty in the morning, they wanted to prepare him for the operation, shave his genitals and do all the stuff that they do for major operations. Gary and I had to leave, and as I'm walking to the door, I do it very theatrically—you would have been very proud of me—I go to the door, I put my hand on the door, I open it, leave a beautiful gap, turn around and say, "Hey, if you leave me with Stills, I'll fucking kill you." My last vision of David before he went into the operation was of him holding his belly to try and stop laughing.

Then I was prepped again, and taken to the operating room, where Dr. Busuttil and his team opened me up and did the deed.

You wake up from a transplant operation knowing you've been cut in half, split up the middle, and stapled shut. You don't feel better, and you're wounded. You're not sick anymore, to be sure, but the overwhelming impression is that someone's hit you in the stomach with a Chevrolet. There was difficult pain before, and immense pain after. They'd opened me up and moved my organs around, putting one part aside so they could get to another. It hurts to even think about it. I was unconscious for ten or eleven hours while they operated, and there was no defining point when I woke up and said, "Oh gosh, I had an operation, how's everything, hi there!" It doesn't work like that.

Getting general anesthesia is essentially like being benignly poisoned, just this side of dead. Machines keep your lungs breathing and your heart pumping for as long as it takes for them to do the job. Coming back to complete, functional consciousness took ten more days, in recovery and the ICU (Intensive Care Unit). While I was in the recovery room, I recall hallucinating that my donor's soul was still around, watching what was happening. I saw him understand it, and the words that came were something about him slanting up or sloping upwards and outwards, with my love and gratitude following him. Later, when I was more stable and conscious, I wrote to an online community called The Well about the experience.

There would be times when I thought I was awake and I wasn't, and I couldn't be sure I was awake or asleep. I couldn't control my hands enough to pinch myself. I couldn't do anything except lie there and wonder if I'd draw my next breath. My past lifestyle gave me a lasting high tolerance for pain medication, but I was coping. Then complications set in. I developed hugely painful pancreatitis, and they doubled the amount of painkillers. I was totally fogged.

JAN:

David was in a private room, but it wasn't big. Larger than your normal bear; room enough for me to have a cot at the end of the bed and still have room for a nurse to walk around us. And, amazingly, for every fear there's a positive opposite force for good—Dr. Marrs made sure we had an ultrasound of our baby's heartbeat, and we had a TV set with a video player and we'd play that image of our unborn child, over and over again. It was a great motivating force for David's recovery. And we'd show it to anyone who came in the room and sat still for it. I had a lot of personal support from close friends. David had tons of support from all over the world, but privately, the people that kept us hopeful on a daily basis were Graham and Susan Nash, and Jackson Browne and his girlfriend, Deanna. Susan and Graham came and gave me a mini version of a baby shower in my hotel room, to help elevate my spirits, to help make me feel I had someone I could lean on when my man was down.

The hospital was deluged with fan mail, flowers, and get-well cards and messages from all over the world. David's transplant was international news, and the reverberations were reaching to unexpected places with miraculous consequences. Mail was brought to David's room in boxes, and he and Jan would sift through the correspondence, taking comfort from the generous emotions of thousands of strangers. In one basket of cards and letters, there was a particular message that caught their attention. It was from a middle-aged married man in San Bernardino, south of Los Angeles, named John Raymond. He and his wife, Madeline, had raised three children, two girls and a boy. The son was adopted in 1961.

JOHN RAYMOND:

I wrote, "We've never met, [but] my wife and I raised a boy that you gave up for adoption thirty-two years ago. We want you to know that he was raised well, in a very loving and caring home, and that he's very, very talented." I enumerated several of our son's professional accomplishments, and I said, "I would never intrude upon your privacy except that the news of your health is so ominous that, as one dad to another, I could not be quiet about our son." Those were the words I used in quotation marks: "Our son."

I had a grown son whom I had never met.

CUT TO:

Nine

"YOU DON'T KNOW ME, BUT . . ."

While I was in the hospital, recovering from my operation, there were at least three letters that Jan and I saw, all from different people, on the subject of my "lost son." The first letter we opened said, *I know who your son is, I know where he is, and I'll tell you if you give me money.* Another one said, *I'm a musician too, and I never got any breaks. If you get me a recording contract or get me a break in the music business, I'll tell you who your kid is.*

I said no to both propositions, but not because I wasn't interested in my son. I'd known he was out there somewhere, and I'd always wanted to find him, but I didn't want an experience tainted by adoption bounty hunters, people who would sell me an identity and location for money. In hippie terms, that would have been bad karma. In practical terms, there was no way of verifying the information that was being dangled in front of me by avaricious strangers. More simply put, I was sure that wasn't the way it was supposed to happen, and I tore up both letters.

The third letter was from John Raymond, who said, in effect: "Hi, we're John and Madeline Raymond and we raised your son James." Jan and I both had the feeling that this one was genuine; it had the ring of truth, and we believed in it. There was sincerity, there was a decent background described, a family with deep ethical and moral values, and no mention of compensation or reward. The Raymonds were driven by altruism and concern. I was desperately, perhaps terminally, ill, and they wanted to afford me the opportunity to meet my son.

The fact that I had an unknown son wasn't a secret. I had already written about it, although not in a way that was flattering to me. In 1961, I was a young folkie, playing little clubs on the coffeehouse circuit in and around Los Angeles and Santa Barbara. I hadn't traveled much, and when Cindy told me she was pregnant, I bailed. Left town, and went as far as Denver, the farthest I had been from home, where I worked the whole winter and never looked back. Nevertheless, I always knew that this kid existed but I didn't know where, and I felt guilty for not being there for him, for not raising him, for not being his father. I didn't know him. I didn't know if he was okay. I worried about it a thousand times. All I knew was he was a boy. I didn't know who he was with, and didn't know anything else about him. Cindy gave the baby up for adoption, and eventually moved to Australia.

"Cindy," Celia Crawford Ferguson, resettled and married in Australia, and pursued a successful career as a painter and artist. Her recollections were reported by CBS News in 48 Hours—Mystery *in a segment on reuniting adoptees and their birth parents. Celia's memories of the Sunset Strip in the sixties, reported on the show, recall the times:*

CELIA CRAWFORD:

We were on Sunset Boulevard going around listening to different bands and people playing. [David Crosby] was an absolutely physically beautiful young man . . . very self-confident and always very talented, and we really just hit it off. [When he learned I was pregnant] he was even more shocked than I was. Basically, his reaction was, "I've got to go now." I was devastated and heartbroken. . . . I saw a little blanket being carried out of the room by the Catholic nuns, and that was it."

California is a complex state in which to research adoptions. Some of the more populous counties in the liberal northern half of the state (Marin, Alameda, Contra Costa, Napa, and Santa Cruz, for example) have "open records," which means the parents of an adopted child can have access to the adoption file on the original family. Los Angeles is not an open county. For adoption decrees issued before 1984, the state maintains a "passive registry"; adoptees or birth parents can write to the Department of Social Services, Adoptions Branch, in the state's capital in Sacramento. If there's a match, the department will notify both parties. John Raymond had pursued the issue with his adopted son long before David's illness.

JOHN RAYMOND:

Talk about coincidences. I was a broker at the time and I had to leave the home very early in the morning, about four-thirty, to get down to the office by six and, because that's when West Coast brokers go to work, when it's nine o'clock in New York. . . . I used to listen to a religious program, I guess for some inspiration. It wasn't my particular denomination but it didn't matter. The fellow was talking about being adopted and how he never felt complete until he was able to make contact with his natural parents. That got me to thinking. James was thirty, not married, and one night when he was at the house for dinner, I asked him if he had any interest [in knowing who his birth parents were]. James said, "In deference to your and Mother's feelings, I never wanted to ask you. But I have no objection." So I wrote the Bureau of Adoption and . . . explained that we had no objection to James having the information. I gave them the case number, which was the only thing we had. After more than a year, we got a call late one evening from the Bureau of Adoption. . . . His birth mother had come in from Australia, and would like to make contact with him. . . . He went and they opened up the file, which described the natural father at the time of the baby's birth as: twenty years old, five feet, eight inches tall, weighing a hundred and thirty pounds; he had completed a year of college and was employed in the field of music. James came back from examining the file and said, "Mom and Dad, I think my birth father is David Crosby." We didn't know who David Crosby was, but our daughters knew. I later told David, "We're Crosby fans, but it's Bing Crosby."

There are a lot of Crosbys, even David Crosbys, but only one David Van Cortlandt Crosby. The middle name was the giveaway, and it was the name on the birth certificate. Celia didn't write "unknown" for the father on the adoption papers, and I always owned up to the fact.

James didn't act on the knowledge immediately. He was aware that his inborn talent seemed larger and more complex than anything in his adoptive family. They sang in church groups and had some instrumental skills, but nothing that approached his innate ability and the skills that led to his work as a professional musician, composer, and arranger. He was also completely aware of Crosby's name and reputation, and could make the assumption that his talents were hereditary, from his biological father. By the time David was in the hospital for his transplant, James was married. He and his wife, Stacia, were expecting a child of their own at the same time as Jan's pregnancy was progressing nicely. James arrived at the decision to reach out to Crosby, but John Raymond, his father, beat him to it.

JAMES RAYMOND:
When the news came that David was sick, I talked to my dad about it. I knew David was in danger of dying, and I'd be ashamed if he wanted to meet me and it didn't happen. Unbeknownst to me, my father had already written and mailed his letter to the hospital. I didn't want that to happen, you know. He went over my head. While he was

doing that, I was trying to get to Crosby through musical channels, people I knew who might know him or anyone who knew him.

Steve DiStanislao is a drummer, one of James's best friends from early college days, they still play together. DiStanislao, known professionally as "Stevie D," recalls their first meeting, and where it led them both.

STEVE DISTANISLAO:

I heard about this band that was being put together and I went to audition for it. I'm setting up my drum kit and I remember James, sitting at the piano, and looking at me. We just started playing. It's was really that simple: he looked at me. There was a band at the time called the Yellow Jackets, which we both liked, and he just whipped right into it, I knew the tune and there we were—boom. By the end of that day, I knew I'd met a friend for life. I'd go out to visit at his parent's house, I'd bring my drum kit, we'd set up in their den, and we'd jam all weekend long. We used to go up in the hills and overlook the valley, young men dreaming "One day we're going to be in some really cool band together." Eventually he met Stacia, and we stopped dogging around together, and fell a little out of touch.

Then he calls me out of the blue and says, "I know I haven't talked to you in a while, but I have a couple of things I want to tell you. First of all, I'm engaged and I want you to be the best man at my wedding." Of course, I was near tears at this point, and happy for him, and honored that he'd asked me. Then he says, "Oh, yeah, and by the way, I found out who my biological parents are. My mom's this woman from Perth, Australia, and my dad's David Crosby." I almost dropped the phone. And I just said, "Whaaat? Come on, man, don't pull that shit, Jackson Browne maybe, because of the look—that boyish kind of handsome thing . . ." But James had contacted Mike Finnigan, who plays the D3 organ with CSN, CSNY, whatever, and figured if he contacted Croz through someone Croz works with, it wouldn't be such a shock. . . . So he called Finnigan and told him the situation. Mike went down and talked to Croz about it and Croz said "Okay, I'd love to meet him."

Mike Finnigan is a longtime friend and musical colleague of Crosby's. A gifted, lanky keyboard player, his professional debut was on Jimi Hendrix's legendary album Electric Ladyland. *A blues man by inclination, he's toured and recorded with Big Brother and the Holding Company, Dave Mason, Rod Stewart, Crosby, Stills, and Nash, Etta James, Dr. John, and Carlos Santana. He won a W. C. Handy Award for his work with Taj Mahal, and played behind Stephen Stills's solo act for years. Mike was recently off drugs and alcohol himself when David got out of jail and started to tour again, and the two supported each other in sobriety for years on the road together, while Finnigan was the regular keyboardist for Crosby, Stills, and Nash.*

MIKE FINNIGAN:

I was newly sober and I kind of helped Croz come to AA. He was funny. He goes, "I'm not much of a joiner." I love that. I said, "Hell, me neither." That's the funny thing—you're not required to take an oath. One day I got a call out of the blue. I answered the phone, and a voice said, "This is James Raymond, I'm David Crosby's son." Then he very calmly laid it out for me: "I was given up for adoption," he says, "and I recently found out he was my father and I want to get in contact with him."

It's been a while back, but what I remember is that after he told me the story, I was sure it was true—it just sounded true. James said, "I think I would like to meet with him," and he was very sensitive about the whole thing, because he said, "He may not want to meet with me but I would like to meet him, if it's all right with him. . . . I thought it might be best if I called you because I know that you're a friend of his and that you know him pretty well and maybe you could act as a go-between," and I said, "Yeah, I will and here's what I'll do, I'll call him right now." Which I did. Told Crosby about it and he said he would like to meet James. He was in the hospital and he was more than agreeable.

JAMES RAYMOND:

Mike said: "I'll talk to him about it, but I don't want to kill him," so he waited a few weeks until David was out of the woods, then he broke the news and gave him our number.

STACIA RAYMOND:

James was in the shower and I knew [who was calling] the second I heard his voice. I was kind of like in a trance and just held the phone into the shower: "Your father."

CUT TO:

Ten

GETTING TO KNOW YOU

David and James talked and they finally met for the first time, as described earlier. The bonds were formed almost immediately; there was no question that the Crosby family had suddenly expanded to include the young Raymonds. David's new son was expected soon—Jan was in her third trimester—and there was still no income to relieve the financial pressure. James and Stacia were a young couple with limited resources; he was a working musician and composer, but not at the level of his newly discovered birth father.

JAMES RAYMOND:
At that point I was off into a lot of jazz R&B kind of stuff. What I grew up on was the Beatles, but I didn't own any CSN records. I knew their music from the radio. Like, I'm sure I sang along with their songs as a kid because I was glued, stuck to the radio. I knew the hits, but none of the ones I knew were Crosby songs, so I embarked on a roots trip and sought out his music. When I heard "Déjà vu" and some of his other songs, well, there it was! His harmonic sensibility is right

where I live. When I heard his weird tunings, I felt totally connected to David's songs and their harmonies, because I always loved to sing harmonies, especially the hidden part, which is usually Crosby's part in the middle.

I was concerned that he would hate my music. I think he appreciated the first batch of things that I gave him, but I sensed that he wasn't knocked out by it. Before our first collaboration, I think he could sense that I was a good musician but I don't think he thought I was in his world. Then he brought me those lyrics to "Morrison" and said, "See what you can do with this." He had the lyrics completely done. I don't think he had any melodic ideas. He just said, "See what happens." I emptied my mind, started thinking of Joni Mitchell, and it just came out.

We met as father and son, but the truth is he was already a full-grown man in his thirties with a family, and when he met me he had been a musician for twenty years. The more we got to know each other, the more it became like brother to brother. He was making a living as a musician, and he didn't need fathering. We became brothers of different ages: we had children at roughly the same time, and we shared a lot of background without knowing it, including tastes in music. I've always been tilted toward jazz and so was he. I still can't believe I got that lucky.

The first thing James played me were some tunes that he had written a while back. They were little jazz tunes and they were pretty good. Then I gave him some words, the words that I had written about Jim Morrison. I'm one of the only people who didn't like Jim Morrison, but I think I understood him quite well. He was a very lost guy and I have some experience with lost. I wrote what I thought was a pretty insightful set of lyrics about him.

James took those and called me after a while, says, "Can I see you?" I went by his house in Altadena, and he had a cassette, which he stuck into the dash of his litter-strewn little pickup truck. We sat in the front seat and he played me this song. It was so good that I realized he was way more than a good musician. I had no idea what was in store for us in terms of our writing, and I was stunned. We got to the end of the tape, and my jaw was just hanging open. It was a startling and absolutely joyous moment for me. From that moment on, I knew that I wanted to write with this guy and I wanted to be in a band with this guy. I'm grateful beyond words for his being alive and being so good at what he does.

STACIA RAYMOND:

I remember the day Croz came over for James to play "Morrison" for him. It was funny to me to see Crosby in that setting, in our house, which was modest and kind of rough and because we didn't have a great sound system, James had to play it in his truck. I'm watching them from inside the house and they're just sitting in the driveway, James has it cranked up so loud I could hear it from where I was, and I'll never forget the look on Crosby's face. James was so nervous. He played it for me, and of course it's incredible, I love it, but he really never played me anything that I didn't like, so I don't know how good a judge I was. But in this case, there wasn't any conversation after the song ended. Crosby was like, "Play it again." He was all smiles, just beaming from inside the truck.

MORRISON

He was lost and I don't think
he wanted it that way
like a gull blown inland
on a stormy day

Lost in round one
spitting out pieces of his teeth
lost in a Paris graveyard
carrying his own wreath

And I have seen that movie and it wasn't like that
He was mad and lonely and blind as a bat
to the bridge and the falling tree
too deaf to hear his own song you see, yeah

Oh, how does anyone get to there
We may never know
oh, how they got that far
or what made them go

But he had flown from his homeland
you could see him there
a gull circling
in the high desert air

And I have seen that movie and it wasn't like that
He was mad and lonely and blind as a bat
to the bridge and the falling tree
too deaf to hear his own song you see

And somehow I have to learn from this
'cause I can hear him cry and feel the hiss
of the wind in his feathers and the sand on his feet
as he dies in the desert on that Paris street

And I have seen that movie and it wasn't like that
He was mad and lonely and blind as a bat
to the bridge and the falling tree
too deaf to hear his own song

And I have seen that movie and it wasn't like that
He was mad and lonely and blind as a bat

to the bridge and the falling tree
too deaf to hear his own song

I have seen that movie and it wasn't like that

The resulting collaboration eventually led to the formation of CPR (Crosby, Jeff Pevar, and James Raymond) with James's old friends and partners Steve DiStanislao and Andrew "Drew" Ford on drums and bass, respectively. They've known James Raymond for many years, since they were all youthful musicians, playing San Bernardino jazz clubs together long before the Crosby connection was made. Jeff Pevar is the "P" in CPR, the third corner of the isosceles triangle. Pevar came to the band after years of experience as a singularly talented guitarist and performer. He'd been Marc Cohn's guitar partner for years, and had played with Ray Charles, James Taylor, Rickie Lee Jones, Joe Cocker, Jimmy Webb, Carly Simon, and Chaka Khan. He had also shared the stage with Crosby's best friends in music: Jackson Browne, Shawn Colvin, Bonnie Raitt, Phil Lesh, David Grisman, and Art Garfunkel. David says Jeff Pevar is one of the best guitarists out there. With "The Peev" in the band, CPR was complete.

I've always wanted certain things. I want people who are not playing their instrument, they're playing the song, and I don't think that there is a better rhythm section than James and Stevie and Drew. We just connect, and they have an attitude toward the song that's a joy to play. I never felt so much communication and so much support and so much willingness to lean forward into the thing, to lean forward into the possibilities, to be unafraid to explore. These guys, you can tell them, "This thing is just too ordinary, can we try it in five or seven?" And they play it for you right back. You can say this fucker needs a bridge and two minutes later, there's a bridge.

I think Stevie is probably the best drummer I've ever played with, anywhere. And I've played with most of the great drummers. But at that level, it's apples and oranges. He and James are so close, really tight. In the middle of a solo, James would go for a syncopation and Stevie would land on it, from the first beat. Just telepathic. Every time we play together, we have an unbelievably good time.

I didn't have an expectation for CPR to be a hit. Not that I wouldn't have loved it. We came close a couple of times. "Morrison" got a lot of play, but CPR is too sophisticated and too good to be a hit as far as I'm concerned. For me, it was about making the best music I could make. At first we went out, it was just the three of us, and Gonzo and Rance [Caldwell] helping us with monitors and Paul Dieter mixing the house and that was it. That was us, all on one bus, and that's what produced the CD from Cuesta College [*CPR: Live from Cuesta College*] that we owned and put out as our first record in 1998. It was a live recording of a concert in San Luis Obispo, and I would have loved it if it had been a success.

I will say something controversial here: if CPR had been more of a success, I would quite likely have done far less with CSN or CSNY. But I like to do the exact same thing that Neil's done, which is to continually cycle through different iterations of what you're doing, so you don't get stale with it. So I think that part of cycling between CSN, CSNY, Crosby-Nash, and CPR has been healthy, and the two CPR studio albums are some of the best work I've ever done.

Noah Wyle and his wife live with their children near the Crosbys in their idyllic valley on a sprawling, working farm that used to belong to Bo Derek. Wyle's best known for his ongoing role as Dr. John Carter in the long-running series ER. He wears his celebrity as a television series star comfortably, and the ranch is a place of refuge and retreat. His home isn't far from the Crosby house, and the two families share domestic concerns and an interest in local issues. Noah also has the leisure time to be available at odd hours of the day.

NOAH WYLE:

I'll tell you my absolute favorite memories of David that I'll take to my grave. Three times he called me up and asked me to come over to his house, and when I got there he called me back into his bedroom and sat me down at the end of his bed, and three times he wanted to play what he was working on for me. He'd take his guitar and sit as close to me as I am to you and start playing and singing right to me, which if you're not a musician and you didn't grow up in big sing-alongs, can be disconcerting—a man invites you into his bedroom and you're sitting on his bed and he's serenading you with a ballad that he's just written. That made me really uncomfortable, and while I was un-comfortable I kept thinking, This is one of those great moments, I'm sitting here, listening to an artist in process, who's so uninhibited about what he's working on that he's actually appealing for input and for advice from anybody who he can get to listen to it. It was profound on many, many levels, and as intimate I think I've ever been with a man in my life.

There are a thousand different ways that songs can come about. Sometimes the words come first, sometimes the music comes first. Some-times the word becomes better, and sometimes you see a scrap that you wrote twenty years ago when it didn't have any relevance to anything else. Then one day you look at it and realize, "That goes with this," and then there's a lot of different ways it can happen.

One of the things that I've noticed over the last few years is that just as I'm going to sleep, the busy mind, the verbal personalization level of your mind, the one that's talking to you right now, is going to sleep, and other levels of your mind get a shot at the steering wheel for a very short moment. It's before I actually go all the way out that I get a lot of lyrics. Somehow a level of my mind gets access to the controls and all of a sud-den, I'll think of a line or a phrase that flashes me, I'll grab the paper and the pencil that I always keep somewhere near the bed and start scribbling. I'll wind up writing page after page of stuff. And the fascinating thing is none of it is something that I've thought before. There's no kind of tab A, slot B process that goes on. It's not an intellectual exercise. It's definitely something more visceral than that. I write and write and write and write and I look at it and realize I'm into it. Then I enter it immediately into the computer. Immediately.

Computers make you a much better editor of your own work, because you try things—take this paragraph or these three lines and put them at the top—and the whole thing takes you two seconds. You can improve your work a lot that way. Then I'll try to fit the lyric to music, although once James came on the scene, if I wrote a lyric I liked I would just ship it to him, because he'll do something mentally I wouldn't have thought of or that I'm not capable of playing. That process has given us a dozen of the best songs that I've ever been involved with in my life. What we do is mess with it until we have a song. What I've always done then is start singing it to my friends. You call up your buddies and you say, "Hey, check this out." That's a joyous process, the song is like a new kid. You can go around and show it off to all your friends and see what connects. When you sit down on the edge of the bed and sing it to your buddies, if it doesn't make you feel anything, then it's not good enough yet.

Songwriting skills intact, and recovering from his surgery, David soon experienced two blessed events. The first was the birth of his son Django in May 1995, which was preceded by a baby shower for Jan that was a grand exercise ("very LA," in Donovan Crosby's assessment) that elicited a huge turnout and a truckload of gifts for the soon-to-be new arrival. Susan Nash was the inspired organizer of the generous event.

STACIA RAYMOND:

Donovan's such a talented great girl; the first time I met her was at Django's baby shower at Nash's. He wasn't born yet and that was quite a moment. Oh boy, that day. It was a pretty spectacular event. I came away just reeling, especially from meeting a sibling and we had instantly kind of hit it off, but there were people watching so it was a little strange. The thing that was cool about it is that even though Donovan had grown up around all that, she felt just as awkward as we did, in that setting. Like the three of us—I had Grace with me—we would have been just as happy to leave and go somewhere else to talk.

Even James hadn't been exposed to that many famous musicians all in one place. I almost fainted and fell in the pool at one point after I saw Jackson Browne and Michael McDonald. I'm not starstruck; it was just that I love both of those artists so much, it was too much for me to be in a casual setting with them. Where do you even begin? How do you start a conversation? There was also this thread with all the extended family that I've met, an instant welcoming—especially with Betty. I just love her to death. She's sharp as a tack and just has the greatest stories and makes me feel like I was there. She fills in the other parts that Crosby doesn't.

Betty Crosby is David's stepmother, who was seventy-seven at the time. A former script supervisor on films, she met David's father, Floyd, on the set of a film on which they were both working. She keeps contact with her ever-increasing family circle. Shortly after the shower, Django was born; after that, another blessed event followed, an unexpected gift that finally lifted the huge financial burden that had been crushing the Crosbys.

Eleven

SILVER LININGS

FADE IN:

INTERIOR — LAW OFFICE — DAY

There was one benefit from my motorcycle accident four years earlier—though it was hard to see the silver lining at first. In the crash I suffered multiple fractures, dislocations, and orthopedic trauma of all sorts, and spent a long time in the hospital at Cedars. Make no mistake, I had damages: not only the medical and recovery expenses, but a missed opportunity to tour in which I lost almost a year's income—all because a carburetor stuck wide open on the motorcycle. It was a Japanese Mikuni, and I sued Mikuni with the help of Buddy Herzog, a top litigator, the former president of the Consumers Attorneys of California, and a specialist in personal-injury torts and product liability.

As we learned, we had a strong case. The problems of hooking a Mikuni carburetor to a Harley were common knowledge in the biker community, sort of a dirty little secret. You can go online now and find dozens of articles about how to make them work together. Our consultant was a guy who had written the Mikuni manual in English, and he had told them that the model of carburetor I had *stuck*. He told them they ought to do a re-call, and they didn't; it was all documented. When Buddy Herzog got a look at that information, he became a very tough customer. I'm sure we could have won a huge amount at trial, but lawyers prefer a settlement, which can be controlled. In a trial, you surrender control to judge and jury.

BILL SIDDONS:

The lawyer I found for Crosby won a million and a half dollars or something, on which, by the way, I didn't get the commission, even though I did all the fucking work for the trial.

Debbie Meister was working in the office. She was the one who had to haul out all the old contracts and the offers for the cancelled dates. The good thing about proving damages is showing exact figures for financial loss. With salaried people who miss work, it's easy: you just multiply the weeks out sick by the wages and you have a total. With artists, it's more difficult—who's to say how much you could have written or performed, or what income you missed from lost creative opportunities? In my case, we had hard numbers from tour promoters, advances, all kinds of paperwork showing what that accident cost me in actual dollars.

Faced with the paperwork and their alleged negligence—their failure to resolve the mechanical carburetor problems and recall defective units—Mikuni eventually settled for a million-two. I took that money and paid the IRS, the State Franchise Tax Board, and my lawyer's fee. There was nothing left, of course, but we were at least solvent and out from under the gun, and I could resume earning without the tax collectors haunting the box office or trying to repossess my liver. Most of all, I could revel in the care and nurturing of our baby boy.

Django, all the way along, since he was born, has been the kind of kid that prompts you to ask, "Jesus, how do you get one of those?" Everyone says they love children. Well, people who love all children obviously haven't had much experience with children. Children are just like the rest of the human race, there are some great ones and there are some not-so-great ones. Django, from the beginning, was a happy kid. It was in him to be happy. He also had love poured over him by the bucketload from the day he got here. Still does, and I believe he deserves it. But his early days, as a child, he was just the sweetest, best little kid that you could ever hope for in a million years.

Just hanging on to Django is like trying to ride a tiger because he's smarter at eleven than I was at nineteen. He's gotten so much more information because kids do have more information thrown at them than they used to. He's brilliant, and he doesn't do mean things. I've never seen him be mean to another kid, and he doesn't lie to me. He's honest and I'm so over the top in love with him that I can't really talk about him without sounding like a complete fool.

One could assume that Django, the only offspring of an older couple, would be a spoiled child of privilege. One would be wrong. He attends a good local private school, works with his father on projects around the house, and poses no discipline problems. On tour as a primary-school kid, he pedaled his Big Wheel happily through the cavernous corridors of arenas where his father was playing, and delighted in piloting remote-control cars around the tour buses and trucks in parking lots across the country. He's never been spoken to in baby talk; from the beginning his parents addressed him as an adult, which leads him to preternaturally mature speech for a kid of his age. He also favors tacos and pizza and spaghetti like other eleven-year-olds and is comfortable ordering them in any restaurant, even when he's the only kid at the table. And, much like his father, he's happy behind the wheel of any vehicle he can drive.

Django Crosby:

I've got the best parents in the world. For me. Other kids' parents are good, and they're probably the best to them. Every person has their own perception of the best. It's very different for different people. My mom and dad are very kind, very loving, and always there for me when I get hurt or something happens to me. We have a riverbed nearby and my dad and I go down there and pick up rocks. We have a Gator, and a Quad. The Gator is a four- or six-wheel vehicle made by John Deere. It's usually a farm vehicle but you can make it be anything you want, whereas the Quad is a four-wheel ATV and a farm vehicle, but you can make it be anything. It can also be a race vehicle and a lot of other things. They come in very different weights and sizes and strengths and engine sizes. Mine is more of a working Quad rather than a racing Quad, designed to allow you to load stuff up on the back and the front, and have a trailer on it.

David and Django personally collected several tons of river rock over a period of months, which were used to construct a massive bedroom fireplace in the Crosby home. They did it without mishap. Asked how they stayed safe, Django offered this advice:

DJANGO:

Don't go too fast. Don't go like maximum speed. . . . I love cars. When I was a little kid I loved to play with them. I played with Hot Wheels and I would get tracks and I would make them fly all over the place. I would have so much fun with them.

David is rebuilding a vintage sixties muscle car, a Shelby Mustang. Django's part of the process. They'll be getting their hands dirty together, and in time Django will be driving grown-up vehicles. I think he'll be a careful driver, if only because his father's vehicular history is a classic of impetuous and impulsive (albeit skillful) driving: boats, cars, motorcycles, and even a turn at the wheel of the Goodyear blimp, the airship America. *That was in the bad old days.*

FLASHBACK:

Twelve

OLD TIMES, HARD TIMES,
GOOD TIMES

EXTERIOR OF HUNTSVILLE PRISON, TEXAS, 1986 — DAY

I stepped into the sunlight, short-haired, overweight, and without a mustache—no facial hair allowed inside, by order of the Texas Department of Corrections. I was on my way to a halfway house in Houston after a year in incarceration, most of which was at the Texas State Prison in Huntsville, the result of an arrest for possession of a firearm in a licensed premises. And drugs. They take the Old West "no guns in saloons" thing seriously in Texas. I went into jail an addict and a fugitive from justice, having reached the lowest point of my life in 1985, when Jan and I fled California to avoid a "show cause" hearing in Dallas for violating the terms of my appeal bond.

Crosby had been arrested in Dallas in 1983, while playing for drug money as a solo act with a backup band in a cheesy nightclub called Cardi's. His association with Stills and Nash had been suspended in 1984 (if not ended) when his recurrent substance-abuse problems strained their creative relationship to breaking point, and he had written no new music in several years. Jan was equally devastated by her helpless codependency with David, addicted and isolated. Tried and convicted, he was out on probation while his case wound its way through the appeals process. For the next two years, David stayed out on an appeal bond, which he repeatedly violated. The Dallas district attorney stayed in touch with the authorities in Marin County, where David and Jan lived like rats under siege in his rapidly decaying house. Jan was arrested a year or so later on similar charges during a CSN tour. It happened on a plane in Kansas City, Missouri, when she took responsibility for a handgun and some cocaine in luggage that David asked her to bring on the plane after it had been loaded as checked baggage. It was a federal offense, and in exchange for a guilty plea, a judge imposed a harsh five-year probation, which included the absolute condition that she not see or associate with David Crosby.

The judge in Kansas City was punishing Jan for what he saw as Jan's lying to protect me, which is what she did, although the charges never officially acknowledged that. It's an indication of how low I had sunk that I could leave her in jail in Kansas City while I continued on the tour, getting high. I'm not proud of that period in my life, and it's painful to recall it now. We were both subject to the terms of our probation and appeals, and I kept fucking up. I'd get busted in Marin for some drugs or weapons or traffic offense, at the same time I was ducking in and out of drug rehab and treatment facilities, having promised the Dallas judge on every occasion that I was working on my recovery and trying to turn my life around. It was bullshit; I was helpless, hopelessly addicted.

Finally, Judge Pat McDowell in Dallas ordered a "show cause" hearing at which I was supposed to explain why I should not be incarcerated for repeatedly violating the terms of my bond. I knew that once I walked into that courtroom through the big doors in front, the only way I'd leave was through the little door in back—in handcuffs, remanded to custody. So I just didn't show.

Instead, David sold his last remaining possession of value, a grand piano. Using the money to pay some outlaw biker/dealers, he bought enough drugs to last the journey as he fled in a small plane that hopped across the country. He was fleeing to Florida, where he and Jan had fantasies of boarding the Mayan *and sailing to some Latin American country without an extradition treaty. Of course, as soon as the crew saw them, they fled. Nobody wanted to be around when the FBI showed up with a fugitive warrant. The boat was an unseaworthy shambles, stripped of necessities that had been sold by the unpaid skipper and crew to sustain themselves in the absence of any pay from the absentee owner. The crew who'd jumped ship would occasionally drop by with a pizza or some takeout burgers to feed Jan and David, who were running out of money, drugs, and hope.*

That was the bottom. I turned myself in, was extradited to Texas, and forced into withdrawal—cold turkey—in a Dallas County jail cell where I was in solitary confinement for months. The sheriff would maintain that this was for my own good, because who could tell what terrible thing might occur if a well-known rock musician mingled with the inmates in a normal incarceration. If anything happened to me, it would attract attention, and if there's anything that jailers and prison wardens don't need or want, it's public or media attention of any kind. So there I was, in "administrative segregation," which is the bullshit jailhouse euphemism for solitary confinement, alone in a cell, 24/7, with the lights on all the time, and no exercise or fresh air.

Jan, strung out as bad as I was, was left in Florida, where she had family. They took her in and helped her get home to California, where she went through withdrawal and recovery while I went through the justice machinery in Texas.

After months in solitary, I formally requested to be moved into "general population," which would mean a transfer from the Lew Sterrett County Jail in downtown Dallas to the state prison in Huntsville. There, I took up residence in the Wynn unit, an old-fashioned brick rotunda with cell blocks radiating from a central tower, a dirt yard with double razorwire fencing, gun towers and a "dead line" (so called because if you cross the line, the guards in the gun towers are authorized to shoot you).

I was assigned a cell and a job making mattresses. There was little in the way of counseling or therapy, and even if I wanted to get high again, nobody would tell a "new fish" like me how or where to score, because they didn't know if I could be trusted, or if I'd been rolled over, or if I'd been promised special treatment in exchange for ratting a fellow inmate. Which was okay with me. There was a gentle evangelical Christian who led a small therapy group. I learned about Alcoholics and Narcotics Anonymous and the twelve-step programs, and even joined the prison band.

After a year in various confinements, I was released on good behavior, not because I was that good, but because the Texas system was overcrowded and they were discharging the people who hadn't murdered anyone. I was released to a halfway house in Houston. A few weeks later, who should come through on a tour but my pal Graham Nash, playing a show at a local club called Rockefeller's.

GRAHAM NASH:

David is standing at the airport waiting . . . We're having a good time and he knows I'm playing a show, he knows I'm going to ask him, so we just sang a couple of things. I was doing two shows that night. It was the "Ménage à Tech" tour. At one point in the show I was doing "Wind on the Water," which begins with "Critical Mass," during which I'd take the lights down and play it in the darkness, then fade up the blue lights when we hit the down chord of "Wind on the Water." During "Critical Mass," which is David's composition, he opens the curtain and walks out. The place went bananas and we did a great show. David had that same fire that I'd loved him for in the past and he wanted to be there. You couldn't get him offstage—he was bathing in the adulation, he was loving the spotlight, he was singing with his friend. He'd done his time, he was clean, he was straight. It was a momentous night.

The friends and fans out there who obsessively collect our material have a recording that circulates in the trading community from the show we did at Rockefeller's in Houston on August 21, 1986. Was that a joy! The first show I did after I got out, the first public appearance outside the bars, the first time that there was an audience that wasn't composed of inmates, and the first time that I played with anything except the prison band for over a year. Nash knew he was going on tour right then, and he made sure that he had a date near where I'd be when I got out. When I got onstage, he says, "I've got a surprise for you all. Direct from the Texas Department of Corrections here's . . . David Crosby." They went crazy and we sang "Wind on the Water." It was spectacular to be singing with him again.

You have to understand, if you're a harmony singer or a guy who loved the Everly Brothers and that kind of thing, singing with Graham Nash is heaven on earth. I believe he's one of the best human beings alive, and he's definitely the best harmony singer. I tell people that I am, but I can confess here that it's him. That night in Houston, I was free. I was clean and sober onstage for the first time in twenty-five years. I was able to think, and I was in front of a microphone again, singing with Graham Nash. That's as close as I can get to heaven on earth; it reaffirmed my absolute devotion to playing music, and got me higher than any drug ever did, or ever will.

By all accounts it was a magical evening, and the number of people who swear they were there is about ten times the capacity of the hall. Great performances tend to attract impossibly huge audiences after the fact, because fans and friends passionately wish they could have shared the experience. "I should have been there, so I was" is the adjustment the mind makes as it implants a benign false memory of a treasured moment that it covets. Soon after Houston, David was back in Los Angeles, resuming his life as a singer, songwriter, and performer.

MONTAGE: CATCHING UP, 1986–1991

One of the first shows I did after being free to leave Texas was opening for the Grateful Dead at their annual New Year's Eve show in Oakland. It was the late Bill Graham's tradition to join the band onstage at the New Year countdown, usually in some outrageous costume or making a spectacular entrance. This particular year [1986] he flew in from the rafters over the arena, suspended on wires, dressed in a complete American eagle costume, descending from the heavens to the stage while a psychedelicized audience watched in stunned, stoned disbelief. There's a picture of us together commemorating that moment, so I know I didn't imagine it, and I know I wasn't high at the time. Jerry Garcia helped get me the gig, for which I'm eternally grateful.

I was there, and it was a memorable night. Joel Bernstein, a photographer and archivist—an intimate associate of David, as well as of Joni Mitchell, Neil Young, Bob Dylan, Bruce Springsteen, Stephen Stills, Graham Nash, Prince, Jackson Browne, Laura Nyro, and many others— was also there. Joel's been a close friend and musical collaborator, playing and singing on albums. His work as a photographer and archivist is included in the permanent collection of the Rock and Roll Hall of Fame and Museum, and he continues with these artists as archivist, editor, and pro-

ducer of their CD boxed sets and DVD retrospectives. The San Francisco Chronicle said Joel's multi-CD boxed sets of the work of Neil Young and a history of his sixties band, the Buffalo Springfield, set "new standards of excellence for archival CD releases." His work on these authoritative collections continues. He's working on the Crosby material now. As we say in the vernacular, Joel knows his shit.

JOEL BERNSTEIN:

I was at the bottom of the stairs leading up to the stage at the end of David's set, and toward the end of the set, Jerry Garcia, who had at that point survived his own near-death experience, his various addictions, who had edema, had heart failure and all the things that happened at once, came to where I was standing, waiting for David to come down after his set. David came down the stairs, Jerry came up to him, and they looked at each other. They hadn't seen each other in years . . . to my knowledge this was their first encounter after David had actually gone through everything that he did. He got to the bottom of the stairs and they hugged each other—which they could barely do because their stomachs were large at that point, each one was reaching out to get the other guy's shoulder, and they hugged each other like . . . survivors, as if to say, "My God, you lived!" It was very moving . . . one of those down-to-the-core moments of life.

A few years after that memorable meeting, I had occasion to talk with Jerry about his history with David, and his feelings about Crosby's rehabilitation and recovery.

JERRY GARCIA:

When David [first started visiting] our place in Ashbury Street [in the sixties and seventies], he was like visiting royalty. He carries his royalness with him. . . . He'd have all kinds of wonderful treasures to show you and he's always been sort of a patron-of-the-arts kind of guy. He always had good stuff. Knives, belt buckles, beautiful work he would love to show you and turn you on to. When David came around, it was always like a cause to celebrate—royalty's in town, break out the cookies. I've always had a lot of affection for him. He's one of those guys that I really love and it's great to see him doing so well.

If I had to elect one musician to represent musicians in the Galactic Congress of Beings, it would be Jerry Garcia. He didn't just tell you what he learned from somebody else, he had his own thoughts about everything, and it was his original concept. Musically, it was a fresh synthesis of everything he had listened to. And he was brilliant. There's never been another guitar player like him and there probably never will be. I've never even heard anybody who can copy him. They can imitate his technique, they can imitate his sound, they can imitate his guitar, that clean-sounding guitar instead of the raspy way that everybody else plays. But they don't have his head. That cat was spacious. He had the big head; there were some big thoughts going on there.

For me, Jerry Garcia's greatest support was all the time he spent in the studio with me making *If I Could Only Remember My Name* in 1970. He was there almost every night, a wonderful friend to me, and at that particular time I was very shaky. I'd just lost [my girlfriend] Christine Hinton, [in a car crash] and I didn't know quite what to do with myself. The only place I felt safe was in the studio; it was the only place I could still function. Jerry was there for me, time and time again. He was just wonderful. I never needed to return the favor, he never asked me. Jerry had his own band to play with, but we did a number of gigs, with Phil Lesh on bass and Bill Kreutzmann on drums, and there are some cherished tapes floating around somewhere of a band with two names, depending on who got to the microphone first. It was either Jerry and the Jerks, or David and the Dorks, and it was fun.

Jerry Garcia died in August 1995, while in a residential treatment facility where he was addressing serious health issues, many of which were related to or exacerbated by substance abuse. The musical spark between David and Jerry lives on in a song called "Kids and Dogs," a playful, engaging tune recorded by Crosby and Garcia in San Francisco in 1970, when If I Could Only Remember My Name *was being made. A dedicated fan and friend, Steve Silberman of* Wired *magazine, kept after David for years to include it on a record, and it will be part of the soon-to-be-released boxed set produced by master archivist Joel Bernstein. It was a more innocent (if not drug-free) time. Felicitous collaborations of surprising quality have always defined and informed David's music; his career has been a history of involvement with leading figures in popular music for the last half century.*

In the summer of 1987—a year after David's release from prison—Crosby, Stills, and Nash toured the United States and made more money than they'd ever before earned as a group. Without having a current hit record, they sold out almost every venue. The tour was economical, David put aside money to help repay old debts and settle outstanding claims by the IRS for taxes delinquent during the jail years. Everywhere they played, reviews and audience response were satisfying, encouraging, and approving. At the conclusion of the tour, there was an added bonus: on November 11, 1987, the Texas Supreme Court sustained Crosby's appeal, and concluded that the original search and seizure of his dressing room at Cardi's in Dallas was illegal. That destroyed the Dallas DA's evidence and David's conviction was finally overturned by the highest court in the state of Texas. The time he spent incarcerated was punishment enough for all the bond violations and flight to avoid prosecution, but the legal basis for the jail sentence was gone. He was no longer a felon.

What basically happened with Crosby, Stills, and Nash was that we didn't talk about what happened to me. We got on with it. Nash was terrifically supportive, I was straight and going to meetings, and Stills was

Stills, and we knew what to do. It's an old and well-oiled machine. We got the band on the road and it worked. Then a really interesting thing happened. While I was in the depths of my mess, Neil offered me a place to stay, a minder, and a refuge to get straight. He said, "Come to my place, I know you're scared to go to the hospital. I've got a cabin where you can stay. I'll stock it with food and I'll hire Smokey [Wendell] to watch you and you can be there, you can go for long walks, you can eat, read books. You just can't take drugs. And if you can stay straight for a year, I'll make a record with you." Shortly thereafter, I went to prison, and never took him up on his kind offer.

Then, after I'd been straight for a year, Neil called up and honored his promise. With no instigation, no pressure on my side at all, he just called up and said, "Okay, let's do it," and we made *American Dream*. It wasn't an easy album; Stills was toasted and didn't have songs, but Neil wasn't toasted and he had songs, and so did Nash and I. It was very cool of Neil to do it, and I still ask myself why anybody would be in a band with Stills if they didn't have to. This summer, as I write this, I think I have an answer: when we do a killer show together, it pulls Stephen out of his shell and up to being the guy that we loved and the guy who can really play like that. We just did a show at Red Rocks in Denver and it was one of the best we've ever done. Much more about that show later. Stills played unbelievably well. Oh, man, was Stephen happy. He's got his bro's—he's back to feeling like we're his friends, so he's all of a sudden feeling strong and he played like it in Denver. Neil walked up to him afterward and whispered, "Man, you played some shit."

Returning to that winter of '86–'87, I played concerts and benefits as a solo artist, in duet with Graham Nash, in trio with Crosby, Stills, and Nash, and the quartet: Crosby, Stills, Nash, and Young. We did a Greenpeace benefit in Santa Barbara in 1987 that reunited Crosby, Stills, Nash, and Young. It was joy to play with everyone again, even if only for a single show, and it hinted at the potential we had. I recorded a solo album for A&M Records, including songs I wrote in prison and after, and completed a brand-new CSNY album that we recorded at Neil's ranch. And back in '87 and '88, my autobiography *Long Time Gone* was written, reexamining the darkest and highest moments of my life.

There was more: in October 1986, the group had done the first benefit for the Bridge School, a school for kids with special needs in the Bay Area. It's a favorite charity of Neil's, whose son has cerebral palsy. The concert is devoted to acoustic music and it's gone on to become one of the most prestigious and musically powerful annual events in the business. There were Byrds reunion concerts with McGuinn and Hillman. The American Dream *album, released in 1988, was a much-awaited reunion of Crosby, Stills, Nash & Young. It went to number sixteen on the* Billboard *charts. David's solo album, entitled* Oh Yes, I Can, *came out a few months later in 1989. David sang and recorded "Another Day in Paradise" with Phil Collins, getting significant airplay and video exposure. David went out on a lecture tour on university campuses.*

In May of 1988, Jan got a letter from Kansas, officially releasing her from further probation, and on June 13, 1988, the Supreme Court of the United States denied a petition for a writ of certiorari from the Dallas County district attorney, who carried his failed case all the way to the top, trying to keep my conviction on the books. He lost, although I don't know if this court, with new Bush appointees Chief Justice Roberts and Associate Justice Alito, would reach the same decision. Nevertheless, the decision of the Texas Supreme Court stood, and stands to this day: my conviction's overturned, and the lower court was directed to find the defendant (me) not guilty. Even though I served hard time, I don't regret a minute of it. I don't recommend it as a way to get sober—it's a painful process—but it sure as hell worked for me.

From the time we reunited after prison until my motorcycle accident, life was good, and even after the accident, wired and plastered, once I was home and relatively mobile again, it wasn't bad. CSNY played benefits together again over the next dozen years, but never touring as a band, although rumors circulated almost every season. It was Crosby, Stills, and Nash that went out in the summertime, year after year, and we kept recording, as a group, as individuals, and as a duo (me and Nash).

As this is written, Crosby, Stills, Nash, and Young are playing a large-scale national tour; the wheel is rolling forward again. Concurrently, Neil's album Living With War *is raising consciousness and controversy. Songs like "Let's Impeach the President" join "Night of the Generals," "They Want It All," "Ohio," and "Military Madness" as quintessential CSNY material that speaks to our times. A boxed set of David's life work is due soon from Rhino Records.*

DISSOLVE TO:

EXTERIORS — SCIENCE OF LIFE CHURCH; NASH RESIDENCE, ENCINO — DAY

May 17, 1987, was a typically hot and sunny Southern California day, and for the only time in my life I was wearing a cutaway formal coat, striped trousers, a vest, wing collar, and spats. Okay, not spats. But I was in the most uncomfortable clothes of my life, with the possible exception of the too-tight orange jailhouse suicide-watch Velcro-and-polyester jumpsuit and slippers I'd worn a year earlier. Jan and I were at the Church of Religious Science on Sunset Boulevard in Hollywood, in front of friends and family, feeling fully dressed and formally committing to each other by law and custom. We weren't alone. Standing next to us, equally formal, were Graham and Susan Nash, who chose to renew their vows on the occasion of their tenth anniversary. The brides carried bouquets, and there were press cameras and television reporters covering the event out front.

Jan and I reunited after each of us cleaned up. We'd overcome some obstacles, including the ruling of the Kansas judge who allowed Jan to go free on the condition that she not see me for five years. Joe Brandenberg, a sympathetic official and a reasonable parole officer, made it possible for us to reconnect as soon as we could. I was totally delighted to see how Jan had blossomed and grown after enduring her own recovery process, months spent in halfway houses and intensive counseling and therapy. We literally glowed when we saw each other, and immediately became once again inseparable, recovering together from the hell we had endured separately.

I don't remember much advice from my parents on how to live my life, but I do recall one very important, positive piece of information I got from my mother, when I was young and asking about love and marriage. She said, quite simply, "Find someone you can make happy," and I thought she'd gotten it backwards. "No," I said, "you mean someone who makes *me* happy," and she quite clearly answered: "No, your greatest happiness will be that you are able to make someone happy." Half a century later, I am convinced she was as right as rain. It's such a wise and true thing; she couldn't have given me a more valuable gift. I've come to understand it's absolutely so.

Getting legally joined was the next logical step. We talked about it, and once I said the "M" word and I saw the look on Jan's face, I realized how lucky I was. The thought in my head, spelled out, was, "This woman is totally in love with me, I'm totally in love with her, she's one of the nicest human beings I've ever met in my whole life, we are incredibly happy together, I don't want to be with anyone else. Why not just go ahead and do it?" So one night when we were lying in bed, I said, "Hey, Jan," and she said "Yeah?" and I said, "Let's get married," and she screamed.

At this point on the original tape of our conversation, there's a very convincing Crosby impression of a woman screaming, and the tape tran-

scription bears the notation "SFX—SCREAM." No verbal re-creation will do justice to the moment.

It is one of the greatest joys of my life that I can make Jan happy. Marrying her is one of the smartest things I ever did. She's a fantastic woman; I'm incredibly lucky to be with her. I don't think she would have left me if we didn't get married, but I'm glad we formalized the arrangement. I couldn't be happier about it, and we both believe it saved our lives. "Even when David and I weren't married on paper, we were married in our spirit and in our hearts," Jan says.

Ultimately, the wedding was wonderful. The part everyone remembers was when Jan and I and Susan and Graham simultaneously jumped in the pool in the middle of the reception at Graham's house. Essentially, it was because we were bored with just walking around sweating in the heat and we were being silly when we did it, but if you look at it as leaping off the cliff, it's like a great song that Roger McGuinn wrote called "5D" where he sings about that sensation, and suggests that you can still be still floating and never hit bottom. "Keep falling through, just relaxed and paying attention . . ." Jumping off the cliff into life and trusting and grabbing your loved one's hand, you're taking a leap of faith, believing there is something on the other side of the jump. Surprisingly and joyfully, there was!

GRAHAM NASH:

I thought there was an interesting point in that. To me, it wasn't just the joke of, "Okay, let's just jump into the pool as a foursome, as we just got remarried," there was a certain baptismal feeling to me. I'm not a pool lover, I'm not an ocean lover, and I would have loved to stand on the side and watch it, but that moment had its own agenda and I'm not sure I'm brave enough to figure it all out yet. When I jumped into that pool with Susan, it embodied the spirit of "Let's just forget everything in the past and move forward in the future, from now."

David's expressed this spirit of curiosity and adventure in these lyrics:

RUSTY AND BLUE

How can I sweep these words into a cluster
Put 'em in a pile like feathers on your floor?
Voyages and sea forests deep blue and rusty
Sew 'em in a satchel 'n leave 'em at your door

People's lives, people whose lives
They fascinate me
All my life, all my life
I've wanted to understand

There's a man on the corner he's got the moon in his eyes
He just comes here to visit and he wears a disguise
And I wonder if he's looking for friends or for truth
I think he's calling for some in that telephone booth

And the smiling woman answers
She defeats fear with her eyes
She thinks life's fine so I think she's wise
And my heart wants to give her a gift so grand
That it will speak for me and tell her just where I stand

And I stand on a pillar and it's melting like ice
Of years that I've lived and some I've lived twice
And I have all these feathers and leaves on my floor
That I don't want just blowing around loose anymore

And I feel a need to gather, to rummage and fetch
To shake out my life and give it a stretch
To bring shells to the surface, give 'em to you
Gifts from the sea floor rusty and blue

Now these two lives hold my attention quite well
You see lives almost never run parallel
Like the boards in the flooring all deep grained and worn
Fated and fitted long before we were born

People's lives, people whose lives
They fascinate me
All my life, all my life
I've wanted to understand
Understand

DISSOLVE TO:

Thirteen

OUR TRIBE INCREASES

My family has become my life. Jan was always a large part of it, ever since we teamed up, but it's a much larger enterprise now. A quick preview of loved ones who'll be appearing (or reappearing) in later scenes of the movie of my life: my son Django; my daughter Donovan; my adult son James and his wife, Stacia, and their daughter, Grace; another adult daughter, Erika, and her husband, Alex; and their three kids, Roberta, Jorge, and Alexa; and two children—Bailey and Beckett—born to Melissa Etheridge and her then partner, Julie Cypher. Six (count 'em) children of whom I'm the biological father, and four grandchildren. At this writing, that's my "whole family," but that's a flexible concept, and I'm prepared to revise the total upward.

I've learned to become Jan's partner and brought myself to a place where I don't just make a decision and say, "That's how it is, because I say it's that way." Most of my adult life was organized around the principle that "Dave's the boss." I'd lean that way even when I was supposed to be in cooperative situations, or when I was involved in an intense collaboration, as in my music and my marriage. My decision-making process has improved a great deal because it's shared with Jan, because she's bright, because she's got another point of view about things, and because we've worked at this relationship.

This is a pearl beyond price. It's survived hell and high water and we've worked at it, put effort into it and spent time with a counselor when it wasn't working. This may be basic Marriage 101, but the success comes from talking and listening. That's something I still haven't learned. I don't listen properly. I'll interrupt: "You've already said that. I know that." Then I'll see that Jan's hurt, and I'll realize I've screwed up again. If I have the presence of mind, I back it up, rewind, and apologize. "I did it again and I'm sorry, that was wrong . . . would you do me the favor of going back over it again, because I didn't give it full weight, and you have something you need to tell me."

That's an effort, and it wasn't an easy lesson to learn, but a really good relationship doesn't work without it. The truth is, I'll do anything to continue to make this work as well as it's been doing. I'm there for the rest of my life, and happy about it. As I've said before, it's not just about being happy, it's also about making someone else happy.

The lesson was a long time coming. David was a rebellious kid who came of age in the Eisenhower years. His childhood was spent in a classic fifties nuclear family, and although his father worked in the film industry, it was a more ordered existence in those days. David went to private school and public school, and eventually went on the road. He had his first hit record in his mid-twenties. Floyd Crosby went to work at the studios while his wife, Aliph, stayed home with the two boys in post–World War II Los Angeles, on the west side, near the new UCLA campus in Westwood. The older son, Floyd, Jr., went informally by the name Chip and later called himself Ethan, which is how most people knew him. He was something of a loner who enjoyed camping in the woods and played guitar. He had his father's lean build. David was the younger son, chubby-cheeked as a toddler, and favoring his mother's side of the family. The brothers played

music together, and Floyd and Aliph held the values of their eastern aris-
tocratic upbringing. Despite their long residence in California, where
Floyd had followed employment in his chosen profession, both families had
bloodlines straight back to the seventeenth-century colonials who founded
America. Some of the Dutch and English settlers whose names appear in
David's ancestral family tree are Van Rensselaer, Van Cortlandt, Delafield,
Crosby, Floyd, Van Schoonhoven, and Whitehead (Aliph was born Aliph
Van Cortlandt Whitehead). The Crosbys moved from LA to the Santa
Barbara area, where David attended an exclusive prep school (Cate), and
less exclusive public high schools in Carpinteria and Santa Barbara. Ethan
taught David how to play guitar and they worked together in informal
jazz and folk groups before David (the more gregarious and social of the
two) began working solo. Interviewed in 1987, Ethan said:

ETHAN CROSBY:

There's one thing that I remember that has been in my mind that I
wanted to make sure that you got on the tape about our upbringing
that may explain partially why he strives so hard, and that is—he always ended up with the second best. He always had the room that
wasn't the groovy room. That was important. In two houses, man, that
was the case, two houses we built, the one in Westwood and the one
in Carpinteria. I mean, at the time, great, man, I'll take the good
room—but [David] was always in that position. Looking back on it
now, hey, that sucked but that's the way it was. He's a Leo with Aries
rising and he just can't not have a big ego trip going. . . . I was always
ahead of him and better than he was, and I was always a better musician, and I doubt if that's true now, but that was the case. . . . I may
not have been famous but I still played better.

While David pursued a career in music, Ethan chose a more solitary route
living as a drifter and woodsman, first in the ridges above Big Sur and
later on Mount Shasta, subsisting on odd jobs and whatever money David

or his father would send. That support varied; some years it would be a regular cash allowance and a new Toyota Land Cruiser, other years a secondhand VW bus and intermittent small checks.

The family structure disintegrated when Floyd left Aliph for another woman, a vivacious script supervisor and native Californian named Betty Cormack. Floyd and Betty married soon after, leaving Aliph to raise the boys. A poignant verse from David's song "Carry Me" recalls Aliph's passing from cancer in 1973 at age sixty-seven.

And then there was my mother
she was lying in white sheets there and she was waiting to die
She said, If you'd just reach underneath this bed
and untie these weights, I could surely fly.
She's still smiling but she's tired,
she'd like to hear that last bell ring
You know if she still could, she would stand up,
and she could sing, sing
Carry me, carry me, carry me above the world
Carry me, carry me, carry me.

Brin Luther is David's first cousin once removed: her grandmother was David's mother's sister. Brin lived in the Bay Area during the eighties and knew Crosby through intermediaries. Later, they became more closely acquainted.

BRIN LUTHER:

I was curious about my mother's family because my mother died of cancer when I was a teenager, like David's mother. . . . I think it's just a fundamental curiosity to know both sides of your family. My mother would explain, "We were not all Tories," and my father would say, "You sure were." He was a Crocker. Eventually they were the Crocker Bank but the East Coast Crockers came over in 1620. My mom was always proud of David and she was devoted to Aunt Aliph, his mother. When Aunt Aliph was calling, Mom would say, "Ducky, come to the phone, you have to talk to your aunt Aliph," and I'd wonder, "Who's Aunt Aliph?" but I'd get on the phone and this sweet, lovely woman would talk to me. The women in the family were very connected. Unfortunately they just died, both Aliph and my mother. Until that point, all of the families were still connected and then all of a sudden, there was kind of a dial tone on the phone. It was over.

Betty Crosby, David's stepmother, is now eighty-seven and thriving. She lives comfortably alone in the hillside home in Ojai she shared with Floyd. Floyd died in 1985, so she's now the last link to David's youth, the vanished world of Hollywood and old Santa Barbara.

BETTY CORMACK CROSBY:
Floyd and I were married in 1960 . . . he was working with [director] Roger Corman at that time. Floyd felt badly about Ethan because Ethan had a very pretty voice and was a good musician, but never wanted to compete. He didn't have the fire in the belly that David had for his music. . . . When David was flying high later on, whenever we stopped at a gas station where a young boy was working, Floyd would get out and say, "Do you ever listen to rock and roll?" The kid would look at him, "What's with you?" of course, and Floyd would say, "Ever heard of Crosby, Stills, and Nash?" And the kid would say, "Yeah," and Floyd would say, "Well, that's my son." Honest to God, it was embarrassing. But he was so proud of David and so happy for him.

My father died before I went to prison. We were never close—he wasn't an easy guy to know, and he kept a lot inside. He was proud of me, but he watched me slide as he got closer to the end of his life, and it's one of my great regrets that he didn't live to see me free from drugs, married, and with a family of my own.

BETTY CROSBY:

Today I am so proud of Dave and Jan, what they've done and how hard it has been to get everything together, what with David having a liver transplant and thinking he was going to die. But having Django, that adorable child, it's just done everything in the world for them.

When I act like an idiot, the world calls me on it. I'm quite literally a serious case of arrested development. During the drug years, I was so deep into it that I don't think I grew much; I stayed pretty much the same. My values stayed the same, my ability to deal with reality stayed the same, and that often meant I simply didn't deal with it. I had only a modicum of responsibility. However, when Debbie was pregnant, I got my act together and when Donovan was born, I was in the room; I caught the baby and cut the umbilical cord. I couldn't have been more present.

At the time Donovan Anne Crosby was born in 1975, David was trying to be an exemplary unmarried expectant father; he reduced his drug intake, attended childbirth classes with Debbie Donovan, and did his share of domestic chores after the baby was born. Soon after, he returned to freebasing cocaine and spending time with other women, while Debbie went on as a single mother, overcoming all obstacles and raising her daughter without turning her against David. Interviewed in 1987, she recalled the baby years:

DEBBIE DONOVAN:

I could not have made that delivery [natural childbirth] the way that I did if it hadn't have been for David . . . [Later] he would come to visit and see the baby and his stories would change from whenever he would be straight or whenever he would be high. I remember that he would say that as soon as the freebasing would stop, that we would get back together again. Because he wanted to have a family and he wanted to raise Donovan, that kept me going for a very long time. When he came here he wanted Donovan to believe that we lived together. That whenever Daddy would be gone, it was because he was on the road. He wanted her to believe that she had a daddy and a mommy and that there was a nuclear family. I'd hope that we would get back together at some point, but it just got very, very old and very, very stale for me eventually. [It got to the point] where I'd say, "Donovan, Dad's on television," and she'd say, "Is he arrested again?"

DONOVAN CROSBY:

Sometimes I think adults underestimate how much a two-year-old absorbs. I remember a lot. . . . Yeah, it's helpful to have him [now] as much as it was not helpful to have him for [only] those brief moments in my childhood. [The interviewer comments: "Although he's your father, he's not your parent . . ."] That's a good way of putting it. David's my papa. He's an excellent father when he's in father mode. He's given advice. He's given inspiration. He's been very generous and supportive and he's been my buddy. He and I are kind of like old friends . . . long spans of time can go by and you just pick up wherever it was you left off, and we have more of that kind of relationship than a tight bond—I'd say he's responsible for a few neuroses, [but] he's my papa.

I didn't have much connection to any of that stuff that you associate with being an adult: taking care of your own shit, telling the truth, making a strong effort to act in an honorable fashion. I was chemically asleep, I woke up in jail, and over a period of time recovered the full faculties that I was born with. I may not be the world's brightest guy, but my brain has always functioned pretty well, at least when I wasn't throwing chemicals in its path. My ability to think clearly returned somewhere around 1986.

Alcoholics Anonymous meetings helped. Many people look at the twelve-step program as a set of tools; I think that's a very valid way to look at them—not a set of rules, a set of tools. Obvious, useful tools to deal with life. Be responsible. Suit up and show up. If you say you're going to take responsibility to do something, do it. Start with something simple, help- ing with the coffee for the meeting every week. You've got to do it. It can't be "the dog ate my homework," or "the creek rained out the driveway." You simply have to be there, and those baby steps they teach you to take actu- ally work. Just the simple fact of saying to yourself, "Every Tuesday night at this time I'm going to be in this place." I never did that before in my life. Never. Not since I was in school—even then, I cut classes all the time.

In 1989, David and Jan took a trial run at parental responsibility, open- ing their home to one of Hollywood's most precocious and difficult chil- dren: Drew Barrymore.

We were going to AA meetings three or four times a week and it was working for us. We came to know Betty Wyman, who'd been married to Dallas Taylor, our drummer on an early album. She was working as a counselor specializing in recovery from substance abuse, drugs, and al- cohol. Drew, at that time, was pretty much of a pariah in the film busi- ness, where she'd been working since about the age of five. She started drinking when she was thirteen and wasn't in good shape—she was in a recovery center where Betty was working. I think her insurance was run- ning out, and Betty called me and said, "I don't know what to do. We can't keep her . . . we're going to have to cut this girl loose."

People magazine, in a long cover piece on Drew in January 29, 1990, said she "spent another three months at an unlikely locale—the home of friend David Crosby, the musician of Crosby, Stills, Nash & Young fame, and his wife, Jan Dance, both survivors of their own harrowing odyssey of alcohol and drug abuse." The article also quoted Drew as saying, "Emotionally . . . I hit the biggest bottom ever. Everything just collapsed on me. Everything," and also said she shared "a stormy relationship" with her mother, Jaid.

I said, "If you send her back to her mother, you might as well just cut her head off and put her in a coffin because she's guaranteed to go down the tubes." Drew's mom was probably one of the lamest mothers I've ever encountered. She competed with her daughter for boyfriends, lived on Drew's money, and always wanted more. To compound the problem, John Barrymore, Jr. (her dad) would call up and demand money, take it, and spend it on drugs at a dealer we both knew, an old supplier of mine. It was a complete mess . . . Then Betty said, "I don't have a place where she can go—what about you and Jan?" Boink! The ball's back in my court. I talked to Jandy about it and we agreed she could use a halfway house where there would be some consistency, serenity, even normalcy.

As Todd Gold, Drew's biographer and author of the People *piece, wrote in the article:*

"It was good for Drew," says Wyman, "to be in a more conventional kind of house." She had to adjust to curfews and a set dinnertime. "Drew tests limits," Wyman observes, "but if she sees you're unbending, she conforms to limits very well. My sense is that she thrived and blossomed at Jan and David's in a way I hadn't seen before." Drew's stay with the Crosbys was the first time she had ever been around a strong paternal figure. "At first I didn't know how to deal with it," she recalls. "I wasn't used to having to answer to a man, but eventually it was really great."

Betty Wyman comes from a long line of public-spirited Californians, has a degree in criminology, and learned about addiction and recovery firsthand when she was briefly married to rock and roll drummer (and addict) Dallas Taylor. Taylor got sober, had a liver transplant, and established a new career counseling and treating recovering addicts. Betty does the same sort of work (though unaffiliated with her ex-husband) and she was Drew's counselor at ASAP, the recovery center that treated her.

Absolutely rigorous about maintaining professional confidentiality, she refuses to discuss any current or former client, beyond what was quoted by Gold in his magazine piece. When asked about the broader issue of finding a nurturing environment for any child in a difficult home environment, she had this to say:

BETTY WYMAN:

It's not just Alcoholics Anonymous that has a foundation of supporting those that suffer. I like to believe that the rest of us help friends in other ways, whether that would be taking in a friend's child who was a runaway until they could get their bearings . . . None of it's revolutionary. You always see parents, or friend's parents, who will take in somebody, help somebody, or give the family a time-out. It's not a foreign concept. Maybe the dynamic is too powerful. Maybe someone can't afford treatment as a time-out. The surrogate family might lend support, or a friend might. At the end of the day, it becomes about love and compassion and boundaries, and the ability to set boundaries with love and compassion. Kids will live today with a grandparent or an aunt or uncle, or perhaps switch from one primary custodial parent to another. It's not uncommon.

JAN CROSBY:

We had been interacting with AA. We would talk to kids, tell them our stories, trying to help them understand that [addiction] was a bad choice to make. Drew was in a place where we were speaking and they asked us to befriend her and asked me to sponsor her. I had already figured out at that point that I didn't really want to be a sponsor to anyone yet because I didn't feel I had the confidence to know how to do it. What I wanted to be was her friend. It was like Drew was the parent and her mom was the child and I don't know what all the issues were about and I probably wouldn't say if I did, but I had a feeling that Drew just needed a break from everybody's intensity.

The Crosbys always kept a room in their house for Donovan's occasional visits, although she was away at an eastern boarding school, and otherwise lived with her mother, Debbie, and stepfather, Steve Earle. Donovan would occasionally visit David and Jan. Donovan's room was a perfectly maintained teenage girl's space, light, feminine, crisp, and clean. For the time, it was where Drew Barrymore would be living.

She needed to go to school, come home, do her homework, and not spend all night in a bar, not at age fifteen. She agreed, and came to live with us, right out of treatment. And I think we helped, I'm pretty damn sure we did. We didn't try to be very authoritarian. But we did give her normalcy for a while. It may have been the first time it ever happened for her. I don't think anybody really had hung out with her to that point who wasn't either trying to get in her pants or get her money. We just wanted to help her, pretty unreservedly, without any tricks.

The arrangement lasted for three months. When approached about interviewing Drew for this book, Drew's publicist said simply, "The 'wild child' thing is over; we don't talk about that anymore." However uncooperative her representative may have been, he had one thing right: Drew Barrymore was a wild child. I attended her eleventh birthday party, at a very adult club called Helena's that flourished in the early eighties. Drew had assumed the role of gatekeeper, holding the clipboard at the door, happily piping in an authoritarian child's voice, "You're not on the list, you can't come in" as she turned people away. Nobody guarding the velvet rope anywhere today could improve on her 'tude. This girl became the teenager the Crosbys took with them on their annual Christmas vacation.

JAN CROSBY:
We took her to Hawaii with us for a vacation and I had a beef with her on the island. When we were in the rental house, I had drawn some guidelines that I wanted her to abide by to be a part of the fam-

OUR TRIBE INCREASES

ily, as any teenage daughter would probably have to do—clean her room, not stay out till two or three in the morning smoking joints on the beach with boys, those were my guidelines. And she wouldn't follow any of them. She'd sneak out and do whatever the hell she wanted. She was probably one of the freest birds . . . never knew anything about authority, or anyone controlling her, or doing anything for any parent. Of course, I didn't know this when we took her in, but eventually she went off on me, saying where did I come off thinking I could tell her what to do, I wasn't her mother and I was never going to be her mother and on and on and on. Then she went after David verbally, started to say some not so nice things to him about the whole situation, and that triggered me and I just went off on her.

That's when it ended. I hope that in the long run it was part of her recovery, because she certainly did recover. I told her, straight up, "If you do this, Hollywood will beat a path to your door. You're a brilliant actress." The *People* article quoted me as saying, "It's kind of like watching your baby walk off into traffic, but I have a feeling she'll make it." As it turns out, I was right. She recovered. She got straight. She was so fucking good that she's had a string of pictures ever since, has her own production company, and is doing fantastically well.

Drew runs Flower Films with her partner, Nancy Juvonen; their skill and acumen at picking properties has made them as successful as any independent production team in town, and Drew Barrymore's acting skills are a model for a generation of young leading women and comedians.

DISSOLVE TO:

Fourteen

THE BEGATS

FADE IN:

EXTERIOR — KAUAI, HAWAIIAN ISLANDS, SUMMER 1998 — DAY

Graham Nash has lived in both Los Angeles and Hawaii for decades. The Nashes are settled on the north shore of Kauai (the "Garden Island"), and find it a peaceful, joyful home. The blue skies and world-class surf make Kauai an idyllic place, and the Nashes have deep community ties there. They are also gracious hosts to David and Jan Crosby and good companions to other friends and musicians visiting the island.

One year, Jan and I were on Kauai for the Christmas holidays, visiting the Nashes, as we've done for years. We were enjoying the beach and the perfect weather; Django was a toddler playing in the sand. Did I mention that Django was a spectacular baby, and very happy? When he was born, he did his normal amount of crying, pooping, and peeing in the air—the fountain trick—crawling around and licking the floor and eating his shoe and doing the unsavory, unsanitary things that make parents crazy, but he was fun all the time. The first time he put his arms around me and held on to me, I felt exalted. I felt a level of joy in my life that I had felt only once, when Donovan was born. There is something about having children that is better than anything else in the world. It's just a joy, and Django was a joy to raise. The bittersweet side effect of raising Django was that it made me wish, over and over again, that I had raised my other children somehow. It really pointed out to me how much I had missed by my own stupidity, not realizing how valuable that experience was, and how much fun it was.

Truthfully, raising a child can be the most fun thing on the planet. I'm fond of saying that I thought I had a PhD in fun but I didn't know what real fun was until my kid said "Daddy." Your heart goes right out through your chest. I would look at Django in the middle of us doing something totally joyful and I would think, "Oh, boy, I blew it. I only wish I had done this with James. I wish I had done this with Donovan. I wish I had done this with Erika. I wish . . ."

I try not to spend much time with regret. Regret and guilt are not really very useful. They're learning tools. They're useful while you're learning the lesson but they're really not much use beyond that. One day, I was watching Django while Jan was deep in conversation with two other women, talking about babies and conception and the difficulties of starting a family. The women were Melissa Etheridge and her then life partner, Julie Cypher. Julie was an adopted kid, like my son James, and had been exploring her own background at the same time as she and Melissa were seriously considering parenthood. Dr. Marrs's name came up, along with the great experience and success Jan and I had with his blessed intervention.

The pregnancies of Julie Cypher, as the partner of one of the music industry's most outspoken and visible lesbian performers, were widely publicized and the source of endless speculation in the tabloid press. Julie bore two children within three years, a girl named Bailey Jean, born February 1997, and a boy named Beckett, who was born in November 1998. The identity of the father was kept a secret, and Julie and Melissa were a light-ning rod for media and public attention. Highly visible pioneers in the struggle for gender equality, they were lauded by gay and lesbian parent coalitions and denounced by social conservatives.

JULIE CYPHER:

We were on vacation, [and] we had the same travel agent, who mentioned that David and Jan were going to be there too, so we got in contact with them: "Let's go visit each other because we're all going to be in the same place." They were at the Nashes' place and Django was just nine months old or something, and we were talking about babies and how we wanted to do it and it was important that the father be a known entity. I was adopted and I had a really strong feeling about that. And that's when Jan blurted out, "Well, what about David?" It was so shocking and overwhelming; I would never dare to assume that someone would give such a huge gift, and I wouldn't be capable of it, I don't think. Of course, in the position I'm in now, if David and Jan wanted a baby, I'd be there for them. You betcha. I'll trade back . . .

It was an overwhelming offer and Melissa and I talked about it and I did the research on addiction and how that plays out. If people believe there's a genetic component to addiction, what would that look like? Because my birth father was an alcoholic and, if there's a gene to it, then we'd be creating children that have a potential for it. I don't know if it's nature or nurture, how much of either, or a combination of both—but the heart and soul you see in somebody's eyes far outweighs anything that I would ever read in a book. Even then, it was like, "Yeah, if you're serious?" They were.

Melissa and Julie had decided on the general, but hadn't gotten around to the specific. That meant they were still looking for a sperm donor. I've learned firsthand that there are plenty of people in this country who disapprove of gays and lesbians raising children and who are also arrogant and judgmental enough to think they have the right to prevent it. Some of these people are so square, they have corners. To them, my being the biological father of a lesbian couple's children means that I'm somehow promoting the breakdown of the American family. Of course, I understand that there are people who legitimately question the wisdom of it. Fine, that's their right. But as I see it, their right ends when it becomes more than an opinion. When they try to deny Melissa and Julie's right to be parents or my right to help them realize their dream, that's where I draw the line.

To me it's a no-brainer. If two couples care about each other and one couple wants to help the other couple have kids, why wouldn't they do it? All that matters is that the relationship is a loving one and that it provides a good place to plant the seed of a child. I wasn't trying to make a statement, and neither was Jan. We were following our hearts, and our hearts told us that these were good people and that this was the right thing to do. Django was probably another key part of the equation, a large part of the reason they decided to accept the gift from Jan and myself, because they saw him and probably concluded, "You can say what you want about Croz, he certainly has his ups and downs, but he makes beautiful babies." I'd be the first to agree; this child is stellar and he was that way from the git-go. Right out of the gate. It wasn't about me. It was Django. They saw him and said, "Man, that one! Give me one of those!" I don't blame them because he was a great little baby.

It was very plain Julie and Melissa were in love with each other; there wasn't a question in my mind. They'd been together for many years, and we felt that the love was much more important than who had which kind of plumbing. It really didn't matter to us if they were both girls, or both boys, or girls and boys. All that matters is the presence of love. That was the critical and deciding factor for me and Jan: we believe in love and we believe it's crucial. Yes, you've got to keep kids fed and clothed and a roof over their heads, but that's not what they live on. Kids live on love, the same way flowers live on water. It's vital nourishment for their infant souls, and the proof is in the pudding: Bailey and Beckett are healthy and wonderful kids.

JULIE CYPHER:

You just can't believe it's happening to you. . . . I consulted Jan and David's doctor about how to conceive, and asked him the old turkey baster question: "Is there any reason we can't just do it at home? Would we have to do it in the office?" Dr. Marrs said there wasn't any reason not to try, and suggested that if it didn't work, we could always do it in the office. I knew exactly when the time was right, and called David. The first time, we were having our house painted and this big black Suburban pulls up while all the painters are eating their lunch. It's David, dropping off a paper bag with the sample in it. He's wearing dark glasses and he looks like a drug dealer, comes in the door with the bag, gets back in the big black car and he leaves. I felt for sure that the painters thought it was a drug deal.

That encounter was the first of two tries to achieve the goal. The second try was a little more of an adventure.

JULIE CYPHER:

David and Jan were staying with Jan's mom in the valley, and David needed to get to rehearsal and asked if I could come over and get it, so I said, "Sure," and drove down. As I turned the corner there's David nonchalantly standing on the corner, in the valley, eating a Popsicle, with the bag that has my future in it. He leans into the car and asks if I can take him to rehearsal, so I say, "Sure, no problem," and he gets in the car and says, "Graham called and he needs a ride, do you mind if we pick up Graham?" Okay, still no problem. So I put the paper sack with this little thing of sperm in it between my legs to keep it warm and we go pick up Graham, and I was (and am) still in awe of CSN, for crying out loud, and I'm driving with two-thirds of CSN in my car. I'm driving really carefully because the car is full of history if I get in an accident, *and* I've got this secret paper sack tucked between my legs as I'm driving them up to Stephen's house. And they're, "Why don't you stay and listen?" and I'm, "No, gotta go, I got things to do." Things to do. Babies to have.

The result was the healthy, happy girl named Bailey. It was a tough time for the parents; Julie was at home, Melissa was on the road, and it led to tensions, according to Melissa's account. In her autobiography, she says that a song she wrote at the time, called "Breakdown," was really about what was happening in their relationship. Nevertheless, they were still working at their union, and agreed to have a second child. Since the little girl had turned out so well, there was no reason to tamper with success, and again I agreed to be the secret donor. The logistics remained the same; it's not rocket science, despite the obvious jokes about "liftoff" and "we have ignition." Julie would be ovulating, and I'd have to stand by to make my contribution. This time, it was more of a challenge.

JULIE:

David was on tour and trying to hook up with him was hard. Whenever it was time for me, I had twenty-four hours to find him. Once, he returned my call but we were already asleep and I woke up at five or six in the morning and got the message, but he was getting on a plane to New York. I couldn't believe I missed the call. I was distraught, and I said, "I'm going to New York," called him and left a message on his cell phone: "I'm chasing you, tell me where you're staying because I'm going to be there, and I hope you don't have any plans tonight."

I was at the Carlyle Hotel in Manhattan, one of the great places to stay in that great city. I called Julie, and gave her my location, as requested. She was already on the plane from LA and landed that night.

STOCK FOOTAGE: NEW YORK SKYLINE — SUNSET

EXTERIOR — RUNWAY — SAME TIME: A JET IS LANDING

JULIE:

I checked into the Carlyle for six hours and as soon as I got to my room, I called David's room. Twenty minutes later he shows up at the door, knock, knock, knock, "Nice to see you, how are you?" hands me the paper sack, the door closes, and Beckett was conceived, just me in the hotel room. I still have the robe; she should have been named Carlyle. I slept for four hours, got up, and got right back on a plane and headed home, because Bailey was real young at the time and I didn't want to be away from her at all, so it was about eighteen hours, door to door, to get the goods from David. We were fully clothed all three times, much to David's regret. And no kitchen utensils were ever used.

Which led, inevitably, I suppose, to the onstage line from one of my partners, introducing me as "the Sperminator." Some guys will say anything for a cheap laugh. It wasn't easy for Julie and Melissa at the time. They were having their own problems, and would ultimately split up. Bailey and Beckett remain in my life.

On the other hand, my old partner Chris Hillman said that I was committing a mortal sin by helping Julie and Melissa have those kids. He's been in my life a long time, we started the Byrds together forty years ago, and he said that. Fascinating. Archaic and mildly insane, but fascinating: "Mortal sin."

Hillman was absolutely serious: from his perspective, this assistance con-
stituted a mortal sin. Chris Hillman's a hero of American bluegrass music.
He has a website where you can read the insight that "Traditional family values have worked for thousands of years, and I think a lot of people
my age are embracing a more conservative outlook on things. Once they've
actually been married and have children, they say, 'Wait a Minute, Mom
and Dad were right!'" In another online location, www.roots66.com, he
characterizes his present belief system: "I'm a Greek Orthodox Christian.
I converted about eight years ago. My wife is Greek. I was a Protestant,
evangelical Christian, in the early 80s and baptized and all that, born-
again Christian. It wasn't really fulfilling me. I'm not saying it's right or
wrong but it wasn't what I was searching for; I got comfortable in the
Orthodox faith, which is the original church." In our conversation, Chris
could not have been clearer when discussing the bonds he shares with
David, as well as their deep philosophical differences.

CHRIS HILLMAN:

I mean, here we are at the age we are now and I really love Crosby. I
think he's a stand-up guy. He's got a real good soul. I don't agree with
him on every level. There's very little I have in common with him . . .
[but] he's been there when I've needed him, always, to help me when
I was ill, and I hold him very dear to my heart. Yet, he can be the most
arrogant, aggravating human being on the planet. I don't have a lot in
common with him, I'm in a different place musically, and politically—
certainly not!

Like it or not, the reality is that almost a third of kids today grow up
in homes without both a mother and a father. My experience with Melissa
and Julie has helped bring the problems a gay or lesbian couple in
America faces into much sharper focus for me. There are lots of families
with a mom and a dad, only there's no love. Remember the Menendez

brothers? Nuclear family, working dad, stay-at-home mom, shotguns in the night, and the boys turned out to be murderers. The "traditional" American family is a little rare on the ground now, and it's getting redefined all the time. That's not the fault of gay people. If anything, it's a measure of how hard it is to make any relationship work whether it's straight or gay. What's important is not the gender of the parents; what's important is that their children are loved. If you give it to them, they flourish. It's really as simple as that.

The problem is that the Catholic and Mormon churches, fundamentalist Christians, and fundamentalist Wahabi Muslims have institutionalized homophobia. They've dug in real deep and they resist any global change. But change is inevitable. They can delay it, but they can't stop it. Which is why I know that, eventually, things will get a whole lot better—if not in my lifetime, then in my son's lifetime. He's almost twelve years old as I write. Growing up, playing with Melissa and Julie's kids, he's never questioned the fact that they had two moms. It's perfectly natural to him. It's been a part of his life growing up and nobody has ever told him it isn't perfectly normal.

When you raise white and black kids together, they don't know anything about racism. It just doesn't occur to people on their own—it's learned behavior. And the same is true of how people form opinions about gay relationships. You have to teach them homophobia or racism in order for them to grow up as gay bashers or bigots. And we're successfully changing that paradigm. When children aren't taught to hate, then they learn to love. And in the long run love is going to win. It always does.

Sadly, the Melissa Etheridge–Julie Cypher relationship ended. Following the breakup, Julie happily entered a heterosexual marriage that has produced another daughter; she and Melissa have shared custody of Bailey and Beckett. Melissa is also happy in a committed relationship with

Tammy Lynn Michaels. The Melissa Etheridge website offered this in April of 2006:

We are thrilled to announce that Tammy is pregnant, and expecting our twins sometime around this fall. To answer the obvious question: we used an anonymous donor from a bank. These are our first two babies conceived together, but not our first time mothering together. For the past five years, we have been parenting two children, from a previous time in Melissa's life. The twins will be a joyful addition to our loving home.

Would I be a sperm donor again? I don't know. It's such a personal thing, and so much depends on the individual person. It's discouraging how this worked out because one of the main reasons that we did it was because of the love between Julie and Melissa, who have obviously transferred that affection to new partners. Seeing that love fall apart after such a long time made us think twice about trying to do it again.

JULIE CYPHER:
It was an amicable split. It took a long time to happen. Having children rattles the cage of any relationship; it either withstands it or it doesn't. And I think having children and Melissa's lifestyle . . . on the road had a lot to do with [its] demise, among other things. I remember feeling so horrible in terms of letting [Jan and David] down . . . that these kids would be raised in a different way, and now it wasn't a nuclear family.

Both women have brought the kids up here, and been with me at different times. It's very kind of both of them to let me spend time with the kids, because our official deal was that I signed papers relinquishing parental rights of any sort after I made my gift. I have no authority to tell them anything about how to raise the kids, no "ownership," if you will, which is what we always understood and agreed to. Julie, who lives in Southern California, has made every effort possible for me to be included in their lives, and that's a great kindness. It matters a great deal to Jan and I that Julie feels that's appropriate, because they're great kids: super bright, extremely nice, beautiful, happy, wonderful children. I have to control how I show affection for them, I made a promise, but they're very special people in my life.

JULIE:

He's their dad. They have two dads, and three and a half moms. Jan's the half mom. Django and James are their half brothers and Donovan's a half sister. They have a picture of Grace and they like having a niece that's older than them. We've been sailing with David; we get together with them three or four times a year, as often as possible, [but] I only have the kids every other week, so sometimes it doesn't time out. Last year when Crosby, Stills, and Nash were at the Hollywood Bowl, we went to visit for a sound check and all the kids—little Crosbyites— were running around the bleachers, and Graham Nash looked out and said, "It's the fruit of David's loins, don't worry about them. There might be some more hiding around here. We're never quite sure."

CUT TO:

INTERIOR — SOUTH FLORIDA HOME — DAY — 2000
A WOMAN IS AT A COMPUTER

ERIKA KELLER:

I knew I was adopted since I was a little girl. I always wondered and had weird dreams all the time. I just didn't know what to make of them. And as I got older I just let it go. When my son was four years old, he had surgery and they had to remove a kidney and they asked

me if it was something genetic. That's when it hit me—I had to tell
the doctor I didn't know. Fortunately, the Internet happened and I
found this thing called ICQ, it had a message board for adoptive parents and I had put a message there. Of course, nobody answered and
I gave up. And then, while my husband was watching some movie for
the trillionth time that I didn't want to watch, I went into the computer and I started playing with ICQ. They had new things on it and
one of them was adoption.com. I knew my mother's full maiden
name, and I had bits and pieces of [other] information. I had seen my
original birth certificate, which stated her name. No father. "Left the
state," it said. I put in what I had and found her. And she told me who
my dad was.

*Needless to say, "Dad" was David Crosby. "Mom" was a woman named
Jackie Hyde, a long-haired blond beauty who was Miss Malibu back in
the early sixties. She had conceived David's child, a daughter who was
given up for adoption. The infant went to a couple who lived in Mexico,
a Polish émigré named Keller and a Roman Catholic mother with dual
citizenship in both Mexico and the United States. They named their new
daughter Erika, and she was raised in Mexico City. Jackie Hyde married
folk singer Arlo Guthrie, the son of legendary folk singer and songwriter
Woody Guthrie, in 1969. Arlo and Jackie remain happily married, with
four children of their own, and their extended family continues playing
and recording music. Crosby's connection to "the folk tradition" was deeper
than he knew.*

Erika came as a surprise package. She found her mother through a
website somehow, and got in touch with her first. Jackie had my e-mail
address. It's a very odd thing, almost every woman I've ever been with is
still my friend, despite the fact that I used and abused some of them. Erika
eventually called me and said, "I think I'm your daughter," and I said,
"Fantastic. Let's do a DNA test and find out." Sure enough, the DNA

match was absolutely conclusive: Erika Keller's my daughter. She successfully and legally came into the country from Mexico, and she settled in Florida with her second husband. She's an amazing woman. Within two or three years of getting into the United States, she had both kids speaking English well enough to go to school and deal with everything.

ERIKA:

I found Jackie, and the day that I spoke with her for the first time she told me about David. We did all the tests and it all came back positive. I didn't need that confirmation—all I have to do was look at my baby pictures and David. We all have his eyes. I have a baby picture where I'm smiling and chubby, I was probably six, seven months old. I did a little Photoshop and I scanned that picture into one of the pictures from David and it's like a Xerox. But when I first got the news, I had no clue. I had to go on the Internet to look up Crosby, Stills, and Nash, and I didn't know who was who. I had dial-up back then and the pictures came out first before the names did. And I saw Stephen Stills, I saw blond, and I said, "He's my dad." My sister was standing right there with me and she indicated Crosby and said, "Oh my God, Erika, you cannot deny, that's your dad right there." I was like "Really? You think?" Then I got it. Oh my God, okay. It's very weird and people might think I'm crazy but I've always dreamt of David, not knowing who he is. I knew that he was somebody important, I thought he was maybe in a company, like a CEO-type thing. But that's a feeling I've always had. He's always been in my life. He just didn't have a name or a face.

Erika has three children of her own. At this moment, they include seventeen-year-old Roberta; thirteen year-old Jorge; and two-year-old Alexa. Roberta was and still is getting straight As. Jorge is doing almost that well and playing sports. Erika's bought a house and a car and was supporting the entire family when we connected. She's tough, she's a hardworking woman, and I'm very glad she found me and I found her. And she's funny. Unfortunately, I haven't spent as much time with Erika as I'd like. I've gone to Florida to meet and talk to her, and the best times have been around a pool at a hotel when I was touring. She'd bring the family and we'd get a cabana by the pool and would all hang out all day, swim and play with the kids and talk. Every time I go to Florida, I see them as much as I can. I like it that she calls me Dad; it was the first thing she asked me when we first spoke: "Can I call you Dad?" These days I'm more Dad-like than I've ever been, and loving it.

Elliot Roberts is a wryly cynical man with a keenly developed sense of irony. He's been David's manager since 1968, and has seen him through good times and bad. He's dropped him as a client, and been replaced as a manager; at present and for the foreseeable future (which is a fungible concept in show business), Elliot is managing Crosby, Stills, and Young, and his management company is booking the Crosby, Stills, Nash, and Young Freedom of Speech '06 Tour. Elliot's speech is both vulgar and direct:

ELLIOT ROBERTS:

You have to get on with your life and make music for people and play and tour and do what you should do and when you should do it. David's happier [these days]. He's nicer. Again, he's in the twilight of his life. He knows it. I'm in the twilight and Carl, please forgive me, but you're in the back end too. To be assholes at this point, you'd really have to be a fucking moron. Especially David, who is so blessed at this point in his life to have people around him who love him. He's got most of his possessions back that he lost. He's got his boat, he's got his house, he's got his boys now, he's got James in his life, and four grandchildren. He's got Django. Again, a lucky motherfucker. He's got Jan, and I think even he senses he's way luckier than any one man has a right to be. I couldn't have dealt with him four or five years ago. There was a time when they said "David's on the line," and I went, "Oh, fuck. Can you tell him I had a stroke or something?" But now he's a pleasure to deal with, he's changed a lot in his life.

And who knows, there may be another child out there, someone who doesn't know that I'm his or her genetic father. And if that person has children, that's more branches of the family tree, growing into an absolute jungle of nieces, nephews, and cousins crossing generational lines, another chapter of ghosts and memories.

FADE OUT:

Fifteen

PUTTING THE PAST TO REST

FADE IN:

INTERIOR — PLAZA HOTEL ROOM — NIGHT — 1998
DAVID AND JAN ARE WATCHING TELEVISION

Before I transferred my allegiance to the Carlyle, I usually stayed at the Plaza Hotel on Fifth Avenue and Fifty-eighth Street; it was convenient, traditional, and luxurious. Then it started changing ownership, eventually closed, and will reopen as a hotel and condo combo. It's a great piece of real estate, a New York landmark, and the place where I almost lost my mind.

Jan and I were watching *The Fisher King*, a movie that has two of my friends in it, Jeff Bridges and Robin Williams. Robin plays a homeless man, a guy named Parry, whose wife gets killed, blown apart with a shotgun as an innocent bystander in a restaurant. He can't deal with it; he becomes deranged. He can no longer face a world that includes that experience, so he goes completely batshit crazy and lives on the streets of New York and in Central Park, in a fantasy world. Every time he tries to return to the world of sanity and reality, he is driven back into his fantasy by a terrible vision of a red knight on a red horse, a menacing figure who embodies his awful experience. The man's fantasy includes a search for the Holy Grail, a chalice, which he believes will free him from this awful situation. Jack Lucas, the character played by Jeff Bridges, becomes Parry's friend, and Parry begs Jack to get the chalice for him. Jack gets the cup out of the castlelike house where it lives in New York and brings it to Parry, who's been beaten and is in a coma, in a hospital. Parry wakes up, sees the chalice on his chest, and says, "Oh, is it all right now? Can I miss her now?"

It's an emotional point in the film, and hearing the line started me crying. Not too unusual—I can mist up and get teary-eyed watching movies—but this time I couldn't stop. Robin's reading of that line pierced my armor and went straight to my heart. I wept. I cried harder and harder. Within minutes I was wailing, scaring myself with the intensity of my reaction. I've never cried that hard in my life, not even when my mother died. I was weeping, moaning. I felt as if a wave had broken over my head and I couldn't get to the surface. It was an absolutely primal experience, and I was frightened. I thought, "Oh, my God, we're going to have to get me to a hospital and get me a shot of Valium because I can't deal, I'm completely overwhelmed." I was a sobbing wreck. Jan said, "What is it?" And then she named it, and this is an exact quote. "What is it you're looking at that you can't bear to see?" she said. I couldn't answer. She pressed on: "Is it Christine?"

Of course it was. Jan knew. The minute she said it, I realized what was happening. There was a direct connection between the movie I'd watched and something I'd seen a quarter of a century earlier.

FLASHBACK:

EXTERIOR — MARIN COUNTY, CALIFORNIA — 1971

David, Christine Hinton, and Debbie Donovan had set up housekeeping in Novato, California, in Marin County, across the Golden Gate Bridge. Christine Hinton had been the original organizer of the Byrds Fan Club, when they were first getting started. Barely of age, she and her nubile friends took it on themselves to provide pleasure and support for their idols. There were no apparent limits to the sex enjoyed, the drugs consumed, and the hedonistic lifestyle that has been memorialized in every book and movie of the time. Christine started as one of many, became first among equals, and eventually was the significant other in David's life, although she put up with his practice of enjoying multiple partners, as well as his ongoing relationships with other women. Debbie was the junior partner in their domestic arrangement. Elliot Roberts recalled the situation this way in 1988:

ELLIOT ROBERTS:
David was known as Twofer, "Two Fer" Crosby. If there was one woman around him, that meant that he had sent the other one on an errand. . . . He was never without two women; he was the envy of all the guys because they were all beautiful women, and they were all devoted to the Croz. Christine at that time was the Thoroughbred of them all. Although he had had a lot of women and harems in LA and harems up north, Christine was his main woman and she'd come down to LA and run his LA trip and when he'd go up north, she'd go up a day early and make sure his Marin trip was together. She was the captain of all his scenes. And there was no question that he loved Christine a great, great deal . . . of all the other women, she was his love.

Part of the lure of Marin County and the San Francisco scene was the fact that the local bands, the Jefferson Airplane, the Grateful Dead, and Big Brother and the Holding Company (Janis Joplin's group) were making original music in an original way. The street theater and the Fillmore and Avalon Ballrooms were their palette and inspiration, and they shunned "plastic LA" and the corporate music business. The Grateful Dead had a ranch in Novato, just north of San Rafael, and David was relocating there, eventually bringing the schooner Mayan *up from the Caribbean to anchor in Sausalito. Grace Slick had this recollection of the Crosby lifestyle when she visited the boat in the Caribbean:*

GRACE SLICK:

What I saw . . . was an amazing situation where he was able to have a couple of girls who were living with him in a sporadic chronic permanent way . . . long blond-haired lovely young human beings running around, sometimes with no clothes. . . . I thought everybody was happy with the arrangement. David was with several girls, people were running around with no clothes on, making food and pouring wine and singing songs with an acoustic guitar in the back of this boat with the sun going down and absolutely dead-clear water, and it was one of those amazing periods . . . David was always pretty good at keeping those balls in the air, or wherever balls belong, so to speak.

I was embarrassed because these women all had perfect figures, no tan lines, and long blond hair . . . [I said], "No, I'm not taking my clothes off." Not for moral reasons, but because there would be no comparison here, thank you very much. Female singers, with the possible exception of Stevie Nicks, were not the best-looking of the lot. The groupies were generally better-looking than any of the singers. Christine was with David, and there were about eight other people aboard, and it was very pleasant and unreal and you can't keep that way of life going forever. We were naive enough to think we could.

David, Christine, and Debbie had been living in Marin for only a few weeks when Christine took a friend on a short drive to the veterinarian with some of the house cats. By all accounts, the kitties were rambunctious and hard to control; one of them got away and was climbing loose in the front seat. Christine's attention was diverted as she struggled to recover the cat. The van swerved across the center line, into the path of a school bus traveling in the opposite direction. There was a head-on crash that killed her, and badly injured her companion, Barbara Langer. There's no record of any injuries to the driver or the occupants of the bus.

Christine loved animals, as Jan does now, and she left the house to run to the vet in my little green Volkswagen van. A little later, I got a phone call from someone at the Grateful Dead's ranch. Someone had seen a wreck by the side of the road, and recognized our van. The voice said, "Christine's been hurt, she's in a bad accident, I think you better get to the hospital." A friend took us to the hospital in Novato. On the way, we had to pass the wrecked VW, which was completely demolished. I remember saying, "Jesus, I hope she's still alive."

At the hospital, there was an ambulance pulled up to the back and the inside of it was covered with blood. An attendant was mopping it up with a sheet and I asked him, "Is she still alive?" He looked at me kind of strangely and didn't answer, so I turned around and started inside. A doctor asked me if I was related to the victim, and I said, "Yeah, she's my girlfriend." He said, "We're sorry to tell you. She's dead." I had no way to deal with that, nothing in my life had prepared me for it. I just said, "No, no, no, no, no." I think I screamed it, really. The doctor asked me if I wanted to see her. I was haunted for years after by the vivid mental image of Christine dead. It was horrible.

On the way out of the hospital, I had to see the ambulance again. It looked as if someone had blown somebody up in it. Blood was dripping out of the back onto the ground and the attendant was trying to hose it off, and he looked up at me and he knew that I must have been her husband or her lover. He was embarrassed, caught trying to wash the blood away so I wouldn't see it. My friends loaded me in the car and took me back to the house. The next day a local newspaper ran a short squib on the fourth page, "Girl in hippie commune on Indian Road dies in auto wreck." That was Christine's epitaph.

Afterwards, I remember Graham and Joni Mitchell came up from LA, I cried constantly, and a friend I loved dearly gave me some heroin to dull the pain. It was bad choice for him to bring it, a worse choice for me to take it. Sadly, it was the only thing I found that gave me any relief. In retrospect, it was probably the crucial fork in the road that led to my eventual addiction to hard drugs. Heroin may be a good anesthetic, but doesn't do shit for your psychic well-being. I know now that by self-medicating for my emotional pain I prolonged and protracted my suffering immensely.

I had no mechanism, no way to deal with it, nothing. This was before any of our friends had died; Christine was twenty-one, I was twenty-eight, and in those days, nobody died at twenty-one. I was lost, made a bad drug mistake, tried to suppress a brutal, nasty, awful experience, and stuffed it completely, after a year of recovering from the initial shock and grief. Failing to process an experience like that is a terrible mistake. The emotions fester, the grief gets worse, it stays inside and poisons you.

ELLIOT ROBERTS:

> After Christine died, David changed his lifestyle considerably. He had much less interest in women and group scenes . . . he became guarded, afraid to give of himself; he became much more morose, and he couldn't focus very well . . . you couldn't have very many long meetings with David. They had to be very short and concise and to the point and he didn't want to make decisions anymore. He gave up making decisions. It used to be I would only talk to David and then we would tell Graham and Stephen what the plan was, and ask if they

had any objections. After Christine's death, David didn't want to be the main guy anymore.

When I came out of the initial shock, Graham stuck close to me because he and my friends were afraid I was going to commit suicide, I was that depressed. Graham and I flew to Florida for a bit, then went to London. We drank. I've never been a drinker, but the pain was so intense that I would do anything to dull it, to make it go away for even a short time, until I could pass out.

After England, I decided I wanted to bring my boat to California. I had the romantic notion that I'd scatter Christine's ashes at sea, outside San Francisco Bay, beyond the Golden Gate. I asked Nash if he wanted to come along, and he did.

David, Graham, a pick-up crew, and some friends flew to the Bahamas, and after a few personnel changes in Miami, sailed the boat past Jamaica and down to the Panama Canal, crossing the Isthmus of Panama and making their way up the western coast of Mexico. After a series of adventures, the Mayan *and its crew sailed into San Francisco Bay and found a mooring in Sausalito. David lived aboard the boat and recorded his solo album* If I Could Only Remember My Name *at Wally Heider's studio in San Francisco. He made the Trident (a local restaurant and bar) his personal watering hole. Built on pilings over the water on Sausalito's main street, it had a deck with an expansive view of all of San Francisco Bay and the most gorgeous waitstaff north of the Playboy mansion. No airbrushing and no implants, Trident women had rings in their noses and tattoos of flowers and butterflies where you could see them, and sometimes where you couldn't. There was no house uniform, so waitresses could wear anything from Victorian velvet to see-through Indian gauze. Some shaved, some didn't; the line between staff and clientele often blurred: beautiful women would hang out waiting for an interview or a job opening, and female staff would stick around after work, fraternizing with guys who could afford the tab (it was not a cheap place to eat). If sex, drugs, and rock 'n' roll had caused a revolution, the Trident was its Reign of Terror. One of the busboys was a drama student at Juilliard who loved the San Francisco improvisational comedy scene. He was comedian Robin Williams, and he'd witnessed the scene aboard the* Mayan *from afar. In response to my statement that David is more comfortable on his boat than anywhere else, Robin responds, both as himself, and (typically) as characters that he channels, including Robert Newton's memorable growl as Long John Silver in* Treasure Island:

BACK TO THE PRESENT DAY:

ROBIN WILLIAMS:

You can see it in pictures, even in the pictures [from] the fucking nut days. [You see] pictures of him on a boat and all of a sudden, you say, "He looks in control there. He looks like he is the master and the commander." I never knew him then, I just knew that they parked their sailboat and all of a sudden, beautiful girls would be picked up in a dinghy and taken out to the boat. It was like shore leave. Shore leave with caviar and coke. Take on provisions and two sultry women in batik . . . [Long John Silver pirate voice]: "Grab her, aye, have her washed and brought aboard. Fire a couple of bongs over the bow, Johnny . . ." [As Robin again]: He'd actually park it right there. Drop the sails, and then drop trou.

I know that Robin worked at the Trident, but the synchronicity is still amazing, that he was watching me during that time. It's hard to connect those days to the profound experience his movie performance in *Fisher King* brought on so suddenly; it was like an IED: an Improvised Emotional Device that went off unexpectedly in our hotel room. Bang!

What was the trigger? What was going on? Jan sat with me like a psychiatric nurse and talked me through it for hours. She brought me gently to the surface, she got me out of the mire where I had been stuck and drowning. She talked me through from one side to the other, and by morning I had written a song about it, without sleep, a set of lyrics that gave voice to what I had just experienced. I wrote the lines, "They say a wolf in a trap will chew off his own leg, I guess I did the same, it's what you do with a thing you just can't handle, a picture you just can't frame."

MUSIC CUE:

SOMEHOW SHE KNEW

As the room slid into focus and he woke up
with room service at the door
And he wondered why he never spoke up
about all of that fear before

It was standing just an inch behind him
a shadow stalking by his side
A thing he was afraid would find him
and wash him away in the tide

And somehow she knew why I was crying
She knew just which fears I had not faced
In her eyes I could see where I was lying to myself
and a path that she gently traced
to where the man in the movie said,
"Is it all right if I miss her tonight"
And the man felt just like me

They say a wolf in a trap will chew off his own leg
I guess I did the same
It's what you do with a thing you can't handle
A picture you just can't frame

And from somewhere deep in that movie
she opened a door in my chest
And delicately took out a death
that had never been laid to rest

And somehow she knew why I was crying
She knew just which fears I had not faced
in her eyes I could see where I was lying
to myself

And a path that she gently traced
to where the man in the movie said,
"Is it all right if I miss her tonight"
And the man felt just like me.

When it was over, I felt triumphant and joyous—I had finally been able to look the thing squarely in the eye and cross to safety. It was like an exorcism where you don't die, a tremendous turning point for me, because I had been carrying this pain around, the agony of Christine's death, for more than twenty years.

When you make mass-media art in this world, whether it's music, books, or movies, it's a little like writing a poem on a piece of paper, folding it into a glider, and tossing it over the top of the Empire State Building. You haven't the vaguest idea where it goes or who gets it or what they think about it or what effect it has. None of us really know. We get reviewed in the press, but most of the time that's some asshole trying to make his bones by being critical. Most of the time, we never know what effect we have.

This time, with this film, I knew I could communicate with the artists. Robin Williams and Jeff Bridges are friends of mine. Jeff and I have been acquainted since we were kids. His father and my father (Floyd and Lloyd!) both worked on the same memorable film, *High Noon*. My father was the cinematographer, and Jeff's father was Lloyd Bridges, the actor playing Gary Cooper's deputy. Jeff and his wife, Susan, live in Santa Barbara County, relatively close, so I went to their house for dinner one night, a month or so after my exorcism by *The Fisher King*. I told them I needed to sit down and sing something to them, because I wanted them to know that this piece of art that Jeff made had changed my life. Then I sang them "Somehow She Knew."

JEFF BRIDGES:

He came over and played that song for us and told us how much the movie affected him. It's wonderful to have something that you've done have an effect on someone like that. What's so great is that he's so relaxed and has such ease up there on the stage and makes everybody there feel like he's just like sitting in your living room, like he was the other night.

Then I sought out Robin Williams and his wife, Marsha, and did the same thing: sent them my song and shared the experience.

ROBIN WILLIAMS:

That song he wrote, which was so beautiful, he sent it to me . . . I was going, "Gosh, man, thank you." That movie, in a weird way, had a power over people in a similar way to *Dead Poets Society* but *Fisher King* touches people, I mean, those of us who have been beyond and back. Who've had the hard life and then come back and gone, "Wow,

I'm alive again." And I think that kind of struck him as this character who is so damn introverted, yet found love. I think it touches him that he's reborn on that level of a guy who has seen the flames of hell and inhaled them and then come out . . . David being in prison and all that other shit, he comes out and has this second life, and then comes out again and has a third life after the transplant.

I couldn't stop there. When I was in England, I found the director, Terry Gilliam, and told him the story. Then I went to Richard LaGravenese, who wrote the screenplay. Just cold-called him in New York, and said, "Hi, you don't know me, but I'd like to talk to you for about fifteen minutes, please," and he graciously came to the Plaza. We went upstairs and again, I sang him the song and blew his mind, he said. In all, the momentary trauma of releasing a suppressed memory not only generated one of my best pieces, but also freed me from a tremendous weight. It was entirely due to Jan's compassion and insight. She was right there, in the moment: she saw me crack, she knew what was happening, she didn't freak out, and she was wonderful. That's another reason why we're life partners; she understands the complicated comedies and tragedies that make up our family histories.

Sixteen

MORE IN SORROW

FADE IN:

EXTERIOR — TRINITY NATIONAL FOREST, MOUNT SHASTA,
CALIFORNIA — NIGHT — 1997

The homemade house in the woods that my brother had called home the last year of his life was cobbled together out of bits of plywood and plastic, nothing that couldn't be carried in from the trailhead by hand. A very basic shelter. He was used to living alone in the woods. It was in the middle of November 1997, and it took a skilled charter helicopter pilot to get me this far. There'd already been a snowfall, and Ethan was missing.

A few days earlier, while driving with Jan, I got a call from an old friend and high school classmate named Jeff Palmer. Jeff was friends with Ethan and lived on Mount Shasta, where Ethan had been for years. He told me they had found a suicide note. "I think he's gone," Jeff said. The sheriff's department confirmed it. The note said, "By the time you read

this I will be dead. . . . Please do not search for my body. I want to return to the earth unmolested by uncaring officials . . . Give my deep love
and gratitude to David and all my friends . . ."

I still love him. There's a complicated family dynamic—my brother
had it much rougher than I did. My dad was still working when we were
in school, and my mom and dad were trying to keep their marriage going,
so they put Ethan in boarding schools. Parents do that—they make mistakes with the first kid that they don't make with the second one.

I owe Ethan a lot. He gave me my first guitar, showed me my first
chords. He's the one who turned me on to music. He had been a working musician for years in little tiny dance halls and bars working for scale,
and all of a sudden his little brother is in the Byrds making zillions of dollars and on the cover of all these teen magazines and all that bullshit. If
that wasn't bad enough, here comes Crosby, Stills & Nash and then on
top of that, Crosby, Stills, Nash & Young. Somewhere along in there, he
just got out-competed, and he finally decided that the only way he could
handle it was to stop. He just dropped out. Ethan, of course, saw things
very much from his own perspective:

ETHAN CROSBY:

> I was really into reading and I was sort of a loner and I was always off
> reading a book instead of interacting with my peers, and my parents
> began to think that I was going to develop a complex or something
> and so they said, "You need a hobby, tell us what do you want," and
> I said, "Buy me a guitar." So they did and that was in like fifth or sixth
> grade. [Every summer] we went to the same camp, out here in
> Northern California, called Camp Trinity, in the Trinity National
> Forest near Hayfork . . . When I first went there it was '45, man, and
> there was no electricity and it was like drip coolers and kerosene lamps
> and the chainsaw hadn't been invented and they did all the farming
> and everything with horse-drawn equipment, horse-drawn hay mows,
> they butchered their own meat, they did the whole thing, man. That

was one of the major impetuses in my movement toward nature, having that experience every summer for like eight years. I was a camper, then a counselor, and David eventually came, and that was part of his intro to it.

The camp is still in business, as Camp Trinity on the Bar 717 Ranch. It's been operating since 1930 under the same family management, with the same emphasis on rugged independent outdoor life. Its mission statement says: "We believe that the pioneer traditions of the family—cooperation, resourcefulness, and sharing—still apply today, and strive to pass these on to our campers." The camp published a small newsletter, "Campservations," and it notes for the record, in 1948, "the guitar trio of Tilley, Winans and Crosby [this would be Chip, aka Ethan] appeared and gave forth with several appropriate songs and the dance got rolling . . . the younger campers and others who remained near the campfire had a good time singing. David Crosby made a fine song leader." Even then. From 1949 through 1951, there are numerous references to Chip playing guitar, participating in skits and talent shows, and being an energetic and enthusiastic participant in camp life, as both camper and counselor. The last entry says, "A note from Chip Crosby gives his address, 358 Padaro Lane, Carpinteria. The Crosbys have purchased an avocado grove and Chip has room to expend his unbounded energies. He likes Carpinteria High School."

I enjoyed my time at camp: I had a big brother who could look out for me; he was a musician and played in groups, we made music together, he was a counselor. I've always had a much wider concept of what constitutes a family than most people. I once got caught by my mother reading my favorite comic book with a flashlight under the blankets. It was about a group of orphaned kids who had somehow found each other and joined to live on a ranch together and survive. Some adults took over the father-figure part and the mother-figure part. I remember thinking that that was all how it should be. Then I read Robert Heinlein's *Stranger in a Strange Land*, and it changed my life, changed the way I think, especially about family. The family that you inherit is one thing, but what about the family that you choose? And *Stranger in a Strange Land* made me realize there was a much wider kind of family possible than other people have in their heads.

The science fiction that inspired David to write "Triad" and "Wooden Ships" was prescient and compelling. One of the genre's towering figures, Robert Heinlein, predicted (in 1948!) a postapocalyptic society dominated by fundamentalist Christian church theocracy. His view of the end of the postindustrial world is eerily similar to Ethan Crosby's expectations of societal collapse.

Ethan and I were raised thinking there was going to be a nuclear holocaust. We were the first generation of kids that grew up with a full stop as part of our psychic vocabulary, in which the human race could come to a bitter end, a screeching halt—and within our lifetimes. Ethan really felt that it was going to happen and that he was going to come down from the mountains afterwards and help us start it over better. That was a big dream of his. When it didn't happen, I don't think he knew what to do, it took the wind out of his sails. People with kids, people who live in the world, generally can find something to convince them it's going to work out somehow. There've been many nights when I've gone to bed seriously depressed, but Jan or my friends would say, "Croz, it's going to look different in the morning. Go to sleep, it's going to be okay." Ethan didn't have that.

ETHAN:

I gave college a good shot and finally realized they were not going to educate me. They just refused. Junior college in Santa Barbara and then Cal Poly for a quarter because I wanted to live out in the hills. I thought I'd study agriculture. Ha ha, come on! I totally mistook what they thought agriculture was. It's scientific agribusiness and totally alien to what I was trying to do, which was to get next to the planet. After my mother died I had a little inheritance coming so I started living in Volkswagen buses, and I got the flash that the thing I needed to do was create a music temple. I decided that I should go back to Marin and try to turn on David and his friends to the Light and to what is going on in the planet because they were spokesmen to the New Age. If they said it, people would hear it, and so I wanted to expose them to it and work through them to get the message out.

I spent a bunch of money and actually got a wind organ built on Mount Tamalpais and recorded some of that. David was in and out, and we had another period of pretty good relationship . . . but there was a tension between me and David and competition and probably deep down in his most secret little place, it's probably still there, and I was, in a sense, trying to jump into his territory, which is the music business . . . And I discovered that rock and roll stars are not interested in the Light, at least not at that point. They were interested in pussy and cocaine and the fast lane and all that, so, basically, I crashed and burned and went back to Big Sur. I was a hermit for a couple of years and finally got run out by the overwhelming tourists. It was like traveling in Yosemite. I found myself up in a guy's face with my rifle one day, some trail biker who was tearing up my ridges, and I thought, "Hey, Ethan, wait a minute . . ." so I moved north, to Mount Shasta.

The last time he ever came down to see me for was my wedding. Before that, he would just call me; it was usually friendly and nice. Occasionally he would ask for more money. My dad and my mom supported Ethan for years. When my mother died, my father sent the checks, and when I started being the one in the family that had all the money, I took over the financial responsibility, but I would send the money to my dad and let him send it, so Ethan didn't know where it was coming from. When my dad died, I took it over completely. I was frustrated with Ethan, wanted him to stop being a mooch and go out and get serious. Get a job. It was a mistake to support him like that, for any of us to do it. It allowed him to entrench himself in the idea that he couldn't live any other way and that it was always just a matter of getting somebody to give him just a little extra.

I wish that I could have influenced him more. One time, before I went to jail, he wasn't doing well and threatened to commit suicide if I didn't give him more money. So I flew up there and said, "Listen, you can't do this to me. You can't threaten to kill yourself to get me to give you more money, and as a result of you doing that, I'm going to stop giving you money. I'm pretty sure it's the right thing to do, it's an unhealthy situation," and his response was that he was absolutely going to commit suicide if I stopped giving him the money, and though I didn't think he'd really do it, I knew I'd feel pretty shitty if he did, so I went on supporting him, for years.

Nothing stopped him from asking. He even sent me a letter when I was in a cell in Texas prison. I'd been a junkie for a while. I was at the absolute bottom of the bottom of the bottom. I was in Huntsville, with murderers and rapists and unpleasant people of all colors, and I got a letter from Ethan saying, "I think I can get a small boat and go up the Inland Passage to Alaska, and it probably won't cost more than about fifty thousand dollars." I wondered—in what world was he living? I was in *prison*; I didn't have a quarter for a candy bar. What was he thinking? That's when I realized he wasn't always connected to the real world. When I finally got out of jail, I visited him up in Shasta, and he had built a house out of poles and timbers and Visqueen [polyvinyl plastic sheeting]. That's how he said you should build a house. "You build the poles and the frame and the atrium kind of thing for the bed to be above the ground. You get your stove, your wood, your little kitchen, and you staple real heavy Visqueen all around it." That was his house, wrapped like a tree stump. It looked pretty funny but it worked. By that time, I had given up on trying to convince him to get a job.

On Mount Shasta, Ethan retreated further and further into the isolation of the forest, so similar to the summer camp where he first discovered the wilderness as a child forty years earlier. He eked out a living doing odd jobs, and eventually became a watchman and caretaker for clandestine marijuana patches hidden deep in the inaccessible mountains of the Northern California national parkland. Before he died, Ethan circulated a densely worded fund-raising document to all his friends and family, describing his vision. For brevity's sake, a condensed version is reproduced here. The original is more descriptive, rambling, and apocalyptic.

"THE SEED PEOPLE"
THE COMMUNITY IN THE WILDERNESS

It is clear to anyone who is watching closely, that this civilization is destroying our planet . . . It is gobbling up resources much faster that they can be renewed. Soon we will have nothing to eat but each other. Why is this happening? Because humanity is disobeying the Laws of the Universe.

The death throes of civilization will be terrible. It is likely that there will be few survivors. From those few will be chosen some very special people to lead the way to a new kind of civilization, one based on Universal Law and a deep reverence for all life.

They must be willing to give up and leave behind comfort, security and the illusion of safety. They will be criticized and ridiculed and often lonely, but they are urgently needed. Their reward will be the knowledge that they are living in accordance with Universal law, and furthering God's plan.

These dedicated "SEED PEOPLE" will form small groups and communities and GO WILD. . . . We will be gentle nomads, moving quietly through the wilderness, blessing and healing, and living our lives as we go. Offering our special skills and gifts to all the lives we contact . . .

His suicide note also said, "By the time you read this, I'll be gone and I'm going to recycle myself. Go into the woods and let the bears have me." He concluded his suicide note with the words "Go wild." The sheriffs were obligated to search for him, but winter was coming on, and they didn't have any success. I had a long conversation with the sergeant in charge, a very nice guy. He said, "We'll look, but I can't give you a whole lot of hope. If he committed suicide out there like he says in the note, we won't find him until springtime, because there's been a couple of feet of snowfall since he went missing." The official manhunt lasted three days and they couldn't find anything. Of course, none of the locals who knew what Ethan did for a living would say anything, because the searchers were, after all, law enforcement. I went to Mount Shasta to make sure there wasn't something funny going on—if Ethan had been tending a big patch, somebody could have knocked him off in order to swipe it. A big patch could be worth millions of dollars. You don't get them easily, and people kill people for that amount of money all the time, so I wasn't sure that he had committed suicide and I wanted to go look for myself. Eventually, I was convinced.

In the spring of 1988, they found him, and he had done exactly what he had said. He killed himself in the woods, shot himself, and the bears had been eating what was left. The sheriff asked me if I wanted the gun, and I said no. His friends up there sent me all his papers and stuff and I have them somewhere. I miss him. I wish he was still alive. I could be a better brother to him now than I could then, and I think he would love his nieces and nephews, he'd be good for them to meet. I'd love to have taken Django camping with Ethan. He would have been a great source of woods lore, he was a real outdoorsman. We could go right now. And sadly, I understand now how his fascination for reading, his disappointment with the music, and his personal isolation led him away from civilization and into the deep woods, forever.

FADE TO BLACK:

Seventeen

MUSIC AND BUSINESS

FADE IN:

EXTERIOR — STADIUM, ARTISTS' ENTRANCE — NIGHT —
AFTER THE SHOW
MASSIVE BUSES IDLING, READY TO ROLL
INTERIOR — BUS — NIGHT (SAME TIME)

When you're back on the bus after a show, it's a good feeling. It's also a good place to talk about what just happened, what's going to happen, and how I feel about it. Sometimes it's a conversation about politics or science fiction, two areas that seem to be overlapping more and more these days. Sometimes, it's tech talk: stagecraft, recording technology, cars and engines, sailing and navigation, or computers. More often than not, it's about the music; what we've played or written, or what we're going to write, or what we've heard recently that we like. From there, it's a short jump to the subject of the music business.

I'm convinced that if you took the original Byrds to a record company right now and said, "Hey, these kids are great," you'd get a big yawn, or worse. Same with the guys I'm with now. If you could get any busy executives in suits to put down their Crackberry Palm Pilot Treos and actually listen to Crosby, Stills, Nash, and Young, in any combination or all together, they'd say, "Sorry, these guys are too weird, that's too inflammatory, too political." That's the truth: we wouldn't get a contract.

The music business changed dramatically, to the point where I'm mad, angry, pissed off, outraged by what's happened to it. I've always been very antiestablishment about the business side of music. I can't help it, it just comes naturally. All I have to do is look at a copy of *Billboard* or any music-industry magazine and I get mad and froth at the mouth.

The structure of the music business was revolutionized by the arrival of Bob Dylan, the Beatles, the Byrds, Joni Mitchell, Jackson Browne, and a host of others. The tidal wave of singer-songwriters swept away the old business models of Tin Pan Alley and the Broadway musical in a tsunami of new talent and new deals. In some ways, the growth of the music business paralleled that of the movie industry. It was founded by groundbreaking independents exploiting a new technology. That power was later consolidated by giant vertically integrated conglomerates that owned the talent, the means of production, and the channels of distribution. Lasky, Goldwyn, Mayer, Zanuck, the Warner brothers, Laemmle, and Zukor invented the movie business, owned the theaters, and ran the studios. Jerry Wexler, Ahmet Ertegun, Clive Davis, Goddard Lieberson, and Berry Gordy did the same with the record business: they found the talent, embraced the recording process, commissioned songwriters, and marketed the product. The same way black-and-white went to color and wide screen, the 78 became the 45, which became the 33⅓, mono became stereo, and FM replaced AM. The new Goliaths are already through the gates—one of the Goliaths is Gates. Cable and satellite broadcast, the iPod, the Internet, TiVo, CDs and DVDs—new technologies and business models are evolving with massive rewards and hugely unpredictable, unintended consequences. Some of David's comments below are from an interview for PBS's Frontline *in March 2004, and although they're published on his website, they bear repeating. We've included elaborations and fresh material as part of the text that follows:*

At some point in the last forty years, when the overall take from the music business crossed some sort of threshold, some multiple of a billion dollars, the really big boys got interested. They said, "Oh, wait a minute, that's some serious cash. I better go over there and rake off some of that." There were changes in attitude and changes in latitude, nothing stayed the same, which is an oft-quoted line from Jimmy Buffet, who's been around long enough to know. There were changes in management, even entirely new managements, and we were dealing with different people. You'd go to a meeting with a record company and it wouldn't be a guy there who knew that you had written a new song and thought that was cool, it would be a guy who knew that he had moved forty thousand pieces out of Dallas this month, and he had no idea what you were talking about: "Pieces of what?"

Today, record companies are run by lawyers and accountants, which is the definition of soulless managerial efficiency. The people who run record companies today wouldn't know a song if it flew up their nose and died. They haven't a clue. And if you tell, their reaction would be, "Yeah? So, your point is?" They don't give a shit, they don't care, and they're proud they don't care.

Look at it this way. A decade ago, somewhere between a fourth and a third of the record business was owned by a whiskey company that was notably inept at running a record company. And they sold it to a French water company, who knew even less. Now, those guys didn't have a clue. And they didn't care about having a clue. They are still trying to run it as if they're selling widgets, plastic-wrapped widgets that they can sell more of. And they want easily definable, easily accessible, controllable product that has a short shelf life, so that as soon as it spoils (which is no surprise, given that it was crap to start with), they can create some more.

You see manufactured acts every day, with puffball hair and black leather, fondling guitars and squirming sexy for the videos—there's a hundred groups like that, a thousand of them, boy bands, girl bands, trans-gender bands, all with shocking pink names and all without any conception of how to write a song. None whatsoever. There isn't one song in anything they've ever done. The process, as I imagine it, goes something like this: "Get me a lead singer. He's androgynous, blond hair, very pretty. And a guitar player, sort of hatchet-faced, wears a hat, plays very fast, must be very dramatic. Then get a pound of bass player, a pound of drummer. No keyboards; I think we look good. And we'll call them the Bosco Bombers . . . no. The Bad Dogs, that's good! I like that!" The people in those bands can't write, play, or sing. They make them sound good with Pro-tools [a computerized music software program], and if they sing out of tune, someone will say, "Oh, punch the button. Put it in tune." Which is very frustrating to people like me, who've spent the last forty or fifty years learning how to sing in tune in the first place.

A month later, the Bad Dogs, or the Bad Band, will benefit from a million dollars spent on promotion and marketing. They'll be everywhere you look and listen, and they'll bring in enough to justify the process and start it all over again with some pubescent girl in low-cut jeans with premature breast implants. Everybody wins, except the audience. Let's face it: music is magic, and the music business of today is dirt. It was corrupted by people with no talent, no sense, no brains, and no knowledge. Early on, there were exceptions, the occasional John Hammond or Ahmet Ertegun. There are some conscientious people in the music business; some of them are musicians. Herb Alpert at A&M Records comes to mind. It's hard to fault musician-executives, but you can count the good ones on the fingers of a gypsy guitarist's left hand—they're a rare commodity.

Ahmet is the guy who signed Crosby, Stills, and Nash to Atlantic Records. He heard us sing, sent us into the studio before we even had a contract or a deal in place. He saw Aretha Franklin when she was signed to Columbia Records and they were trying to turn her into a lounge act. He said, "These guys don't know what they have!" and hired her away. Six months later, she was the biggest star in the country, because she could sing like God on a good day. It took people with the ears and balls of Ahmet, Jerry Wexler, and Tommy Dowd to make it happen. It doesn't happen now. Every once in a while, there's an aberration, a crack in the pavement. Somebody like Shawn Colvin will have a hit like *Sunny Came Home*, because it's just so good, and it slides in, avoiding all of the meaningless, tasteless, cardboard cut-out crap around it.

There was a moment in time when music and pictures came together, when music videos started showing up on television. We all thought it was great, we could tell the story in pictures, while we're telling a song. Crosby, Stills, Nash, and Young made videos—I made one myself that Sean Penn directed after he contacted me and asked to do it. It was a song called "Hero" that Phil Collins and I wrote. But it didn't get played. I'm not cute. I can sing, but I'm not cute. And so, of course, it didn't do anything. The focus had shifted from what you can do to what you look like. It meant that anyone who came off well in an interesting video was suddenly at the top, whereas hugely talented people who might be great musicians but didn't have a charismatic or even interesting visual appearance barely got any notice at all. We singers went from being a musical experience to being a theatrical experience.

The music video arrived in 1980, a key element in the success of a fledgling cable service called MTV. Ironically, the thing that helped kill the business first made it strong. Producer Trevor Horn's band The Buggles made an album prophetically titled The Age of Plastic. *The hit song on that album was "Video Killed the Radio Star." No shit! According to most sources, it was the first song played in the first hour of the first day MTV*

went on the air. The visually compelling video precisely outlined the prob-
lem and predicted the future. The director was Russell Mulcahy, who
went on to shoot classics of the genre (remember Duran Duran?) before
graduating to feature films. The Buggles' lyric refrain has a sad echo ef-
fect: "In my mind and in my car, we can't rewind, we've gone too far.
Pictures came and broke your heart . . ." MTV and, from 1985, VH1,
caught the public's attention, especially the viewers in the much-coveted
youth market demographic. There wasn't any evil intent; it was pure mar-
keting, an idea whose time had come. It was a cultural turning point that
led to massive unintended consequences.

None of us saw what would happen, and ultimately, the business de-
volved to make stars out of people who looked great. Unfortunately,
many of them had no vocal, compositional, or technical skills whatsoever.
The current ethos in the United States of America is all to do with surface and nothing to do with substance. It doesn't matter that Britney
Spears has nothing to say and is about as deep as a birdbath. What matters is that she has cute tits. She doesn't sing in concert; none of them do.
Push a button, out comes the vocal. Do you ever notice, when you're listening to the new pretty girl acts in a live concert—any of them, Janet
Jackson included—that they're not breathing hard? Even when they've
just been dancing like crazy? Running across stadium stages and climbing risers? That's because you're not hearing what they're singing. You're
listening to a tape.

Here's a perfect recent example of technology run amok: movie and video
hottie Jessica Simpson has an equally hot kid sister, Ashlee Simpson. Barely
in her twenties, Ashlee has a successful career as a singer, as that's defined
these days: multiple chart hits, concert tours, and plenty of media atten-
tion. She's a gossip-column favorite, because of her lasting contribution to
music industry lore. Her moment occurred on Saturday Night Live, *in*
2004, live on network television. An audio malfunction cued the wrong

lip synch tape for Ms. Simpson and she couldn't sing it. Her band played, her voice was heard singing the wrong song, and rather than catch on and move her lips and pretend she was singing, all she could do was goof around for the camera and do a little clog dance, making herself forever the poster girl for the drawbacks of pretaped performance, i.e., "lip synch" (or "lipstink"). Shades of Milli Vanilli.

In 1988, our great good friend Michael Hedges, a genius who died too soon, struggled to sell less than a hundred thousand records for a boutique label, Wyndham Hill. It reinforced my belief that talent and brilliance and music often have very little to do with show business; they're completely separate. When you first get involved in the record business, it's a total mystery and it takes you a long time to find out how it works, how they're cheating you, where they steal the money, what to do and what not to do, who to trust and who not to trust. It takes a great deal of time. You pretty much have to make a few mistakes before you can get a grasp on how to hold out making your living in the music business. I actually came home from a tour once where the manager made more money than Graham or I did. We made him give it back. It wasn't Elliot Roberts.

Elliot Roberts is the guy who shook hands with David Geffen and started a company with a name that could be seen either as a protective beacon ("We're looking out for our clients"), or a shout of warning ("Look out!"). In truth, Lookout Management was named for the street in Laurel Canyon where many of the principals lived: clients Joni Mitchell and Graham Nash, Elliot, and more. My ex-wife, Allison Caine, moved the files from Elliot's home office and set up a new office in a small place on La Cienega Boulevard called the Clear Thoughts Building. The name was actually emblazoned on the modest façade; it later became one of the many interior designer/decorator dens that line the street. Lookout Management became the Geffen-Roberts Company, and had one of the

most impressive client rosters and bank accounts in the music business.
When they became a record company, they chose the name Asylum, be-
cause part of their huge profitability and success derived from a fiercely
protective and nurturing management style.

ELLIOT ROBERTS:

We still do the same thing today. I don't talk about any of these deals
with Neil [Young]. He knows what none of these deals are. He assumes
that I'm not fucking him, he's wrong, and one of these days I'm going
to go to Brazil and never come back . . . They did the covers, they did
the music, they wrote the songs, they did the albums and we did the
deals. . . . They trusted us to always look out for them, to never be self-
motivated, and kill the corporate pig who had been fucking us because
we all made such bad deals when we all started. Everyone gave their
publishing away. Even when I made Joan and Neil's first record deals,
they were like seven [percentage] points. I didn't know. I didn't know
what you could get. I thought seven points was like real good, and we
paid the producer out of our seven points for the first album . . . Then
we found out [we were screwed], and they went, "Well, you signed it,
man. After that we [said], "Okay, fine. If that's how you play, that's
how we'll play," and so we did. That was the philosophy and we were
very protective of the artists because we loved them.

David's publishing was all over the place. He was badly exploited and
overdrawn on advances given during the drug years. His catalogue was
bought by Graham Nash, who held it safe from predator creditors and the
IRS. He and Crosby have settled the debt. David's new music and CPR's
catalogue are more carefully managed, and the CSNY/Atlantic Records
deals are among the legendary Gordian knots of the music business; it took
decades to sort out album commitments from thirty years ago.
  Eventually, David Geffen sold his record company to MCA and re-

ceived a significant number of shares in the company, which multiplied in value as MCA was sold to Matsushita, which sold it to Seagram, which sold it to Vivendi. The Geffen MCA shares contributed to a personal fortune that made his name synonymous with major philanthropy, including a $200 million donation to establish the Geffen School of Medicine at UCLA; his name is all over the building where David Crosby has experienced multiple surgeries. When asked, "How does it feel when you're trudging up the stairs or being wheeled into UCLA and every other wall has the name Geffen on it?" David replies:

It doesn't bother me at all. I called him up and thanked him when he gave the two hundred million to UCLA. I told he did a fantastic thing that almost nobody in his position would have done, and I really appreciated it. I'm perfectly ready to criticize him all to pieces for the things that he did wrong, but David is what David is. If you expect something else, then it's your own expectations that are screwing you up. He made his money from music and the movies, he's partners with Steven Spielberg and Jeffrey Katzenberg in DreamWorks. He's always been ahead of the curve.

ELLIOT:

Crosby's a veteran. This is a man who's looked at royalties from both sides now, you might say. But he's pretty sophisticated, David, about the business and so there are periods of great productivity and there are periods that aren't. So the periods when you're writing and you're doing songs, you don't want to hear about what your sheet music problem is or about this licensing deal or that licensing deal. You want to know that we'll make an educated guess, and not put [your music] where you wouldn't want it, and that you won't hear it on some schlock TV show, and call me to say, "Excuse me, please tell me I got a fortune for doing that because it sure wasn't for art."

After the whiskey company and the water company and some others got out of the record business, the remaining record companies and competing labels became part of three global conglomerates. Free market laissez-faire capitalism in action: big fish eating little fish, big companies eating little companies, until only the big companies are left. That's doubly true of the broadcast industry, which once was a glorious anarchic array of thousands of stations in hundreds of markets, each different. Hell, during the twenty-five years between CSNY tours, we were kept alive and introduced to an entire new generation by independent album-oriented rock FM stations and free-form DJs who played whatever they liked. Those days are gone for good.

At KMPX and KSAN in San Francisco, at KMET in Los Angeles and WNEW in New York, the potent combination of no time and temperature announcements, idiosyncratic DJs, stereo broadcasting, and no talking over the music dramatically distinguished free-form FM (alternative radio) from Top 40 AM radio. When Tom and Raechel Donahue started the first underground FM radio on KMPX in San Francisco in 1967, I was hired to fill a Sunday noon to six p.m. slot. Tom Donahue recognized that FM could play album cuts of any length, in stereo; essentially, the station's philosophy was "Play music on the radio the way you play it for your friends at home." In San Francisco in 1967, everyone's friends at home were getting high, playing KMPX at high volume and through headsets, and the unique programming turned heads in every tie-dyed paraphernalia shop, VW garage, record store, and exotic clothing storefront in the Bay Area. The revolution in FM broadcasting had begun. When radio found its new and independent voice, nobody would've predicted that the form would be born, flourish, and die in just thirty years. The phenomenon has completely run its course. Jim Ladd is a veteran of the entire cycle, a DJ in Los Angeles currently heard on KLOS, 95.5 on the FM dial. He is the last free-form disc jockey in a major market in North America, the only person not shackled to a play list issued by station owners and management, and he knows the history as well as anyone.

JIM LADD:

You could buy an FM station for pocket change when that started because there were only foreign language, religious programs, and static. Tom Donahue came along, found an FM station whose phone was disconnected, and, as Raechel puts it, "Tom painted the sky blue for them." They brought in boxes of their own records, and started everything. FM radio created a sense of community that you do not have through the Internet. We took what Dr. King was saying, we took what Abbie Hoffman and Tom Hayden were saying, the antiwar people were saying, and we combined it with what David Crosby and Bob Dylan and John Lennon and the Doors were saying. We put that together and created a third element. Once you combine "I Have a Dream" with "Blowin' in the Wind," once you combine antiwar statements with "Wooden Ships," suddenly you're relating to a broad audience and pulling all of those thoughts together in a way that you can't do anymore. Why? We got too successful. Unbeknownst to us, we were making gazillions of dollars.

Crosby's rule number one is a simple axiom: *The bigger a company gets, the less it gives a shit about you.* Huge companies don't even know who's on their roster. They don't have the time or the money or the inclination, or the ability, to see budding young artists, nurture them, and bring them along. They don't have the wit or even a clue, and worse yet, they don't care about not having a clue.

Marc Cohn is a singer-songwriter, probably the last of the traditional breed. Cohn's first signature hit, "Walkin' to Memphis," made him an instant star—he won the Grammy in 1992 as Best New Artist. Jeff Pevar

*was his guitar partner for years. Cohn and Crosby met at the Grammy
ceremonies, and played together shortly after. He was an opening act for
Crosby, Stills, and Nash, and has a glorious memory of their early times
together:*

MARC COHN:

Crosby, Stills, and Nash played the Universal Amphitheatre and I
think it's quite possible that this is the first time I ever sang with
David, certainly one of the first. I did a song from my first record
called "Perfect Love" and my background choir was David, Graham,
Bonnie Raitt, and Jackson Browne. If that had been the end of my career it would have been fine. I think that's certainly one of the first
times we actually sang, which was incredible.

*Cohn has been supported on tour by his company, and he's also been
dropped from his label. He's survived years of touring and recording, and
he can speak directly to the issues:*

MARC COHN:

I could tell immediately there was something different going on hearing Crosby, Stills, and Nash, Jackson, James, Joni Mitchell, Neil, when
I was twelve years old, sitting in my apartment kitchen in Cleveland,
Ohio, and the Sunday morning FM station was playing a whole side
of whatever it was. Before I even knew what that music was, I knew
it sounded different to me than the music that was being played during the week on that same station. I later found out what was different was that [the artists] wrote it. The authenticity of the delivery and
the rawness and honesty of it was completely earth-shattering to me,
completely. That's what drew me in.

Nowadays, it's all about everybody trying to sound like Stevie
Wonder sounded thirty years ago or the way Mariah Carey sounds
now. To me it's all affected, mannered, over the top, soulless interpre-

tive singing. It has nothing to do with the lyrics. Clearly, these guys didn't write any of what they're singing [and] they're not even good interpreters. They're just wailing away. Not one songwriter has come out of *American Idol* because it has nothing to do with writing: It's complete reflection. It's perfect. I totally get it, and I'm even interested in watching it, kind of like you're interested in watching a car wreck. But it's worlds away from the thing that drew me into wanting to be a musician.

The only relief is that somehow the Jackson Brownes and the Joni Mitchells and the James Taylors and the Neil Youngs and the Bonnie Raitts of this world manage to hang on and still be able to work. And every now and again, there will be a new original voice or talent, like Marc Cohn, or Bruce Hornsby, Tracy Chapman, Shawn Colvin, Jack Johnson, Norah Jones, Nickel Creek, Pink ("Please, Mr. President") who write real songs and create great music, and no one comes to see them dance or work in a G-string and high boots, they come to hear the music because they love the songs. Somehow, good art always prevails, even against overwhelming odds, even censorship and suppression. Ask the Dixie Chicks, whose new record made number one even after Clear Channel (twelve hundred FM stations) banned their music because one of the singers criticized the president in a public forum!

JIM LADD:

How did we go from being the outlaw voice of the counterculture to this boring media outlet? How do you make *rock and roll* boring? In one word: deregulation. Before Ronald Reagan, and throughout the entire history of radio, ever since there was an FCC, there was something called the Seven and Seven Rule: no one person or company could own more than seven radio and TV stations at once. Period. Networks had affiliates, but seven was the maximum you could own. Then they figured out a way around that rule, they lobbied the

Congress to rewrite the law and deregulate the broadcasting industry. Now you can own as many radio and TV stations as you want. Suddenly, Clear Channel Broadcasting owns twelve hundred radio stations. Metro Media has another eight hundred, whatever.

So what does that do? FM radio was making millions of dollars for the owners. They don't want to leave this in the hands of hippies. So they bring in radio consultants because they can understand pie charts and graphs and blah, blah, blah, as opposed to somebody like me talking to them. Now, thanks to deregulation, not only do they own KMET, let's say, or KLOS, but they own all the other rock stations in town. So if Jim Ladd says something about George Bush that the station doesn't like and they fire me for my political views, before deregulation, that was fine. I could walk across the street, and if my ratings and my name were big enough, I got another job and I went to work for the competition. Well, they eliminated the competition because they own it all. So suddenly there is no place to go, there is no alternative voice. You can't go across the street because they own across the street. And that's what happened to FM radio. They sold it. It's a First Amendment issue.

Russ Kunkel is one of rock's great drummers, a survivor of more than three decades onstage, in studios, and on the road. He's also toured with Crosby, Stills, Nash, and Young, as well as Bob Dylan, Jackson Browne, Linda Ronstadt, Lyle Lovett, Jimmy Buffett, James Taylor, George Harrison, Carole King, Steve Winwood, and more. He's also a record producer, songwriter, film composer, and entrepreneur, and an articulate advocate for new technology. Another drummer once assessed the new technology that was changing music recording this way: "The difference between me and a drum machine," he said, "is that if you spill beer on me, I keep playing." On the business of music, Russ is more of an optimist than many—and if you spill beer on him he'll keep playing too.

Russ Kunkel:

Getting something done in the record companies in the old days took forever. Legal Affairs had to talk to Business Affairs, and Business Affairs had to talk to the A&R people, and they were always fighting and somebody's on vacation, and then the president of the company is screwing a new artist and she just got your release date. If you're going to be successful, you have to be on MTV or VH1, and there has to be a video playing on it or you're not in the game and that's that. The truth is nobody's selling that many records anymore. Twenty-five thousand units of a record on Rhino or anything like that, everybody's happy. Everybody's happy with twenty-five thousand. If you look at the *Billboard* charts, there are some weeks where the number one record only sold 120,000 that week.

I remember I produced a record for Jimmy Buffett called "Barometer Two" and it charted at number five, and that week it sold 240,000 copies. That was ten years ago. And that was small compared to Linda Ronstadt and James Taylor. When their records came out, you'd have to sell 500,000 copies to be number one. [The industry] is selling less and less now, and the reason for that is because everyone's getting it on the Internet. Fortunately, the music business has deteriorated to such a point that it has to rebuild itself again; the process has started and in the entrepreneurial spirit that is alive and well in this country is the thing that's fueling it, and I kind of liken it to the Wild West again because there are no rules anymore.

There used to be thousands of little mom and pop record stores. Now, there's only a handful of chains. There are maybe twelve guys who control seventy-five percent of sales in the United States of America. There are possibly eighteen guys who control ninety-five percent of sales in the United States of America. We know their names. We know their numbers. The old-time record companies were like a bank: they gave you a big advance, essentially lending you your own money to make a record, after which they'd take ninety percent of the profits. They did nothing for it, other than hand it over to layers of distribution: rack jobbers and the like, who were like a capillary system that fed small stores. Oh, and "promotion," which mostly meant bribing radio stations for airplay, either directly or through intermediaries ("independent promotion"). The Rolling Stones even put out a song mocking the parasites who fed off the process. Remember "The Under Assistant West Coast Promotion Man"? He and those like him are dead and gone or selling used cars these days. The record business just doesn't work like that anymore. It hardly works at all.

The big companies are dinosaurs. They have a huge superstructure of people who do nothing. In the basement, there are three women who do all the work for the entire company. Upstairs, they fly in corporate jets, they pay CEOs $4 million a year with a $8 million bailout if they fire them. These are business practices that are ludicrous and have killed businesses before, and will eventually kill these guys. They operate on the principle that all product and all artists are disposable and they have no intention of doing anything, no matter what they say—and they promise you everything. What they mean is they're going to take one single off of your album, two if you're Madonna, and they're going to throw that single out there. If it doesn't stick, then you'd better come through with another album because that one's over. It was about the single. Radio was the only selling tool and if you don't sell to the radio with that single, then the rest of the songs in the album were just filler. They don't know that there's any other way to do it. I can't live and work like that; I'm not disposable product and I don't put filler on my albums. It's insanity, and I don't deal with it anymore.

Ani DiFranco formed her own label and successfully manages to rake off sixty-three percent of the gross for herself. She made a distribution deal. She makes her own records. She makes them very simply, and she has a secret weapon—she works 250 days a year. That's why she's able to do what she does—she has a very loyal following because she's very damn good.

In 1997, the Los Angeles Times *financial section wrote an article about Ani DiFranco's record label, Righteous Babe Records, citing the business acumen of a singer-songwriter who opened her own independent company, avoided corporate overhead charged by the major labels to their artists, and made more for herself per unit than Hootie and the Blowfish or Michael Jackson. Ani DiFranco reports that the story was reprinted by the* New York Times, Forbes *magazine, the Financial News Network, and* Ms., *which prompted her to write a strongly worded letter to the feminist publication. It's as true today as it was then:*

ANI DIFRANCO:

I have indeed sold enough records to open a small office on the half-abandoned main street in the dilapidated urban center of my hometown, Buffalo, New York. I am able to hire fifteen or so folks to run and constantly reinvent the place while I drive around and play music for people. I am able to give stimulating business to local printers and manufacturers and to employ the services of independent distributors, promoters, booking agents, and publicists. I was able to quit my day job and devote myself to what I love. And yes, we are enjoying modest profits these days, affording us the opportunity to reinvest in innumerable political and artistic endeavors. RBR [Righteous Babe Records] is no Warner Bros. But it is a going concern, and for me, it is a vehicle for redefining the relationship between art and commerce in my own life. It is a record company which is the product not just of my own imagination, but that of my friend and manager Scot Fisher and of all the people who work there: people who incorporate and coordinate politics, art and media every day into a people-friendly, subcorporate, woman-informed, queer-happy small business that puts music before rock stardom and ideology before profit.

We also knew that we had to be in the real-world marketplace, so my band, CPR, went looking for an independent. There are lots of people who call themselves independents, but what that means is they've got themselves a label deal with a major, which means the major still controls what happens. "Dependent independents" rely on the major's distribution apparatus and warehousing and shipping and inventory and bookkeeping and accounting. Organize the money that way, let the major be involved in the decisions, and the independent is just another front.

The true independent is an entirely different animal: it's responsive, direct, is usually referred to as a "boutique" label, and has its own money. CPR made their record without having found such a home. But our friend Michael Jensen played the record for the guys at Samson Music, which was owned by Gold Circle, and Gold Circle was owned by Norm Waitt. Norm and Ted Waitt are brothers who started Gateway Computers. They had plenty of their own money, and it didn't belong to Sony or Seagram or MCA or BMG or any of the monsters who control most of the record production in the world. Gold Circle was run by an honest guy named Mike Delich, who used to run Gramophone Records. He's the only guy I've come across in the forty years I've been in the music business who has done every single thing he ever said he would do, and more—he's done nothing that he hasn't said he would do. This is a total first! Luckily for them, sadly for CPR, Gold Circle made such a fortune in the film business (backing an independent feature called *My Big Fat Greek Wedding*) that they dropped the music side to concentrate on film production, where they've become a power; I think they still might conform in many ways to that ideal mentioned by Ani DiFranco earlier: people who incorporate and coordinate politics, art, and media every day into a business that puts ideology before profit.

Donald "Buddha" Miller has refined the independent production concept to fit his old friend and management client, Jackson Browne. In the cur-

My brother, Ethan, during his visionary days as a mountain man in Big Sur. *(David Crosby personal collection)*

...ngo as the cutest toddler . . . ...s, no, that's David Crosby. ...etics at work. Resemblance? ...be the judge. *(David Crosby ...nal collection)*

The young, good-looking David Crosby . . . Oh, wait a minute, it's Django Crosby, who almost cut his hair. Genetics again. *(Photo courtesy Buzz Person)*

With James Raymond: father and son, in the family business. *(Photo courtesy Tim Owe*

The wetsuit walrus look, underwa
(Photo by Dana Africa)

Mother, son, and
granddaughter: clockwise
from top, Django, Jan, and
Grace. *(Photo courtesy
Buzz Person)*

With Jan at the
Berlin Wall in 1989.
CSN sang at the
historic teardown.
*(David Crosby
personal collection)*

There's nothing that
feels as good as this.
*(David Crosby
personal collection)*

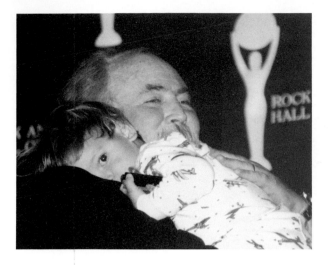

Holding Django before takin
the stage to be inducted with
CSN into the Rock and Roll
Hall of Fame on May 6, 1997
(David Crosby personal collect

Me, Graham Nash, and David Gilmour of Pink Floyd
at the Royal Albert Hall in London, 2006.
(Photo courtesy Buzz Person)

Jan and Django, happy in Amsterdam on our European tour, 2005.
(Photo courtesy Henry Diltz)

The lineup of the band CPR: from left to right, Steve DiStanislao, Jeff Pevar, Andrew Ford, me, and my son James Raymond.
(Photo courtesy Francesco Lucarelli)

Dudes in shades II: Graham and me in 1993, joined at the hip, then as now.
(David Crosby personal collection)

My wise, mature, mischievous loo
(David Crosby personal collection)

Happily between two wonderful women:
Shawn Colvin and my wife, Jan.
(David Crosby personal collection)

Chatting with Diane Sawyer about children, the environment, and campaign finance reform. *(David Crosby personal collection)*

On my Harley without a helmet, which is no way to ride.
(Photo courtesy Buzz Person)

Neil Young and me, standing on our constitutional rights (the stage floor) during the 2006 CSNY tour. *(Photo courtesy Buzz Person)*

Onstage and loving it on the Freedom of Speech '06 tour.
(Photo courtesy Buzz Person)

rent state of the music industry, many artists have had better results re-leasing records independently. Jackson's political activism and instinctive desire to play benefits for worthy causes have made conventional record companies and concert bookers wary. Buddha's response to the changing industry was to create a business model that would connect Jackson's music to his fans. Gerry Tolman was the longtime personal manager of Stephen Stills and Graham Nash, and managed the collective career of Crosby, Stills, and Nash as a trio. He died unexpectedly on New Year's Eve, 2005; Graham, bereft, joined Buddha's management company, Donald Miller and Cree Clover Miller, Esq. Buddha explains the concept, prefacing his remarks with this qualification:

BUDDHA:

On the management side, the challenges are in dealing with record companies, if you deal with them at all. . . . You have to keep from being bitten by sharks that are all around these artists constantly. Record companies are completely out of date and just don't get it any-more. The only thing they can do is capitalize you a little bigger. I hap-pen to have married an attorney. Actually, we decided to get married, and she went to law school. You have to be law literate [because] a lot of these old contracts have language and definitions in them that are interpreted in different ways. Ownership needs to be clarified and protected at all costs. I'm encouraging them [Crosby, Jackson Browne, and Graham Nash] to never, ever sign another contract as long as they live.

Buddha and his wife, Cree, are combining her knowledge of law and contracts with his thirty years of experience on the road with us, and with Jackson, seeing every aspect of the music business from the old days through the Internet era. Their take on the business scene defines the new way music can be made and circulated without being distorted through the prisms and the mirrors of big labels, big business, and big theft. Jack Johnson and the Arctic Monkeys are two new artists who owe their independence and success to the kind of thing we're talking about. ADA [Alternative Distribution Alliance] is an exception to the "no majors" rule because its corporate overlords have no say, and don't meddle in the decision-making process.

BUDDHA:

Jack Johnson, he took that model when Ani DiFranco started. He put out his own record and he is humongously huge. You don't have to reach the success that a record company lives on. That's the thing that's bullshit. A big company thinks that if you sold two million and you dropped off to a million one, you're not successful. Holy shit! That's ridiculous. Now, I just want to be successful amongst the fans. I had to become my own record company for Jackson, not because I couldn't go sign, [but because] there was just no fucking sense in it. You want music, I'll put it on the Web, I'll take it to ADA . . .

Alternative Distribution Alliance was begun in 1993. Its president, Andy Allen, describes it this way: "The thought was to create a system with the same kind of visibility and safety and security of a national major, but scaled for independents." The organization has made alternative independent music distribution not only viable, but profitable for itself and the artists. It's indicative of the bizarre dysfunction of major record labels that this highly successful distribution company was paradoxically financed and set up by the Warner Music Group, a subsidiary of Time-Warner-AOL, one of the true corporate monsters so maligned in this chapter! And yet their artist roster as this is written includes Liz Phair, Nirvana, Better Than Ezra, Postal Service, Arcade Fire, and Death Cab for Cutie. Donald Miller's plan for taking a major artist like Jackson Browne off the major-label treadmill is a classic example of how to do it yourself.

BUDDHA:

We get to ADA and we realize they're front-loading the whole fucking thing for us. They pay for all the retail and they bill back. They pay for manufacturing, all the way down, and they bill back . . . Manufactured, shipped, and positioned in every town is what they do.

Oddly enough, just a few years ago, the advertising and marketing model for independent releases was still under construction. Jackson's company was selling a known commodity; he was an established star, but he didn't have the seven-figure budgets that his old corporate labels could allot to indiscriminate mass-media print and broadcast advertising. The alternative was right there.

BUDDHA:

Andy Allen at ADA, not knowing what he was saying, said, "You know, it's all about the Internet these days. If we get anything going like AOL, we really see units move." And I'm thinking, why in the fuck aren't we going to advertise on it? I took [whatever amount] I could come up with as a budget, I went back to the same TV people who buy and place movies . . . we designed an ad, and—this is the key— *we picked where we would place it.* We had Barnes & Noble, very important to us, and we had Amazon, and we went to the *New York Times, Washington Post,* the *Nation.* We placed [our ad] where people understand who Jackson is. We went to one kind of upbeat rock site where our little banner would pop up and say it's now available.

The Internet has leveled the playing field. It gives artists, singers, songwriters, and innovative bands an alternative and profitable outlet for their work. When we put the band CPR online and sold direct, it cost us a buck, tops a buck twenty-five, to make a CD with case and artwork that a retail store would put in a rack and sell for fifteen to eighteen dollars. When we made our second live album, we owned all the income; we did it with our own money and with our own music, we sold it on the Internet, and we get every damn penny. We shipped quickly, and we got a great rep on the Net because of that. People love it, I love it. I totally, totally dig that. I think that iTunes is the model for the record company of the future.

MARC COHN:

I'm a complete iTunes addict. I'm on there at least once or twice a week. I haven't given up going into record stores. I don't think I ever will as long as they exist, and who knows how long that will be. . . . I go to record stores just to buy something that I think might thrill me and surprise me. And sometimes it's just a hunch; I may know nothing about it. I do that on iTunes all the time, because now you can do it song by song; you don't have to buy a whole record. I'm in mourning too, because I feel that when I go on iTunes, I'm killing the very thing I love, which is the album. But I do it, and I certainly have found amazing songwriters on the Internet.

MUSIC CUE:
"PRE-ROAD DOWNS," REPRISE

Fortunately for us, there's always the road. The music reaches out, and for people who want the authentic experience, without lip synch, flash-pots, light shows, dancers, and glitz, there's always us.

EXTERIOR — HIGHWAY — DAWN
BUSES AND TRUCKS ROLLING TOWARD A LIMITLESS HORIZON
SUPERIMPOSE — A TEXT ROLLS UP THE SCREEN

The fortunes of musicians and the fortunes of music labels have less and less to do with each other. This may be the first stage of what John Perry

Barlow, a former lyricist for the Grateful Dead, once called the shift from "the music business" to "the musician business." In the musician business, the assets that once made the major labels so important—promotion, distribution, shelf space—matter less than the assets that belong to the artists, such as their ability to perform live. As technology has grown more sophisticated, the ways in which artists make money have grown more old-fashioned. The value of songs falls, and the value of seeing an artist sing them rises, because that experience can't really be reproduced. It's funny that, in an era of file-sharing and iPod-stealing, the old troubadour may have the most lucrative gig of all.

"Hello, Cleveland" by James Surowiecki
The New Yorker, May 16, 2005

DISSOLVE TO:

Eighteen

WHAT, AGAIN?

WAYNE, NEW JERSEY, AFTER THE SHOW — NIGHT
INTERIOR — DRESSING ROOM, WITH JEFF PEVAR
AND DAVID CROSBY

The week of March 1–7, 2004, CPR had a tight schedule. On Thursday, they played B.B. King's Blues Club and Grill on Forty-second Street in New York City; the next night they were onstage in Wayne, New Jersey; Saturday they were due in Glenside, Pennsylvania; and Sunday night there was a show in Annapolis, Maryland. Four one-nighters in a row, and Jeff Pevar was feeling a tension in the band, all of whom had deep personal bonds that predated the formation of the group by years.

JEFF PEVAR:

When I have a chance to go out with CSN, or any of these bands that give me steady work, I'm thrilled . . . We're of service to each other and that's one of the things that I feel is beautiful about a band collaboration. With CPR, it feels more like we're all in it together. I'm just really happy and for sure, since the day I met David, he helped get my name out there to the world. A lot more people heard me play music and got familiar with my art because of my association with him, so I'm quite indebted to those guys. We sometimes talk about things that need to be said, and David and I had this huge talk one time in New Jersey somewhere. It took a lot of time, and then I felt shitty, because I looked at my watch. "David, we have ten minutes to get on the bus," I said, and that was the day he left his gun in the hotel room.

Dan McGee is a relatively new addition to the CSNY management family, working first with CSN, later with CPR. Hired by Gerry Tolman in 2003 to fill a temporary vacancy in the middle ranks when lead tour manager Coach Sexton left to manage a Rolling Stones tour, McGee had years of experience as a road manager and tour accountant, working for k.d. lang, Joni Mitchell, the Pat Matheny Group, and Supertramp, the old rocker band that's still huge in Europe. He'd also worked full time as a tour accountant for a New York promoter. Like John Vanderslice and the others in his particular line of work, Dan has a clear idea of his responsibilities.

DAN McGEE:

After the show, David clears the room and says, "Dan, I forgot something, I forgot my bag," and I say, "Oh, that's cool. I'll call," and he repeats it: "No, Dan, I've forgotten my *bag . . .*" and he gives me the look and I don't have to ask, so I call the hotel and they say, "Yeah, we have your bag, Mr. Crosby." Somewhere in between knowing that the bag is actually there and getting on the bus with everybody to go back, with the intention of picking it up, Crosby describes to me what's in the bag. He says it's his gun. And right then, I'm like, "Okay, we don't go. We leave it." David says: "Oh, no, no, no." And then it becomes not a *g-u-n*, it becomes a personal possession, some valuable thing, as if he'd left jewelry or a watch or a pair of shoes. And because we know it's there and we're sure of it, I'm like, "David, we'll just leave it, man. It doesn't matter," and he's insistent. "It's there and I need to go get it."

Well, there's an argument with a sixty-three-year-old man who's my employer who's telling me we should *just do it.* Y'know, [some] tour managers and road managers just cater strictly to the needs of the artist, whether it's going to the drugstore or shining their shoes, or doing whatever's necessary, and they maintain their position without knowledge of the workings of the tour as a whole. I pride myself on knowing everything that's going on so that I can answer to the person who's employing me. I'm a hired professional. These people are my clients, I behave in a professional manner, and I'm disposable.

That's a stark view, but it's the professional ethic, part of the code of the road, if such a thing can be said to exist. Protect the money. There's a spectacularly underappreciated movie called Payday *that captures the seventies, with Rip Torn in a brilliant performance as a substance-abusing country music singer on tour, who gets his tour bus driver/roadie to take a manslaughter charge that should be his. More than one road manager has gone to jail or taken the heat for a client's issues. One of the most senior tour managers for CSNY, Mike Sexton, universally known as "Coach," adds this note:*

MIKE SEXTON:
I say, "Don't get in the business." I told that to my nephew. I told him to get a real job, get married, have kids. The thing about being on the road is that it's tough; if I was married and had kids I wouldn't want to do it. Fortunately, I've had the same girlfriend for twenty-six years; she's happy to see me come, and happy to see me go.

CUT TO:

EXTERIOR — NEW YORK STREET — SATURDAY NIGHT —
FEBRUARY 2004
THE CPR BUS IS ON THE STREET IN FRONT OF THE
DOUBLETREE INN
TWO DARK UNMARKED SEDANS OCCUPY THE PASSENGER
LOADING AREA

There's no excuse for being completely stupid. I made five big mistakes in a row. Road rule number one: never put anything in a drawer or a nightstand, ever. It doesn't matter what it is, your watch or your wallet, your phone, your clothes. Nothing, because sooner or later, you'll forget it. I forgot the wrong thing at the wrong time in the wrong place, and of course they found it. The last mistake in the chain of errors was going back for my bag. They were waiting for me when I walked into the hotel and asked the guy at the desk for it. I didn't have to go back for it, but I believed the guy when he said, "If you have your ID, we have the bag, just come and get it." Did I know he was told to say that by the cops? No. Should I have figured it out? Probably. But as comedian Ron White says: "You can't fix stupid."

Dan McGee:

So the bus pulls up in a zone that's supposed to be No Parking, and there's two cars parked there. If I spent three seconds looking at them closer I would have known exactly what they were. David and I walked toward the elevator and I'm like, "You know, Croz, you really don't have to do this. Just leave it." And he's, "No, man, we've come all this way. We might as well do it." What can I say? "No, David, get your ass back in there. You can't take a chance!" There's nobody in the whole place except two guys sitting on a couch.

191

David goes right over to the counter, pulls out his ID for the night clerk, and says, "I'm here to get my bag." The guy didn't say anything, and I'm looking over at the two guys over on the couch, and I'm thinking Oh, fuck, there's two big guys, they're plainclothes, they look pretty straight, and I don't turn around and tell David to stop. The guy goes into the back and comes out with a short, meekish-looking guy who says: "You're under arrest." I'm shaking my head and holding the counter, and David's like, "Aw, fuck me, you got to be kidding."

Not only was I stupid, I was predictable. One of the cops told Dan he couldn't believe we were actually coming back. The fact is these particular detectives do this at least once a night on a Friday and Saturday night in Manhattan, busting out-of-towners who leave guns in their rooms. It's a routine thing they do at different hotels, although I doubt the Plaza or the Carlyle or the St. Regis or any other discreet hotel would've called the cops on me. But CPR was an economy tour, one bus, mid-range hotels and motels, nothing fancy, and here I was, just another jerk who left a .45 in a hotel room in a city where they have something called the Sullivan Law, which goes back to 1911, and is one of the strictest firearms laws in the country. I asked the guy at the desk for my bag, he gave it to me, said, "Is this yours?" and as soon as I said yes, that was it.

The wire services and national press ran it something like this: Rock musician David Crosby was arrested in a Times Square hotel after an employee found marijuana, a loaded pistol and two knives in his bag. Crosby had checked out of his room at the Doubletree Suites Hotel on Broadway, after performing with his band, CPR, at the B.B. King Blues Club Thursday night, and in Wayne, N.J., on Friday. Mr. Crosby left a suitcase behind, and in it an employee searching for identification found ap-

proximately an ounce of marijuana, a hunting knife, a folding knife, a
.45-caliber pistol, and some cigarette papers, according to police. Mr.
Crosby was arrested when he returned to pick up the bag . . .

After they busted me, the cops read me my rights and cuffed me. Very professional, nice guys, and I have no beef with them. They even took me out the side door of the hotel, so there'd be nobody to see my familiar face and shape being bundled into the backseat of a car in handcuffs. They took me to Midtown North, in the West Fifties, and Dan had to tell the guys on the bus what happened. He took the bus to the precinct and sent them rolling toward the next gig while he stayed in the city to deal with my problems, starting with the medications I need to live. Everything was properly labeled, in pharmacy bottles with my prescription number and my name, so I got to take my medications after the detectives scrutinized everything.

They told Dan they'd keep me uptown as long as they possibly could, because they didn't want to put me "in population" at four o'clock in the morning. That would have meant a trip downtown to the Manhattan Detention Center, commonly called The Tombs, with New York's less-than-finest, in a crowded tank of drunks, junkies, pimps, headbangers, leg breakers, rapists, and thieves, a place where the floor covering is wall-to-wall barf. I was grateful for the consideration, but I still needed to have a lawyer present at my arraignment in the morning, to formally request bond. If I didn't, the judge would have no choice but remand me to custody. Dan's job was to ride for help. He left to make the calls, including telling Jan before she heard it on the news. While he scrambled, I finished the night sleeping as best I could on the floor of the cop shop, just a short walk from the bright lights of Broadway.

Dan started burning up the wires, calling David's management in LA,
Elliot Roberts and Frank Gironda, Jan, in Santa Ynez; Jim Hart; and

anyone else David suggested before they parted ways at the precinct. Meanwhile, the band was heading for the next date without them. Each has his or her own sorrowful recollection of the event.

STEVIE D:

Basically, what happened was we did the show in New Jersey and after the show, David said, "I have to go back to the hotel to get my meds," and we were all "Okay," and we get halfway back and he says, "I forgot something else." I didn't ask; I usually try to stay on the downlow and not to get too involved. We pulled up next to the hotel, he and Dan went in. About ten minutes later, Dan comes running back and says, "They got Croz. They found a gun." I just felt sad. Things get so blown out of proportion and I feel like I know him so well, I know his intentions are all really good, so it broke my heart that he had to spend the night and the whole thing.

DREW FORD:

We're just told that we just have to drop by, do a little detour before we keep going. So we're just kind of waiting for him to come back. And damn, the tour manager comes back by himself and he has this horrid look on his face. He's kind of pacing around, telling us what's going on and man, I'd never seen him like that. And it was like a nightmare.

JEFF PEVAR:

God, I didn't feel good about it. When Dan came out he was so upset with himself, he's beating his head against the wall and he feels like a total idiot. We had to tell him, "Dan, come on, it wasn't your decision to make. It's his tour, it's his bus, it's his life, he made the decision, it's what he wanted. We all tried to talk him out of it." Didn't help.

Jim and Judy Hart were in a hotel in Los Angeles when Jan reached them on Jim's cell phone. Together, they share their memory of frustration and anxiety.

JIM HART:

The phone rings in the hotel room at four in the morning and it's Jan. She doesn't know we're in Los Angeles or has forgotten, and she's hoping we're right up the street in New York, where we live, because David has been arrested and is going to jail and it's really bad. And I thought he got into a fight or he punched somebody out. No. He'd left his gun. They were looking for a lawyer, anything, and I said, "Jan, we're in LA." She said, "Oh, my God," she was devastated, and angry, as she should have been. And we ended up getting a car service to wait outside the door for them at the courthouse. It was all we could do.

JUDY:

We got our car service because we knew they'd be somewhat cool and hopefully not give out information. McGee wanted to sneak David out because he had to go work in Philadelphia or Pennsylvania, someplace they had a gig.

Buzz Person (pronounced "pur-sohn") is a devoted fan, a lawyer whose schedule permits him to go on the road frequently, seeing CSN and CPR shows all over the world. He's a semiofficial photographer for the bands, and his images grace their websites and fan pages all over the Internet. He had gone east from his home in Southern California and met a couple of fans from the UK to see the four CPR shows in and around New York.

BUZZ PERSON:

It's my habit to go to a hotel [after a show] and drive the next morning, while the band and crew may go on [to the next] city overnight.

I woke up Saturday morning, checked my e-mail, and found a note from Dan McGee, saying, "Buzz, call me, no matter what time it is when you read this." So that was around six or seven o'clock in the morning, and I called Dan and he says David got busted last night. I got the guys up and had breakfast and we drove over to Glenside, PA, where the next show was supposed to be. On the road we heard the radio news, that David had been arrested for possession of weapons and drugs. We were staying at the same hotel as the crew, there was a show that night at the Keswick Theatre, and all we could do was wait for David . . . Everybody was well aware that David had probably been up all night, was probably under a great deal of stress, and was probably emotionally drained and so there was a real concern as to whether or not there would be a show.

ELLIOT ROBERTS:

Neil and I got the phone call. I remember us both laughing for quite a while when we heard that he went back. . . . He's definitely hit rock bottom, because that is so fucking stupid that even he, when he looks back on it, will say: "That was my bottom moment." We actually looked at that as a good thing, in some sick, perverted, sarcastic way. He left his gun in the room and he went back for it: "Excuse me, can I have my gun, please?" The only other guy we know who did that was Robert Blake. At some point, David's saying, "Yes, I am a fool. I eventually should be learning from this, I guess . . ." But, again, we thought this was a rock-bottom moment and it would be a good thing.

GRAHAM NASH:

Susan and I were in London and I was just on my computer checking messages and stuff and checking the news and I see Crosby's being busted again, so I immediately get on the phone because nobody knew where I was in London and found out that yet once again, he had made a wrong decision, and it was a silly decision. I mean, knowing what was in that bag, and knowing that there was probably very little else of value in that bag, he admitted to me he should have been smarter and he should have just left the bag and just carried on his way and not gone back for the bag and have them waiting for him. That was not uncharacteristically stupid, that was *positively* stupid . . .

The truth is David is one of my very best friends, and I love him dearly and everything he does affects my life. Unfortunately, I get a little pissed off that I'm so emotionally attached to his guy and he seems to be constantly defeating himself on that level of smoking and making silly decisions . . . yeah, of course it affects my life. But I have to constantly remind myself that it's not me. That it's David. It is somebody else's life—I'm not doing these things. I constantly have to remind myself to maintain a certain distance, but it's very difficult when I care about him so much.

There was nothing Graham could do from London, except to feel a sense of absolute frustration with his wayward partner. Meanwhile, Jan reached Art Garfunkel's house. Since Arthur had been arrested a few months earlier on a simple marijuana charge, she thought he might be able to recommend a good lawyer. Unfortunately, there wasn't much his wife could offer Jan except the Yellow Pages. Surprisingly, they found their man at the second number they called, out of the handful of criminal-defense lawyers they picked for starters.

DAN MCGEE:

He was a twenty-five-, twenty-six-year-old criminal attorney who was willing to jump at it. Daniel Parker, Esq. He says, "Hi, how are you?" and I explain I have a situation: there's someone incarcerated and we need to deal with this and they're going to be bonded today. The lawyer says, "What's the guy's name?" "David Crosby." I can hear him stop writing his notes, and he says, "Wait, David Crosby, who I paid to see at Jones Beach last year?" He was a fan. I gave him the information, and he contacted the detective, explained that he was representing Crosby, and found out David was still in the office, but they were about to take him to arraignment. We met at the courthouse, where Jim Hart had ordered a car. Crosby looked disheveled and pale, you know, but that's how he always looks when he's had a bad night's rest. He didn't look timid. He didn't look wasted. He just looked pissed off at himself, but he was respectful and he answered when questions came up. But it was quick, man. I'm telling you, it couldn't have been more than a minute-thirty, two minutes. It was wham, bam, bing. No comments from the judge, just business as usual. I had cash, the attorney presented the bond, David was released.

David was in a holding cell waiting his turn in front of the judge in the same courthouse where the Martha Stewart stock trading trial was heard. The street was full of television mobile units and bored reporters looking for distractions in the various municipal courts in session that Saturday.

Remember, I said the cops were good guys, and I had already benefited from their good nature. They had let me crash in their office while in custody, then transported me to the courthouse where they signed me over to the bailiffs, who put me in a holding cell until my case was called. The courthouse reporters had learned that I was there, and they were nosing around while I was waiting, taking notes and asking questions. As soon as I was cut loose on bond, the arresting officers pulled me aside and said, "There's another way out of here. We can put you in our car. We're not supposed to do this but we can actually drop you off a few blocks away, if you want to split and meet up with your people." It wasn't a huge deal, four or five reporters, three or four cameras, but it was at the tail end of all that Martha Stewart stuff, and it got me nervous to see all the mobile units until I realized they were just waiting for Martha, not me. I went with the cops, Dan picked me up on the edge of Chinatown, we went to a little breakfast bake shop, had something to eat, and got on with the day.

I'd be lying if I said I felt any better than terrible. Besides the physical stress and lack of sleep, I was truly worried about the effect this would have on Jan and Django. Jan had been through the hard times with me—we knew what it was to have the press dragging out all the library footage and old stories. "There he goes again, drugs and guns." But Django was born after all that, he's only seen me sober. He was just nine years old, and that's a hard age to process that kind of media flap about your dad.

DREW FORD:

David's such a family guy. I remember talking to him and his main concern wasn't himself but it was really what Django might have to go through. The look on his face, he was just floored. I don't know if I can even describe the look on his face. I just so felt for him because I knew, he can be really selfless like that. He had that side to him. He has a harsh exterior, I know you've seen it. But underneath that he's really a softie, not a pushover but really . . . it broke my heart. I had to do everything I could to keep myself together, hearing him talk about what could happen as far as Django or what he would have to go through.

The news story lasted only one cycle, which was a blessing. The story didn't have any legs, so it just went away. But it's a crappy thing to do to your wife and your kid; it hurt Jan and Django, and it took a while to come back from that place. The evening news is not how you want your kid to find out you smoke pot. It could have been avoided, it was stupid. You'd think I would've been smarter than that, but the only useful step was to learn from it and move on. At the time, however, there wasn't time for introspection, or even any energy to deal with the immediate problems of what to do about the show. Dan wanted to know what to tell the guys, who were all in Pennsylvania, waiting on tenterhooks. I just wanted to sleep. So I did.

DAN MCGEE:

He fell asleep in the back of the car and we just drove from New York down to Glenside, PA. I told [monitors mixer] Rance [Caldwell] and the rest of the lads just to move ahead with the show, so they had it all set up when we got [there]. David said he wanted to shower, lie down again on his own. No one saw him. He went straight to his little hotel room, and when he came out, he said, "Yeah, I'm definitely doing it. I want to do it."

BUZZ PERSON:

So we're all up in the hallway, near the lobby, waiting for this phone call, probably eight or ten people just kind of standing around, talking and waiting for the phone to ring. Rance was on his cell phone, and when it rang he said, "Well, here's the sixty-four-thousand-dollar phone call." He takes the call and when he hangs up, he looks at everybody for a minute and he says: "The show must go on."

Just before the show, there was a lot of discussion about whether or not I should refer to what just happened during the show, knowing that anything I said would be reported and prolong the life of the story. Negative press never stops, while the good stuff is barely reported at all. It's the old "Man Bites Dog" theory of journalism. The Keswick Theatre, the place we were playing, is a cool venue and a great place for bands to work. It's a converted vaudeville theater and movie palace just outside of Philadelphia, and it was sold out—never underestimate the capacity of lurid press to generate an audience. Some sick few are there to see a train wreck, to see me wasted, thinking, "Oh, good, he's on the skids again. It's the old drugged insane Crosby, let's go watch." Meanwhile, the rest are full of love, coming to show their support and affection for the band. They're the ones spontaneously shouting "We love you, David!" "Keep singing!"

My friend David Bender, a political journalist and commentator and theorist, was with us. I'm told I wanted to make a public statement, and Bender and the others came down on the opposite side. Bender tells me, "Croz, you don't have to go on record for anyone or anything. Don't do it." I had a conversation with my publicist, Michael Jensen, who's my adviser in these matters, and we decided we were not going to give it any light. So we didn't feed it, we didn't do any interviews, we didn't explain, we didn't apologize, mitigate, spin, or skate. We didn't say it was someone else's gun. We didn't talk to anybody, except McGee says somewhere there's a tape of that show in which I make some obscure reference to my "recent unpleasantness" and get a chuckle from the crowd, but that was it. There was no grand statement to make, it was just raucous and noisy and excited when I walked onstage and we did the show.

It seems anticlimactic to conclude the adventure on a down note, but the fatigue and stress of doing two shows in two nights with a major arrest in between laid David low. The next night's show in Maryland was cancelled, and the CPR tour resumed when David was rested sufficiently, his stress level reduced, and his system stabilized. The greatest damage done was to David's reputation as a clean-living spokesperson and poster boy for sobriety. To this day it troubles him. Not as a drag on his conscience, but on a practical level, as some sort of perceived limit to his ability to work for social justice, and his effectiveness in the political arena and as an advocate for his personal beliefs.

Ultimately, he engaged additional counsel to represent him in New York for the resolution of the arrest issues and pleaded guilty to a single count of felony weapons possession, paying fines, court costs, and lawyers. The case is over, and David Crosby is a convicted felon in the state of New York, with legal constraints on his behavior. As they warned us in high school, "This is going on your permanent record."

STEVIE D:

None of us had any idea that he was actually carrying them [guns and knives] on the bus, but I completely understand how you'd want to protect yourself, and from his point of view, it makes perfect sense. It's like an automobile in the wrong hands will kill somebody. The same with a gun, in my opinion, but if he feels he needs to protect himself and he knows how to handle the gun, it's not like he's wielding it. I respected the fact that he had it, and I didn't judge him at all. I just felt sad because he felt so bad about it. That's what I got from him. He felt like he let us all down. Genuinely. And he was really afraid for Django and his wife.

Whatever personal damage it did to my family is on my head. They're cool. They were worried then, but they're fine now. It appears there was no lasting damage there, but there was lasting damage to my credibility and my ability to do some good in the world, which is distressing. Doing some good in the world, being of service, and speaking out on the issues that affect us all is important to me. The arrest and the subsequent publicity hurt my ability to have people listen to me seriously. After the bust, I could be dismissed as just another gun-toting felon and fuzzy-minded pot smoker. I'll talk about drugs first, and then about guns.

This is a difficult thread to continue. Clearly, Croz "went out," as they say in the program, and he'll argue that he's one of those recovered addicts who can return to a modest use of the least destructive of their addictions without resuming the patterns and behaviors that led to his self-destruction and backsliding into hell. The first step in recovery is to admit you are powerless in the face of your addiction. If you're not powerless, are you addicted? We're not talking about the illusion of control, the notorious "one beer won't hurt me" rationale that sends drunks back into the downward spiral, but some evidence of genuine moderate behavior. In truth, David's sparing use of marijuana and an occasional glass of wine with dinner are not only medically unremarkable, but have not changed in frequency or intensity in seven years. The opinions of David Crosby on the topic are, as always, very much his own.

I started getting high more than forty-five years ago. I was straight for fourteen of those years, and for the whole time the only drug that was ever really a pleasure to me (and didn't bite me in the ass) was pot. I've got a young son who will soon reach an age where he'll be exposed to pot. He knows about me, and I told him what the deal was: it's illegal but that I don't think it should be. I think it's a medicine, and a good one. It makes me feel good generally, and it helps my pain specifically. I'm sixty-five, I live with three fatal diseases (hepatitis C, diabetes, and cardiomyopathy), and the permanent orthopedic damage of multiple traumatic injuries. Anything that helps pain and isn't an opiate or other narcotic is useful to me, and Django's fine with that.

Before my son faces any choices, I will make it absolutely clear to him what the truth is about the substances available: cocaine and heroin are absolute killers, don't go anywhere near them, ever. Might just as well shoot yourself. They're death in a box, the worst thing there is. The same is true for speed, crank, meth, or whatever other central-nervous-system stimulant they come up with in decades to come. If your kid comes to you and says, "Gee, Dad, I'm either going to get a bottle of Jack Daniel's or a half ounce of pot, what should I do?" I think you'd be crazy not to tell them you'll help them get the pot: it's not hepatotoxic (meaning it doesn't kill your liver), it's not full of poisons the way the cigarettes are, and it's much better for you than booze in every way. If you grow your own, it's free. But wait—there's more, and it's about benignly altering or expanding your consciousness without any drugs at all. I think Django might actually choose this path: I will tell him that you can get to the same place that grass can get you without the grass.

There are Buddhist monks who are higher than anyone ever got on any drug, and they can get there any time they want. They can sit down, fold themselves into one of those pretzel positions, clear their mind, and get higher than I ever was. Truthfully, I think that's the best way, and if you want to study the way the monks study, you can get there. I'm confident about the kid, because unlike me, he actually does his homework. He thrives on math and science; school and study are not chores, they're part of his life.

DJANGO CROSBY:

Homework is my worst enemy. I know it's making me more intelligent, but I just don't like the concept of having to bring the work home with you. I don't like that concept. I'd rather stay a little bit longer, do more class work during school, and then have the rest of the afternoon free.

What I will share with my son is that there are appropriate times and places for grass, and there are inappropriate times and places. You don't ever, ever have anything to do with this stuff during the day while you're trying to be a student, because it doesn't help with that. If you want to smoke some, I don't think you need to. At this point in your young life, you're already high naturally. Later on, if you want to try it, smoke with me—I've got better pot.

So, if you're going to get high, the least damaging intoxicant that we have is pot. Having demystified grass, I will leave Django with one last cautionary note. There are two kinds of smokers: people who smoke a little bit and then go do something else, and people who smoke too much and just sit there and stare at their toes. I will remind him that the latter is what happened to my brother, and that smoking grass from wake-up to bedtime is a bad idea. But the idea of taking a couple of puffs and going for a walk or making love or listening to music, that's all good. Which brings me to the experience that concluded my years of sobriety.

Jan and I were with friends in Nevada City who were lighting up. They said, "You guys don't do this, right?" And we said, "You know we haven't, but we've been thinking about trying it again." So we did. I know conventional wisdom and the core philosophy of Narcotics Anonymous and AA and all the other twelve-step programs depend on complete abstinence, and a number of people have expressed their disappointment, and even despair, when they heard I was smoking again. I can only remind them to put principles before personalities. Not to defend myself or my actions, but the reason for that is clear: personalities will let you down. You don't follow David Crosby or anybody else because they're on their own. Don't get sober for someone else, and don't stay sober because of someone else's sobriety, or lack of it.

Although I'm reluctant to make the comment, there are some recovered addicts and alcoholics—admittedly, very few—who use moderate doses of their original qualifying drugs or drinks without suffering immediate relapse. The larger discussion is beyond the purview of this narrative. Those in recovery are urged to remain in recovery, and nothing said here should ever be used as a recommendation or excuse for breaking sobriety or "going out."

I don't see the harm in my smoking pot. I like it and it helps me in a number of ways. It's a great painkiller and it helps me go to sleep at night. What happens with Jan and me is that we take a couple of puffs and put the thing back in the box and then we talk. We talk a lot at night, before we go to sleep. We might make plans and get dreamy, or just walk around, holding hands, looking at the sunset. It's a pretty nice thing for us, a good tool for nonverbal communication. It doesn't lead us anywhere else, and we have never even thought of about doing anything else. I don't think I could. As for the folks out there who condemn me, if I've rattled their world or shaken their confidence, I'm sorry for it, but again, don't base *your* sobriety on someone else's.

MIKE FINNIGAN:

Crosby appears to be one of the lucky few who, having been brought to a hopeless state of mind, body, and spirit by drug addiction, has been able to partake of milder drugs, in moderation, without any negative results. This is akin to Russian roulette for the addict. Having escaped once from the grips of a progressive illness—and even been given a new liver—the choice to try the desperate experiment again, is, in a word, insane. Obviously, I'm pleased that he hasn't been drawn back into obsessive use of the other more powerful and destructive chemicals which almost killed him. It is also gratifying to note his acknowledgment of a certain loss of credibility. There's a price to be paid for once being a highly visible miracle of recovery, with the ability to help some others as perhaps no one else can, and forfeiting that rare gift in exchange for a joint.

Despite the fact that I'm still smart and may have something to say, and be a perfectly valid spokesman on a particular issue, I can be discredited as a felon, or a pot smoker. That's a loss of credibility, which might affect my ability to participate in meaningful debate, to have my say and effect on issues of importance to me, and that's a loss I take seriously.

MIKE FINNIGAN:

I don't think he truly realizes the profound impact his sobriety had on scores of others. I can't count the number of folks, over the years, who have told me what an inspiration he was to them, how much his own battle for recovery helped them, how—even though they had never met him—just knowing he could recover made their own seemingly impossible quest seem somehow more attainable. As he notes, he didn't ask to be the poster boy, and those who place inordinately high expectations on others walking the path are being foolish. We're taught to place our ultimate trust in the Higher Power (whatever that is) rather than on people. But we're also instructed that that power speaks through others and we should listen closely to the sober experience of the other men and women who travel with us. Ultimately, I only wish him well. He appears to be comfortable with the choices he's made and it's his life.

Bonnie Raitt, the memorable singer-songwriter and performer, has shared innumerable benefits and concerts and recording stages with David since the early eighties. A fellow inductee in the Rock and Roll Hall of Fame, she's won nine Grammys and is an authoritative voice on blues, folk, and American music. With more than nineteen years in sobriety, she has her own perspective on the issue:

BONNIE RAITT:

It's crucial that we take better care of ourselves. Our spiritual, physical, and emotional health have everything to do with whether we can fire on all cylinders at our age. In the old days I used to worry that I would lose my funkiness or my edge or that I had an obligation to be "the blues woman." I was carrying on in that tradition and thought that I would become somehow neutered if I became sober. I learned from the people that went before me that it's possible to sober up and actually do your best work and get more and more edgy, and more funky, actually feel your feelings and be more authentic, including being angry and all the other emotions that you might stifle and stuff with drugs and alcohol. So I learned, as we all do, from other people that have gone through it. Other musicians (including Mike Finnigan) showed me that not only were they working better and feeling better, but they were playing better.

A great deal of it is genetics and luck and ambition, and you have to have talent in order to be able to sustain the lifestyle that we live, you have to be strong emotionally, but you have to be strong to put up with the bullshit that is this business. When I heard about the bust in New York, I thought, "Oh my God, what a crazy thing, after all that he's been through." I can't wait to hear the story about this. I haven't had as much background to know where the gun thing would come from with David. I roll my eyes like everybody else and kind of hope he can get out of it okay.

DISSOLVE TO:

STOCK FOOTAGE — BOYS PLINKING AT TIN CANS
WITH .22 RIFLES — 1953

As for guns, I had been a shooter in my childhood, a rifle person. I went through the Junior NRA and was taught how to shoot as a kid. Where I grew up, in Carpinteria, California, when you got to be about twelve years old, you got a .22 Winchester. It was just a normal thing, and 1953 was a different world. You didn't have armed rappers singing on television, or the Columbine massacre as examples. I already have a .22 picked out for Django—he'll be twelve soon, and I'll teach him to shoot, the same way I'm teaching him to read, sail, fish, play guitar, drive, and fight. I'll teach him whatever I can about women and I'll teach him how to be a rifleman.

I personally didn't own a gun until Charlie Manson's creeps killed those people at Terry Melcher's house, half a mile from where I lived. Terry Melcher has been one of our producers since the Byrds. I knew the house. I knew the people. I knew who they were trying to kill, and I knew who they killed instead. After that, I went out and bought a shotgun, which is a wonderful defensive weapon. Later, I got a Colt .45 pistol and started hanging out with some people from a gun shop called the Brass Ring on La Brea Avenue in Los Angeles. The shop isn't there anymore. There was also a pistolero named Charles Tacot, Steve Winwood's ex-father-in-law, who taught me how to shoot. I carried a gun on just about every tour until the New York felony arrest, and frequently had a gun with me when I went about my normal business.

It would be comforting to liberals and gun-control advocates to point to this as evidence of David's indulging paranoid fantasies. Unfortunately for them, Crosby's reliance on personal firearms has prevented serious injury to himself and his loved ones on at least two occasions, including a home invasion burglary in Marin County in 1975. David and Debbie Donovan were woken from sleep by masked armed intruders who were breaking the glass in the French doors leading from the deck outside into their bedroom. Reflexively responding the way they had been taught, David snatched a loaded gun off the nightstand and snapped a shot that narrowly missed the robbers, who shot back into the house. Debbie rolled off the bed, cocked a shotgun kept there, and had a second loaded .45 magazine ready for David in case the firefight escalated, all in the space of seconds. The intruders fled. They were looking for cash and drugs in a rock star's house, not mortal combat. Months later, Charles Tacot, who was something of a soldier of fortune and adventurer, presented David with a homemade plaque welcoming him into the fraternity of men who've personally traded fire with an armed enemy.

The second instance of a firearm used in self-defense is a little less exciting, and not a perfect example of David's wisdom during his addicted years in the late seventies. It was at the Chateau Marmont Hotel on the Sunset Strip, where a parking attendant objected angrily to Crosby parking his car in space reserved for hotel guests. David was staying there and believed he had every right to leave his car in the underground garage. He exchanged heated words with the attendant, parked and locked his car and headed for the stairs. The attendant picked up a four-foot length of lead pipe, and came at him in a rage. Crosby stuck a .45 in his ribs and said, "Do you want to die right now? Do you want to put the pipe down? I think you should put the pipe down."

It was very close. That's the only time I've ever given way to anger to ṭe point where I actually pulled a gun. The only time, if you don't count ṭe occasion I fired a round from the balcony of Graham Nash's house

in San Francisco into the trunk of a guy's car as he sped away after trying to rip off my Mercedes as it was parked on the street. That was at the
time of the CSNY Reunion Tour in 1974. The incident at the Chateau
Marmont was largely due to the fact that I was out of my freaking mind
on cocaine. High or not, if I'd been unarmed in a fight with a lead pipe
I would definitely have suffered serious injury. That was twenty-five year
ago. I'm a felon now, I can't own a firearm of any sort: rifle, pistol, shotgun, nothing, and I can't even keep any guns of my own in my home.
My gun-toting days are completely over.

You're probably wondering, why did I ever carry a gun all the time in
the first place? Remember that ever since I was a kid reading science fiction, I shared a pessimistic worldview with my brother, Ethan. We both
had an unfortunate feeling that the human race was due for some sort of
an apocalypse. Society is out on the end of so many limbs, psychologi-
cally, environmentally, militarily, socially, and medically. I felt there were
such basic flaws and instabilities in the system that opportunities for disaster were inevitable. You know Murphy's Law: if something can go
wrong, it will. I thought something was coming that would take society
and blow it apart. We were the first generation that grew up thinking that
the entire world could get killed.

Whenever I had a vision of postapocalyptic America, the thought in
the back of my head was always: "If it comes unglued while I'm out here
I'm going to need this fucker [the gun] to get home." I'd constantly play
out scenarios in my head where I'd have to get back to California from
somewhere out on the road, and I knew that I'd need a gun to get there
alive. "I'm going to need to steal a plane, I'm going to need to steal a boat,
I'm going to need to deal with people who have gone completely crazy
because society just broke." I'm sure that sounds nuts to most people and
I'm embarrassed to have to lay it out, but to me it made perfect sense. I
thought that this wasn't just possible, but likely.

Nineteen

"WE HOLD THESE TRUTHS TO BE SELF-EVIDENT"

DISSOLVE TO:

EXTERIOR — WASHINGTON, DC — DAY (MONTAGE)
FLAGS FLUTTERING, THE WHITE HOUSE, CAPITOL DOME,
MONUMENTS, STATUES, ALL THE DEFINING LANDMARKS OF
NATIONAL PATRIOTISM

When it comes to the Bill of Rights, I tend to be an absolutist; I believe the founders meant it when they said, "Congress shall make no law respecting an establishment of religion, or prohibiting the free exercise thereof; or abridging the freedom of speech, or of the press; or the right of the people peaceably to assemble, and to petition the Government for a redress of grievances," and also, "A well regulated Militia, being necessary to the security of a free State, the right of the people to keep and bear Arms, shall not be infringed." These are direct quotes of the First and Second Amendments and they seem most relevant to my life at the moment.

The Crosby, Stills, Nash, and Young Freedom of Speech '06 tour was all about speaking out. I believe in the Constitution, the Declaration of Independence, and the Bill of Rights. I think they're the best idea of how people can live together under the rule of law in a representative democracy, and if I'm fighting for anything, I'm fighting for that because I believe in it wholeheartedly. If I lose my voice, it's one man less; if we lose our collective voice as a free people, we've lost everything. When we speak of politics and government, I will do my damnedest to be heard, as opposed to our executive branch of government, which is doing its damnedest to be obeyed.

The bastards in power as I write this would love to do the same thing that Nixon and company did during the Vietnam era, which is to say that if you don't agree with their policies, you're anti-American. They wrap themselves in the flag and pretend they're America, but they're not. They're *Americans*, but they are not *America*, and for them to say it's un-American for us to disagree with them is deeply un-American in itself. Disagreement is exactly what this country was built on, and dissidents are the guys who started it all.

Among David Crosby's ancestors are William Floyd and Philip Livingston, both signers of the Declaration of Independence. His Dutch forebears were among the first European settlers of New York, and Mrs. Astor's famous invitation list that defined the first families of American society (The Four Hundred) included all their names. Crosby's parents, Floyd and Aliph, may have been in the Social Register, but that didn't stop them from being the personification of progressive liberal political thinking in the decade when Ethan and David were growing up. Floyd shot a powerful Zionist film in Palestine in 1947 (My Father's House) and worked on socially conscious documentaries in the turbulent thirties. He shot The River *and* Power and The Land *made by progressive filmmakers Pare Lorentz and Joris Ivens, respectively. Ivens, a Dutch national, later left the United States and finished his career making anti-imperialist films in*

Eastern Europe. Floyd paid the price for his friendships with "premature anti-Fascists" and was blacklisted during the McCarthy era, while working with filmmaking legend Fred Zinneman.

I once complained about having a crappy job when I was a kid, working some stupid gig: delivering cars for the Chevy agency, working in the drugstore, something like that. I remember my dad getting very serious, saying, "Don't ever complain about work. Ever. I don't ever want to hear you complain about having work, any work. You're lucky to have a job. You don't know anything about it." At the time that went by me, but later I got it. I knew my father lived through the Depression and the Second World War, made films about social issues, lost friends in the war, and suffered for his personal and professional connections to documentary filmmakers who made American realist classics.

My mother had gone to finishing school and was a debutante, but she was also liberal and antiracist. She could not abide injustice, and if she'd been younger when the sixties came around, she would have been right there with the demonstrators. As it was, she wrote poetry and painted, and turned me onto classical music. Every Sunday morning we'd hear the Philharmonic on the radio. She's the one who bought me Josh White's records, the Weavers, and the South African folk artists Mirais and Miranda. She's the one who first acquainted me with the realities of racism when she played Billie Holiday's "Strange Fruit" for me and explained the lyrics, which describe Jim Crow lynching in the Deep South in poetic and disturbing ways.

We get our first news at home, from our parents or families, until we're old enough to watch it for ourselves. I grew up watching the news, but a news broadcast today would make Walter Cronkite bilious. Most of the information sources put out a sort of predigested pap, and the perfect example is how they handle war. At some point, after Vietnam, there must have been a meeting between the guys who were going to run the country and the people who manage public opinion, and the new ruling class said, "Give us a war we can like, we can love—how do we do it?" I'm sure they insisted on some conditions: "We don't want them seeing all the wrong stuff and saying it's wrong. We can't have that; it's no good for us."

They figured out how to completely muzzle the news, and that's what they've done. When they won't show you the dead bodies coming home, when they can just say about that footage, "No, you can't have it," that's outright total censorship. They embed reporters with the troops, but the only thing that goes out is what they permit. This is not the American way, and it's not what the founders had in mind when they built this country. They manage news now to a degree that they never did when I was growing up, when there was a much more honest information stream.

Luckily, there's a counterbalance to managed news, the Internet, which can't be controlled in the same way. The thing I love most about the Internet is that it can't be censored. I think it's one of the most valuable things about it. They can't shut it down without turning off all the phone systems, and because of that, there's a healthy underground news medium that I love. A place where anybody can get on and say whatever he or she wants, and some of it may be offensive to me, but it's free to be there and I love that.

When I came to folk music in the late fifties and early sixties, it was the era of what was called "protest" music. Freedom marches were happening in the South, peace marches and the free speech movement in Berkeley, and a growing interest in turning music into activism. It was a phenomenon. Nobody said, "There shall be benefits," they kind of grew up out of the cracks, starting years ago with Woody Guthrie and Pete Seeger and the labor movement down through the civil rights movement. There were people huddled in a church singing "Ain't Nobody Gonna Turn Me Around," and "We Shall Overcome" and they became the anthems of a movement. There was the March on Washington with Dr. King, and when people standing on the Mall in front of the Capitol heard the immense and glorious voice of Joan Baez singing, they believed it and they all felt it together. That's a powerful, powerful bonding force. Music's really good at that.

I can remember the 1950s, when all the folk singers in New York could fit into the circular fountain in Washington Square Park and often did on Sunday afternoons, when they would share songs and tunings. In 1958, at a hootenanny at the Knights of Pythias hall on the Upper West Side, I first saw Pete Seeger. As it was for Crosby when he saw Seeger, it was a transformative experience.

Pete Seeger is a national treasure. I think there should be a class on Pete Seeger in every high school. His point of view in life is to include everybody, to bring people together, rather than to be divisive and try to separate people. He says, "Bring them together and you get magic. You get power for good." He's an inspiration.

Once banned from network television as a Communist, Seeger was a guest on the iconoclastic Smothers Brothers Comedy Hour *in their final season on CBS, as was Joan Baez. I was a writer on the show, and witnessed the way the network pulled the plug when Pete Seeger sang "Waist Deep in the Big Muddy," a scathing antiwar song directed against then-president Lyndon Johnson. ("We're waist deep in the Big Muddy and the big fool says to push on.") It's as relevant now as it was then. Seeger returned and eventually performed the piece on the Smothers Brothers show, much to the discomfort of the executives who had nominal oversight of what the Smothers Brothers did. Harry Belafonte was another guest who made the censors cringe. When he sang "Don't Stop the Carnival" on the show, the Smothers Brothers chose a vivid backdrop of civil unrest, riot, and repression to illustrate the music.*

Bob Dylan and Joan Baez wrote and played and sang inspirational, angry, and poignant songs from the beginning. Baez earned her reputation as an absolute righteous artist; she walked from Selma to Montgomery. She worked with Martin Luther King, and took enormous risks to repeatedly get arrested at the terminal in Oakland talking to young draftees being shipped out to Vietnam, telling them, "You don't have to go. You need to rethink this and reconsider." The draftees themselves would attack her, but every once in a while she'd pull one out of the line. She and her mother and her sister, Mimi Fariña, went to jail together for their work in Oakland.

David Crosby and David Bender wrote a book and filmed a documentary together about music's role in social activism called Stand and Be Counted. *In it, a pantheon of performers testify to their belief in music performance as a tool for mobilizing opinion and working for change, as well as an instrument for raising money for a variety of causes.*

When we did *Stand and Be Counted*, every artist we interviewed about their participation in benefits for positive change and social justice, for environmentalism, for labor unity, for farmers—they all cited Pete Seeger as the single voice they all heard that inspired them to contribute their time and talents to their cause.

The history of benefit shows goes back to the earliest days of the professional theater. In sixteenth-century Europe, the safety net for the ill or injured was simple: the family fortune paid for the nobility and the merchant class, the guilds paid for tradesmen and apprentices, and the Church ministered to the poor and everyone else. People in show business were outside the system, but had a unique, intangible commodity as a basic resource—talent, and the willingness to donate the proceeds of a performance to the welfare of one of their own. A company of players could prevail on an actor-manager to give an extra show, and the purse collected would be given to the one in need for health care, retirement, or basic housing. The system endured for hundreds of years, and in the tumultuous twentieth century, mass media made stars into national celebrities. In World War I, English music-hall stars made appeals for volunteers, sold war bonds, and enlisted relief workers on the home front. When America entered the war in 1917, Enrico Caruso, Charlie Chaplin, and Mary Pickford raised millions of dollars for the war effort. World War II multiplied the levels of appeal: movies, radio broadcasting, and a thriving newspaper industry unified a national consciousness. Once performers realized the power of their participation, there was no turning back. An entire generation of unemployed vaudevillians went back to work in the USO, salvaging egos, garnering publicity, and genuinely serving the audiences of servicemen and women they found around the world. For the record, the legendary Al Jolson died of an illness contracted doing benefits for soldiers in Korea, and orchestra leader Glenn Miller disappeared on a flight carrying him to an unpaid performance for the troops.

The late Bill Graham, a prickly and difficult man, was the promoter who helped put rock and roll back on the national map in the eighties. He was a refugee child who fled the Holocaust, made it to the United States with great difficulty, and understood that a lot of people have a rough go here and there's a lot left to be done when it comes to social justice. Bill was the essential lynchpin for organization. He got into the concert business by throwing a benefit for a little gang of activist actors called the San Francisco Mime Troupe, and that show was the first link in a chain that became the Fillmore Auditorium concerts that starred every major band in rock and roll. He was a man who would say, "This isn't right; we're going to do something about it." He did it over and over again. When the Loma Prieta Quake shook the shit out of Oakland and San Francisco in 1989, Bill Graham put together two gigantic benefits and then wrote a check to match the total that was earned by both of them. He was always willing to put his time, his money, his reputation, his effort, and his work on the line to help other people. When there was a benefit, people would say, "Well, gee, Bill asked me and of course I did it." Benefit after benefit after benefit wouldn't have happened without him.

The modern history of rock and roll and pop music benefits is a seamless transition from USO shows to concerts for charities, and should include Elvis, the King, who raised $65,000 in 1961 in Hawaii for the USS Arizona Memorial. Bill Graham's career as a concert promoter began with a benefit, as David notes, and the early folk protest days were filled with small acoustic concerts and fund-raisers for liberal causes. Country music, which operated in its own sphere until the seventies, leaned more toward conservative issues, but its "outlaw" icons, particularly Willie Nelson and Kris Kristofferson, embraced populist causes like Farm Aid. Today the lines are blurred, if not erased, between political affiliations and the genres of the musicians that support them. In 1969, Crosby and I participated in the Big Sur Folk Festival, a benefit for Joan Baez's Institute for the Study of Non-Violence, an event memorialized in a feature-length documentary my wife and I produced. We were scrupulous about forwarding income from the film, but in the late sixties, accounting standards were flexible.

Monterey Pop, 1967—it's been almost forty years, and they're still waiting for the accounting on that one. John Phillips got a Ferrari, the rest of the Mama and the Papas wound up in the toilet. I don't know if there really is any yardstick you can apply to recognize or justify a "good cause," but you have to do it case by case. It's tough. Here's an example: Graham Nash and I both feel that if it has to do with kids, it's much more likely that we will want to do it. Kids are twenty percent of the population and a hundred percent of the future. If they come to us with something that makes the lives of kids, and particularly the education of kids, better, then we're likely to seriously consider it.

On the other hand, we don't do benefits for big charity businesses that take the lion's share of the money for "administration." That's a rip. The gold standard is Farm Aid. They don't pay plane tickets—if you play Farm Aid, you get there on your own. They don't buy you a hotel room, so performers stay in their buses. They don't use limos, they don't do any of that shit. If you want to help, you come and help. If you don't, you don't. That's how it's supposed to work. They're up front, straight, and they run a good operation, so they deserve support.

The whimsically named Avocado Productions and Guacamole Foundation are unique phenomena in the world of music benefit performance. For more than thirty years they were the backstage organizers, founded by a fiery-tempered ex-folkie named Tom Campbell, who put rock music benefits on the map. Peace Sunday, No Nukes, Doctors Without Borders, Greenpeace, Voters for Choice, Central America, Africa, AIDS—between 1973 and 2001 there was hardly a cause or a foundation that put on a show without Tom Campbell's crews building the stages, finding the sound and lighting equipment, organizing the catering, parking the buses, and attending to the business of putting on a show.

TOM CAMPBELL:

It was about 1963, I was watching television, and it said they were going to kill thirty thousand whales in Antarctica, and I thought, "Fuck, that's terrible. Somebody ought to do something about that." I thought I had some energy and some talent and that I had been a performer in clubs and pizza parlors and Dodge showrooms and those types of things we all go through. And I'd also been on the production side of putting shows together, I thought I was in a unique position to serve the musical community as well as the social change community, so we made it professional sound, professional lights, and most important, accounting. Still the most important.

Making *Stand and Be Counted* was an interesting ride. We interviewed peace and justice activists of all ages and persuasions, from Pete Seeger to Michael Stipe and Eddie Vedder, and everybody in between: Jackson

Browne, Bonnie Raitt, Elton John, Sting, and Don Henley, people from all areas of music, and we got amazing answers when we asked them why did they did it. We got to the heart of what inspired them, and we made a catalogue of the music, which will continue to influence generations. I think a song like Sting's "They Dance Alone" is going to still be around a hundred years from now, and "We Shall Overcome" isn't going to go out of fashion. Jackson Browne's "Lives in the Balance" isn't going to get forgotten next week. There are going to be people singing these songs years from now.

TOM CAMPBELL:

I got involved in Black Mesa, and moved to New Mexico. . . . In those days the coal-fired plant in Page, Arizona, put more pollutants into the sky than New York and LA daily. The astronauts could see the plume from the Four Corners Power Plant [Black Mesa] from space. I went to do a film about it, wrote the music, did the narration. The cinematographer suggested I do some benefits. I called Linda Ronstadt and the Nitty Gritty Dirt Band and Steve Martin and they came out to New Mexico; I was a real go-to-meetings environmentalist. You do one benefit concert and that's it. Since '73 that's all I've done.

Who knows what the future holds? Every day there's another new singer-songwriter coming up, and they are most often people of conscience. They join an unbroken line that runs back more than a half-century, to when Harry Belafonte was a young man coming out of the navy, started a musical craze with calypso, and then embraced a lifelong involvement with civil rights. I admire him tremendously. When we interviewed him for the book he was living history, on point and so lucid—he understood why things had caused other things to happen. You can't help remembering he was at Martin Luther King's side all through the struggle for civil rights, from the beginning, into the next century.

In 1989, the Berlin Wall came down; the ugly barrier that stood for the enforced separation of Germany into eastern and western segments was dismantled and a nation divided since World War II was reunited. Crosby, Stills, and Nash wanted to be there, and miraculously connected with that moment of international celebration. They were even able to sing to a vast audience in Berlin, without a stage, without equipment, without any advance notice. They didn't even know they were going to be there, until they impulsively went, with a little local help.

You have to understand that hippies get very few triumphs out of history. Seldom do humane ideas prevail; more likely, it's the big battalions that prevail. In this case, no group of tanks knocked that wall down, no army shot it to pieces, no artillery, no bombs destroyed that wall. It was ideas going over that wall. People on the other side realized after time that the folks on our side of the wall were not standing in line for a loaf of bread. They had butter. They had BMWs. They had a place to live, they had electricity, hot water, color TV, and that's pretty much what tore down that wall.

I hate to give any credit to Ronnie Reagan for anything, but it certainly helped, him saying, "Tear down this wall." Ultimately, just seeing it there made it inevitable. Watching something that abysmally wrong makes you completely understand: that wall's a huge, physical wrongness. It was like a giant sign saying "Bad Thing."

When we heard it was imminent, Stephen called his European publisher, who said if we would do some press or do something for him, he would get us over there. We didn't have the money to fly there commercially ourselves, so we took him up on the offer. We were only there a few days, but that was long enough for me and Jan to see it, and I got to take a screwdriver and a hammer in my hand and beat some pieces out of that wall for myself. I still have chunks of German concrete with layers and layers of paint on them; it was probably the most heavily graffitied wall in history. But it was a triumphant moment to feel that in some way, sometimes good wins. That was a definite win, *and* we got to sing to the people. We did a show, even though we couldn't get a PA system—maybe there were people who didn't want us to have a PA system. What we did was a very interesting alternative—we got a local radio station to bring mikes and broadcast it live, while at the same time we had everybody in the audience bring radios, and tune it to the station; a thousand transistor radio speakers in the crowd. Amazingly, it worked. A low-tech/hi-tech solution. There's nothing stronger than an idea whose time has come.

There's a chain of influence, an ongoing transmission of democratic ideals: Thoreau affects Gandhi, Martin Luther King reads Gandhi, Joan Baez meets Dr. King when she's fifteen, and so on. I had my personal agenda for ideas, wanting to say to people everywhere, "You can do this!" You can start in your own backyard and change how things are, and pay no attention to "You can't fight City Hall," and "They're too big for us." Gandhi was one lone guy who didn't have two nickels to rub together, looked like a prune wrapped in a bedsheet. He didn't have anything, but he stopped the British Empire in its tracks by simply being unwilling to sit down and shut up. He would not do it. Acts of exemplary humanity by people like Gandhi have resonance, carrying ability, and they sustain as the ripples spread outward. They don't diminish, they increase.

In that documentary and book I wanted to make a point. I wanted people to understand that you can't go a hundred yards in this world without seeing someone whose condition you can make better. Necessity is everywhere, and what are we going to do? Sit there and collect your money and hide in your house, or try to do something and make things better? You do whatever you can. Maybe it's just trying to get the school lunch program in your kid's school to serve better food. Maybe you're trying to stop war permanently. Whatever the fuck it is, you can stand up on your own hind legs and make a difference, and even if you don't affect the rest of the world, or if you run into a complete stone wall and what you're trying to accomplish doesn't happen, it will change your life. It will change how you think of yourself, and it will change your priorities for the better. It changes your life to be a stand-up guy, and I wanted to tell that story. And in Berlin, when the people got tired of running into that stone wall, they simply tore it the fuck down.

These days, people who are in a position to use their talent and reputation for a good cause pick one and make it their own. Sting cares about the rain forest. Paul McCartney's concern was minefields. U2 chooses to work toward ending world hunger. People will say, "I can't do them all, so I'm going to pick one where I can control the circumstances and work my butt off to try and make the world a better place." God bless them for being smart and doing it that way.

There are also people who are proactive instead of reactive. When Barbra Streisand and Don Henley got hit the thousandth time for another benefit, they chose to generously fund foundations. That way, they can examine every request, and if they see something they want to help, their foundation writes a check. They've already got the money. That's the way that Crosby, Stills, Nash, and Young have been doing it for a while. We take a dollar a ticket—every ticket, a buck—and we put it toward charitable causes. It goes into family foundations for the four of us. Sometimes I have more money in my charitable account than I have in my regular bank account, because I'm careful with it and I don't give it out in big chunks.

Bonnie Raitt, who's a veteran of benefits and good work, is fun to watch when she weighs up a potential benefit. Somebody hits her up, says things like, "It's for the kids, it'll be really great fun and you'll have a nice dressing room and it'll be cool, will you do it?" Then Bonnie will say, "Right. It's for the kids, where? Which kids? How many? What age? What did they have for breakfast? Who are you? How much money is actually going to go to the kids? How much money is actually going to go to administration? What are your costs? I would like to see your books." She's not fucking around. Bonnie demands to see what she has every legitimate right to see, which is an accounting of what happens to the money. That's how a smart person approaches benefits now.

There's no shortage of ways that you can help to make the world a better place. What really baffles me are the people who don't do it at all. If you're a ticket-buying member of the public who likes to see live music, I pray that there will continue to be many millions of you, and if you're going to see a show that's advertised as a benefit, you have to do your homework too. That's what Bonnie will tell you. Read. Research. Go on the Net, ask questions, hard questions. Get hard-nosed about it. If Joe Schmo is doing a benefit for woodpeckers, go on the Internet, find out if woodpeckers are in danger. Find out if Joe Schmo has been sued for holding a woodpecker benefit and walking off with the money. If you can't do the homework, at least pick the people you trust have done *their* homework. If Bono tells me that relieving the debt of Third World countries will give them enormous leverage for making a recovery and getting on their feet, that's the benefit I'll go to, because I know he did his homework.

But the whole game has changed.

During the thirty years he worked on benefit concerts, Tom Campbell took little for himself beyond a minimum wage, and his colleagues in the small production office did the same. When the landscape changed, he became redundant, and now works quietly on his memoirs and on the continuing small community and social service organizations that meet his cautious standards.

TOM CAMPBELL:
As soon as they saw what happened with No Nukes and Peace Sunday and Bangladesh and our pro-choice rallies with a half a million, a third of a million, a million people, the big guys wanted to do it, so they took it over and started doing it, which was fine. It's a big wheel, there's room for a lot of hands on the wheel. Everyone puts a hand in. But what happened is it eliminated the smaller community events. Only a few people are going beyond the big television show "Live from

Philadelphia and Around the World," and doing community events in Knoxville and in Ashville and Eugene, Oregon, and places like that. For the most part, they're the people we know, David and Graham and Bonnie and to a certain degree Keb' Mo' and Jackson Browne and Nancy Griffith and folks like that.

Avocado did giant shows, we did little tiny shows, we did the first-ever benefit concert in a football stadium with Linda Ronstadt and the Eagles and Jimmy Buffett in '76. But when the big sharks came in, the benefit concert became institutionalized. Now a benefit concert is in Staples Center with Paul Simon and sponsored by American Express Blue Cards. Excuse me, American Express ain't a green company.

Institutional or not, global or local, I can't imagine not being involved in the world around me, and I'm baffled by people who don't stand up. Is it possible they don't even think about it? There are huge pop stars that have never done a benefit for anything. Their world is about celebrity. They've been so sold on the bullshit idea of stardom and celebrity that they're slaves to the concept. They don't really live in the same world that I do. It's not important to them if the people in New Orleans are being disenfranchised and having their homes and their neighborhoods stolen from them, it doesn't really matter. What matters is that they properly manipulated the paparazzi last night at some club so they got the right shot in today's tabloids. They live a very shallow life, they don't seem to have much of a worldview, and most of them don't seem to have much of an education. They don't read. They don't seem to have a strong interest in social justice or political action.

If you ask Bonnie Raitt or Jackson Browne or any one of a hundred singer-songwriters I could name, "Give me a few well-chosen words on the subject of honor or justice or peace," they'll give you chapter and verse. It's central to their lives, and to some degree central to my life as well. Certainly, there are more important issues than wearing the right clothes and getting a properly subservient limo driver. But some people just don't live in the same world as the troubled victims of repression, catastrophe, or societal collapse.

Grace Slick started working in the San Francisco era that transformed pop music. As the lead singer in Jefferson Airplane, she spoke to a generation that combined a drug ethos with popular music and political consciousness. She's sung and recorded with David Crosby, and done her share of benefits, beginning with those long-ago celebrations in Golden Gate Park in San Francisco. Retired from music and working as a visual artist, she's been painting and showing her work for the last fifteen years, without losing touch with the music, the news, and the world. She notes the next generation's fund-raising technique:

GRACE SLICK:

They have "functions," they don't necessarily play. I see it on VH1 and MTV; they raise a lot of money by showing up and they're usually indoors. Most musicians are willing to do something within their own generation, whatever it happens to be. Like P. Diddy and Beyoncé Knowles and Kanye West; they're top-end hotshots making lots of money and they'll organize these things; it's just a little different. Ours were mostly outside. Theirs are inside, for whatever reason, I don't know. It's very tribal, and kids under thirty can't seem to get a grip on being a unified generation.

The kids that are stars now are a reflection of how big the music business became. The people I admire, the singer-songwriters, did not start out to be stars. They started out to say something. They started out to make music, to emulate peers that they thought were making beautiful music and beautiful statements. Becoming a star was not our primary ambition, although once success arrived, we certainly embraced it. But now, an act arrives full-blown with a costume consultant and a hair blower and they're a production. They're a cardboard cutout, a stamping, and a manipulated piece of stuff that's desperate only to win, and to accumulate the trappings of a winner. There are acts who believe it's more important to have a posse than talent. I'm sure it's a generational thing. Maybe they'll change as they get older. That seems to be nature's way.

GRACE SLICK:

Age? You can't do a lot of drugs because old people are pathetic anyway. You don't have to be pathetic and drunk, which makes you even more pathetic, so there's a lot of stuff you can't do, but you do gain one thing: you're not very good-looking, but you've got wisdom. Young people should be seen and not heard because they're kind of stupid, but they're good-looking. Old people should be heard and not seen, because we're bright but we're not too hot-looking. So I figure we're built for radio.

Not entirely. The Freedom of Speech '06 Tour sold out three nights at the Red Rocks amphitheater outside Denver. The last night of that engagement (July 20, 2006) was as exciting a performance as the audience or the band ever saw. The tour featured much of Neil's album, but the material was surrounded, enhanced, and reinforced by the CSNY repertoire, as well as new songs by all the principals. The concerts averaged more than three hours a night, which is an intense demand on any band, let alone a quartet of men in their sixties, most of them with medical as well as political issues.

Neil and I privately agree that this is the best we'd ever been, ever. Better than '74. Certainly better than 2000 or 2002, and a lot of it has to do with having so many of these new songs that are lyrically, heavily loaded, heavily put-together songs. Neil can really write powerful lyrics, and he wrote very simple music for his new album (*Living With War*). I said, "How come you didn't do any complex changes?" and he answered,

"I'm not giving up any of my good shit just talking about George Bush." The way we're delivering it now gives us a validity that nothing else could. When we can go out there and sing brand-new songs and bring nine thousand people to their feet, singing "Let's Impeach the President for Lying," we've hit a nerve.

There are many, many, many people in this country who feel disenfranchised, who feel that the last two elections were stolen, that the country is being dragged in a direction that they do not agree with, many of whom are Republicans. I know an awful lot of Republicans who feel that George Bush and company have demeaned the Republican Party and dragged it so far to the right that they don't feel like they're part of it anymore. And these are good, staunch Republicans, people who have been in the Republican Party their whole lives and they're not happy, and, of course, the rest of us, who are more liberal than that, feel that we're having our country stolen from us. And when Neil says: "Let's impeach the president for hijacking religion and using it to get elected . . ." hijacking our religion and using it to get elected, man, he's touching a nerve too.

On the 2006 tour, when we did "What Are Their Names?"— something I wrote many years ago—we did it as an a cappella thing and Neil's idea made it a show-stopper:

One of David's songs, "What Are Their Names?," has been on the set list for the whole tour, but performed in a novel way, as David describes it.

Neil said, "What if, right after we get 'em crazy with 'Ohio,' we just start singing, four guys, like this . . . whoa-whoa. It's a whoa-whoa and a clap." So we lead the audience into this rhythmic unison do-wop, and then we started in on the lyrics, with a hand-clap punctuation at the end of each line: "Who are the men [clap] who really run this land" [clap] . . . And on that night, the audience kept singing the intro, repeating it in counterpoint, and they did it in full voice, they sounded like a soccer crowd singing one of their chants.

You know how electrifying that sound is when there are thousands of voices? When we started singing the words in counterpoint to them, it was electrifying. It was a peak moment for me of musical performance in my life. One of the greatest moments, because they knew, the audience collectively understood, what we were doing, they understood what we're saying. They wanted to be a part of it and they did it perfectly. It's one of those quintessential moments that you get in a lifetime of performing when somehow the damn thing just worked. It just flew. The righteous part is that it wasn't just one night. We got a lot of those evenings on the tour, and for me, moments like that are why I came to the party in the first place.

WHAT ARE THEIR NAMES?

I wonder who they are
The men who really run this land
And I wonder why they run it
With such a thoughtless hand
What are their names
And on what streets do they live
I'd like to ride right over
This afternoon and give
Them a piece of my mind
About peace for mankind
Peace is not an awful lot to ask

To me, I can't put a price on it. It's the second most important thing in my life, and there it was, gloriously fucking right, and everybody felt it. Stephen felt it. Graham, of course, has his antennae up all the time and it's like telepathy between us. He and I did "Guinnevere" that night as well as we've ever done it in our lives. We did "Southbound Train" as well as we've ever done it. We did a lot of stuff at the top of our abilities, and, you know, amongst it were all of the new songs and old songs. We did "Rocking in the Free World," and we nailed it. We were on it. I don't think we've ever been better. I think we tore it up at Red Rocks as well as I've ever seen us do it, ever, and it makes me happy because that's what I was born to do.

DISSOLVE TO:

Twenty

9/11, JOHN McCAIN,
AND THE DALAI LAMA

EXTERIOR — NBC TELEVISION STUDIOS

BURBANK, CALIFORNIA — EVENING

After the tragedy of 9/11, the Tonight Show, *with Jay Leno, suspended broadcasts for several shows while the nation mourned and processed the events of that day. When the* Tonight Show *returned to the air, the host had a very specific guest list for what would be the very special show that marked his return.*

Jay called us and said he wanted us to be the show that went back on the air. He had said, "This isn't the time for being funny, I'm not doing it, I'm taking the show off the air for a few nights," which I thought was a straight-up move. When he went back on, he said he wanted Crosby, Stills, and Nash and John McCain. He asked us specifically to come and do three songs. We're the only people who've ever done three songs on that show, ever. We did "My Country 'Tis of Thee," with Michael Hedges's special guitar arrangement. It was an impressive night of television, because Jay and all of us were very serious and because John McCain was the closest thing the Republicans had to a human being. He was very cool, our music was good, everyone there had a strong feeling.

Right after 9/11, this country was one country. It took George Bush to split this country up again, and now McCain's running alongside him. It's one of my great disappointments, because in 2000, I thought campaign finance reform [the McCain–Feingold bill] was the answer to many of our problems.

I liked McCain's courage. I loved that he was willing to take on the entire establishment, including his own party, over campaign finance reform and that they tried to kick him out of the Republican Party for doing it. I like that he's not afraid of anyone, and I figured if he could survive years in a Vietnamese prison, no one in Washington's going to be able to scare him very much. I disagree with him strongly on abortion, and on a number of other issues where he's always been a social conservative. Recently, I've been extremely disappointed in him. He used to say religious extremists were bad for the country, now he's suddenly saying Pat Robertson and Jerry Falwell are great Americans and good for the Republican Party, which lets me down totally.

If McCain's willing to demean himself that way, then he is not as good a guy as I had hoped. Falwell, Robertson, and the others are raving sickos. They sell hatred and divisiveness over the counter, by the pound, and they're a bunch of shit-heels, in my opinion. If McCain feels it's necessary to cater to a son of a bitch like Pat Robertson because of the amount of power that he has, then he's not okay with me. It was a disgusting thing for him to do, he's off my "good guy" list, and I'm not ashamed of saying it. It's a perfect example of "I'll say whatever I got to say to get what I want." And it's a stone complete lie, those guys are not good Americans or good Republicans or good anything else. They're the worst possible influence in Washington that they possibly could be.

I'm not saying the evangelical Christian right shouldn't exist. They have every right to be here and campaign for their beliefs, however fundamentalist they may be. But there's some history they need to learn. The people who started the United States of America came here for religious freedom. They were a persecuted group in England because England had, please note, a *state religion*. State religions are a terrible thing, regardless of the time or place. Whatever your faith, fundamentalist or not, if you want to make your religious belief system the basis of civil government, it's intrinsically a bad idea. Historically, as I read it, fundamentalism has inevitably led to bloodshed and terror: the Crusades, the Inquisition, the Hundred Years' War, the conquest of the New World, the African massacres, the troubles in Indonesia and India and Ireland—the list is endless.

The first place to try the balance of power and separate church and state was here, and that's one of the reasons this is such a great country. The Christian Right in the United States seems to be blissfully unaware of that. They maintain we're a "Christian nation," and there are several things about that that are wrong. It's an "everybody nation." Freedom of religion and freedom of speech were probably the first and most important freedoms here, and they're either ignoring that, or they're unaware of how important they are. They'd like the power, they'd like to be the ones to run things, because they're intolerant enough to believe that if they could just impose their beliefs on everyone, it would be all right, just fine, a greater and stronger nation under their particular God.

Pat Robertson and Falwell would happily run the country. No problem—send all the gays to New Zealand. Jews and niggers, you can have second position, be almost like citizens. Immigrant workers, undocumented aliens, noisy, smelly people of color with different gods— outta here. And women? Back into the kitchen; bear children, no matter what. You know, the Christian Right would love it, while to me, it's an absolute nightmare, and I would fight it with every breath possible.

Nobody likes abortions, but pregnancy, carrying a child to term, and bringing a baby into the world are the choice of the mother. The government has absolutely no goddamn business having anything to say about it at all. Ever. That's how I feel about that. The fundamentalists try to paint pro-choice people as joyfully killing babies. We take no pleasure in abortions or killing anything, but we do believe it's a right of women to control their own bodies and their own circumstances. If they don't feel it's a good pregnancy or it's time for them to raise a child, they have the right to terminate that pregnancy and I will fight for that. I always have. When it got to be a really, really crucial issue, Nash and I went to the largest women's organization and volunteered to do rallies and benefit concerts for them. It was Voters for Choice. We did a lot for them.

Intolerance is not the fundamentalist's only mistake. Self-righteous certitude is another. They believe that theirs is the only road up the mountain, which is patently not true. God has a thousand names and there are a thousand roads up the mountain, that's how I see it. I have no problem with them being Christians, although they should actually study the Bible a little more and act like Christians instead of like Nazis. I will fight it when they try to impose their value system and their religion on me and the rest of the people in this country. One of the distinguishing characteristics of fundamentalism of all sorts is its absolute claim on God's exclusive favor. Think of the German army belt buckles during both world wars: "*Gott mit uns,*" they said. "God is with us," and Bob Dylan memorialized the concept in his song "With God on Our Side."

At this point, it's worth reprinting something Mark Twain wrote at the turn of the last century, after the Spanish-American War, in an unpublished short story called "The War Prayer." Feelings were, as usual, running high and Americans thought God was with them and the Spanish-American War was just. It was a war driven by media, when publishing mogul William Randolph Hearst reportedly wired his field correspondent and artist Frederick Remington: "You furnish the pictures, I'll furnish the war." In that fevered climate, more than a hundred years ago, Twain's "prayer" is a disturbing echo of the Christian Right's exhortations of contemporary campaigns in Iraq and Afghanistan. I've shortened it here, but the point isn't lost:

O Lord our Father, our young patriots, idols of our hearts, go forth to battle—be Thou near them! With them, in spirit, we also go forth from the sweet peace of our beloved firesides to smite the foe. O Lord our God, help us to tear their soldiers to bloody shreds with our shells . . . help us to lay waste their humble homes with a hurricane of fire; help us to wring the hearts of their unoffending widows with unavailing grief; . . . We ask it, in the spirit of love, of Him Who is the Source of Love, and Who is ever-faithful refuge and friend of all that are sore beset and seek His aid with humble and contrite hearts. Amen.

CUT TO:

EXTERIOR — ARLINGTON NATIONAL CEMETERY,
WASHINGTON, DC — DAY
FOREGROUND — THE MONUMENT OF MARINES
RAISING THE FLAG
BACKGROUND — THE CAPITAL CITY

By way of contrast to that dark parody of Christian prayer, I had an experience in Washington that gave me a broader view of humanity. I was at a big, well-known hotel, and as I came downstairs to breakfast I saw two men in suits wearing earpieces standing by the elevators. Obviously Secret Service. They recognized me, I waved to them, and went off to eat.

When I came back, there were four of them, so I walked up and said, "You're Secret Service, right? Who's here?" They said it was the Dalai Lama. I said, "There were two of you before, there's four now, he's about to come down, isn't he?" That drew a suspicious look and an attitude: "You're not supposed to get that information," and I said, "Look, you know who I am, I can't be a threat or a problem, if it's okay with you, I just want to stand over here against the wall and see him. I just want to see him." They said, "Okay. Stand right over there. Don't cause any trouble."

A few minutes later, down comes the elevator: entourage, entourage, entourage, State Department, more Secret Service, his own people, his own security. They start walking down the hall, and I'm just looking at him. He's a lovely man. He's got a great vibe. He's talking to somebody next to him and he sees me and looks right in my eyes, stops talking to them, turns off course, and walks over to me. Full entourage is going "Uhhhh." Secret Service guys are going "Uhhhh." He looks at me, he takes my hand, holds my hand, he looks in my eyes and kind of nods a little bit. Then he walks away.

I start crying.

I burst into tears, and I don't know why. It's never happened to me before but it had to do with the spirit in this man: he was *clean*. This is a guy traveling light. No baggage at all. He doesn't hate anyone, he doesn't fear anyone, not even the Chinese. He doesn't want anything you have, so he doesn't want anything. If you ask him what he wants, it's like, "World peace would be nice." That's it. He's not looking for a new pair of shoes.

A little later someone from his entourage invited me and Nash to hear him speak at the National Cathedral. We went and were eventually seated in the sixth row, behind Associate Justice of the Supreme Court Sandra Day O'Connor. We listened. I usually think it's smarter to believe in principles because people will let you down. ("Principles before personalities.") But if you had to pick one exemplary human being, someone who was truly a pretty clean machine, there he is, His Holiness the fourteenth Dalai Lama, Tenzin Gyatso. I found him inspiring as hell.

I can't be like that. I can't imagine myself having enough time to grow that far, because I've always been pretty much of a kid in my head, but I can see it. There's no final line you cross over and all of a sudden, you're hip: "Well now, okay, I have achieved wisdomhood!" Wrong. It doesn't happen that way, it's not like that. "Here, Dave, sixty-two karma points this month." It's not what you can see you've achieved, or what state of wisdom and cosmic fullness you've achieved. All you can measure is which direction you're going. There isn't an odometer, nothing records how far you've gone in one direction or another, although people can look at you and guess.

You can plainly see that the Dalai Lama has gone a long way. If it was me, I'd be saying that Mark Twain prayer, I'd want the death of the Chinese leadership, I'd want every single Chinese army guy out of Tibet, I'd want ten trillion dollars to rebuild everything that they've blasted into rubble. I'd want revenge and the Dalai Lama doesn't. He's looking for something higher and better. I'm not as furiously angry with politicians and lobbyists as I once was; I'm not exactly embracing them as my brothers in humanity, and I'm not changing my essential mistrust of the system, but I am interested in finding something higher and better if I can. Unfortunately, I'm afraid that it won't be in the national political process over the next few years.

Philosophically, the politics of rock and roll has been characterized as chaotic and unfocused, the legacy of an era that first heard it as the music of rebellious youth. When Crosby, Stills, and Nash met with President Jimmy Carter, one of their party says he made a point of smoking a joint somewhere in the White House, just to say he did. One is reminded that musicians run the political gamut: Elvis tried to get President Nixon to appoint him as a special undercover narcotics agent, while Ted Nugent is a vocal advocate for guns and maintains a part-time residence in Crawford, Texas, where one wonders if he will vote for Kinky Friedman as governor of the Lone Star state.

Kinky, a singer-songwriter who had a renegade country band called the Texas Jewboys and is a successful author of mystery novels, is conducting a serious campaign for governor of Texas. Populist pro wrestler and former governor of Minnesota Jesse Ventura actively campaigns for him. At the same time, Euro-punk nihilists fly the black flag of anarchy, and Christian pop stars wrap themselves in the flag and the cross. In 2004, Alice Cooper said, "If you're listening to a rock star in order to get your information on who to vote for, you're a bigger moron than they are.

Why are we rock stars? Because we're morons. We sleep all day, we play music at night, and very rarely do we sit around reading the Washington Journal. *" One presumes he was speaking for himself, if not the entire rock and roll right.*

After 1986, when I was out of jail and sober, my support was no longer a political liability. I could show up and campaign for people, not just whales and the environment. Chris Shays and Marty Meehan in the House, and Russ Feingold and John McCain in the Senate had my full attention and support before 2000. Then McCain said Jerry Falwell is a great Republican and I was over him. On the other side, there's equal disappointment, because I don't think the Democrats could find their asses with both hands. They handled the last two elections with incredible ineptitude. They picked the wrong guy both times. They keep trying to go back to the status quo, and it's not working. I don't think John Kerry was a good choice. I think he was "business as usual," a purely political animal who didn't have the charisma or the guts or the stones for the job.

Still and all, the musicians in the country, except for one or two country guys, went out and worked for him because he was the only choice. George Bush is doing our country and our Constitution great harm. As for our reputation and our relationships with the people in Europe and Canada, the really close ones, he's fucked all that up. He's gotten us into a war, and all the musicians I know worked very hard to keep that from happening and tried to get him out of office, but we weren't working to get John Kerry elected, we were struggling to get George Bush defeated.

Howard Dean was different. The one time that the Democrats had someone who'd have breathed new life into the situation, the Democratic National Committee started gunning for him the minute he entered the race, because he would have upset the apple cart. They knew that if Dean got in, he'd bring a broom with him and sweep the building clean and frankly, that's precisely what needs to happen. We need new blood and a willingness to change things on a very deep level. Drastically. Otherwise

the Democratic Party is going to continue to get more and more irrele-
vant and further and further away from having an influence on what
happens in America.

If you haven't noticed, I have a very low opinion of most politicians,
because as a class they seem to lack honor. They speak about it, but people can say anything; it's what they do that reveals their true nature.
That's even more true of politicians than it is of most people. We may
never know, but there are a great many of us who feel quite strongly that
the Republicans didn't win; that they rigged the elections the last two
times. Take the Diebold voting machine situation—the electronic voting
station. Some news organization hired a hacker to see if he could screw
with it and change votes. The hacker was alone with the machine for
about a half hour, called the people back in and said "Okay, you can vote,"
and they voted a straight ticket. Then the hacker pushed a button and all
the votes went straight over to the other side. Took him a half hour. Of
course, the Diebold machine has no paper trail, which is what the
Republicans want. I don't think George Bush has ever been elected. I
think what we are enduring here is a long, slow coup where these bastards are stealing our country.

I'm worried about the next elections because the people who should
be mounting a serious challenge are the Democrats, and even with
Howard Dean running the DNC, I don't see anybody out there worth voting for. The only young guy that I see that gives me any hope at all is Barak
Obama, a brilliant man, extremely well-spoken, very knowledgeable, and
seemingly an unusually honorable guy for a politician. But Barak Obama
is too young and half black, which is a handicap below the Mason-Dixon
line. Once upon a time, the Democrats could count on the South, but
they're losing it hand over fist to the Republicans—it's already a lost cause,
as they used to say about the Confederacy during the Civil War.

ABRUPT CUT TO BLACK:

Twenty-one

THINK GLOBALLY, ACT LOCALLY

At some level, all politics is local, and the Santa Ynez Valley is not with-out its particular problems, some environmental, some having to do with the local schools, others rooted in the Chumash Indian Reservation. Fueled by gambling profits, guided by professional consultants, protected by fed-eral law, a modest bingo parlor grew into a massive Vegas-style casino en-clave. The ongoing program of expansion and development is facilitated by the unique status of native American reservations as "sovereign na-tions." Any new lands added to their real-estate portfolio would become "tribal lands," exempt from local taxes and zoning ordinances, regardless of whether or not they were adjacent to the existing reservation, or sim-ply large parcels available for development. Dan Gerber is a poet and for-mer race-car driver who moved into the valley within the last ten years.

DAN GERBER:

When we moved here, Fess Parker and his wife, Martha, were very generous to us, took us in, we were invited to their birthday parties and then this thing came up with the fourteen hundred acres and I

240

was just flabbergasted. . . . Fess and I exchanged some letters; we don't see each other anymore. But, I was just stunned. . . . There were all sorts of rumors about a five-hundred-room hotel and a couple of golf courses and X number of houses and another casino, and in one of our letters, Fess said, "I don't see why everybody's getting so upset. We haven't even announced what we're going to do with the property." I said, "It doesn't matter, if you get it annexed and it becomes sovereign land, you can do anything you want to on it." Of course I got accused of racism [against] the poor Native Americans, but I've been a big contributor to the American Indian College Fund. I've taught on I don't know how many reservations in South Dakota and Arizona and New Mexico. But Fess said the people of this valley voted to allow them to have gambling here and I said if you took that vote again today, I wonder what would happen. These people have not been great citizens. I said that if he thought this was such a good thing for this valley, he should put it up for referendum. He didn't want to go there.

So I went to Washington, before McCain did his awful thing with Jerry Falwell. I spoke to his committee, the Committee on Indian Affairs, hoping to get a sympathetic ear, considering our past support for him. We had a local issue, but what it came down to was that casinos are bad neighbors. Ask the people who live around any casino and they'll tell you they're bad neighbors. They're not working for the casino. Everybody, anywhere near any casino, thinks they're shit.

Mohegan Sun and Foxwoods, both of them in Connecticut, seven miles apart, do over five billion dollars a year between them, and we've played in their theaters, for major dollars. Maybe when they read this they won't ask me back. This one here in our little valley does over two hundred million a year, and the situation is replicating itself anywhere in the country where a group can get certified as a tribe and claim title to some ancestral land. The Pequot Indians learned quickly that they could get a lot more out of their casino profits if they plowed them into political action committees, donations to politicians, and lobbying at every level of government: local, state, and federal. For better or worse, they went out and educated and funded local expansion and development efforts everywhere there were Native American communities. This is what I said to the Committee on Indian Affairs about that, in public session:

I am honored to be here to speak with you . . . this is about fairness and justice. In an effort to correct injustices done to the Native American tribes in the early days of our country, the government gave the tribes the right to have gaming, originally bingo. Smart lawyers saw the opportunity and found financing to build casinos. Whether you think gambling is an addiction or just a minor vice, casinos are not good neighbors. They say they put money into local economies but the truth is that almost all of it goes out of town, out of state, and offshore. They use our schools, roads, hospitals, firemen, and police and they don't pay taxes. They inevitably bring crime to a community. A twenty-year veteran in law enforcement where I live estimated that 75 to 80 percent of all crime in our valley was casino-related. I believe him. As disturbing as all this is, it is not my main issue here. We are now in a situation where the laws intended to give Indians a break are doing unfair and unjust harm to communities all over the country. At the center of this is zoning. I expect you can guess how completely alien a subject zoning was to a singer-songwriter, but circumstances forced me to learn. At the core of it, zoning is a compact between all the people in a town or county to agree on what kind of place it will be to live in, and especially to raise our children in. We in the Santa Ynez Valley, through our elected officials, voted to keep the agricultural and rural character that was the main reason we live here. Now there are about ten thousand of us in this valley and the current laws make it possible for about 180 people in the Chumash tribe to circumvent this zoning agreement as well as building codes completely . . . for profit. We have an unscrupulous developer named Fess Parker who sees this as a wonderful opportunity to evade land-use restrictions and build a very large and completely inappropriate "resort destination," a giant hotel and golf course complex and, although they deny it, we believe another casino. We believe that the tribes have every right to buy any property they want with their money, but if they are allowed to take those lands into the reservations, then developers will be speed-dialing casino operators all over the country to take advantage of this loophole to evade the laws. How can it be fair to give them rights we don't have? . . . to exempt them from laws we must obey? We ask you please to look at this nationwide problem and try to find a fair and just way to let the tribes invest and grow but not destroy surrounding communities in the process as they are trying to do in Santa Ynez.

I should point out that while this section is action-specific, the Crosbys' involvement in local affairs goes far beyond the issues of Indian gaming. They perform benefits to fund school arts programs, Jan is deeply involved in local environmental issues, and their anonymous donations and contributions to the valley's individuals and institutions are substantial. This is beyond "not in my backyard" gentrification.

The specific issue that drew me into this was the question of zoning. These guys want to exempt themselves from the zoning laws the same way they've been exempt from the tax rolls. If they get to take any piece of land and make it part of tribal property, then they can build anything they want, anywhere they want. They can build a casino next to a school. They can build a garbage dump next to a school. They can build a nuclear power plant, a slaughterhouse, next to a school. They can do anything they want and they don't have to play by the same rules as us, and that was the crux of it: this is America, they're Americans, whether they like it or not. They're proud of saying they were the first Americans. Well, they're still Americans. They tell us they're sovereign nations and they're very snotty about it. Bullshit. They're still under the federal government, and they're still Americans.

This country was built on the idea that we all play from the same rule-book, that we're all on the same page, that the essence of America is equality. All men are created equal. Not "All men are created equal but the Indians get special breaks." I know they had a rough time of it, but so did the Irish and the blacks. That was then, this is now. None of the punks that are running this casino were at Wounded Knee and neither was I. They don't want to work with the locals—their idea of community participation is to make sure that they bought a new police car for the sheriff's department so the sheriff's department will leave them alone. The danger is that what we're dealing with here is not so much a tribe as a single family that controls a gang. And frankly, if you want to see them blanch and then get really mad, start talking about DNA testing for who's really an Indian and who isn't. If the guy who's running the tribe here has any Indian blood in him at all, it's a miracle. Ultimately, if some segment of the population operates under a different set of rules in an egalitarian democracy, you've planted the seed for the destruction of that democracy. The disparity will cause it to go awry, tear itself apart, and blow up like an imbalanced engine.

SOUND — AIRPLANE PISTON ENGINES (RUNNING PROPERLY)

DISSOLVE TO:

Twenty-two

THE JOY OF FLYING, AND SOME
THOUGHTS ON TERRORISM

EXTERIOR — SANTA YNEZ AIRPORT — AERIAL
A SMALL PLANE IS PASSING OVER THE CHUMASH
INDIAN CASINO

You can see what a blight the Indian casino is from the air; it's the only unpleasant sight flying in and out of the Santa Ynez Valley. More often than not, you marvel at Lake Cachuma, and the Sespe Wilderness Area, which is the route I fly when I'm going to LA, and when I can enjoy the luxury of a flying my own aircraft. I've always loved planes, and when I was a kid I used to build all the little model airplanes that Revell made, particularly the Second World War fighter planes, and the bombers in which my dad flew as an aerial cameraman.

When I got sober and healthy and was starting to put my life back together after the transplant, I wanted forward motion in my life, new experiences, so I took flying lessons. I took a lot of flying lessons. Because I'm diabetic, I had to provide extra data for the physical exam, but I qualified: I got to solo. I learned how to fly and I flew as a student with other people. I had a half-interest in a Cessna 182, which I flew for two or three years. I was flying home at night a lot over the mountains and in a single-engine plane, and that's just a dumb thing to do. Lose the engine and all of a sudden, you're trying to land in a riverbed full of rocks in the dark. Rather than do that, I bought an older twin-engine Beechcraft Baron, a good one. I put better electronics in it, learned how to fly the twin, and always flew with another pilot. I think it's the smart thing to do and, for me, it was the legal thing to do. I always flew with somebody who was rated as an instructor.

It really worked for me. The music business is still in Los Angeles, and I needed to be there to work with agents, managers, record companies, publishing companies, all of it. It was good for an area from San Diego to Phoenix to Sacramento to Sonoma. I could hit any of that in just a couple of hours, and I used my plane probably more than almost anybody at the local airport. If I had a two-week rehearsal period coming up before a CSNY tour, I would fly down in the morning, rehearse until we were done, then there would be a smoking David-shaped hole in the rehearsal stage. I would fly back and have dinner at home, wake up in the morning, take my kid to school, and then fly off to work again. That took me half an hour. I could get to Burbank faster from Santa Ynez than you could from Malibu. I flew into Santa Monica, flew into Burbank, flew into Van Nuys, all the time. Constantly, if I had an appointment with the accountants, I'd be down there. If I needed to go to UCLA to the doctor—into the plane. Marsha and Robin Williams call, say, "We want you guys to come to dinner in San Francisco." It's nothing, I'm there in an hour.

The *Mayan* prepared me for flying in a very important way. Flying and sailing both take place in an unforgiving environment—you can't be disrespectful. If you sail a big boat carelessly, you'll lose the big boat and your life. You fly an airplane carelessly, you will lose the airplane and your life. Neither of those environments is out to get you. They don't even know you're there, but they *will* eat your lunch if you're disrespectful. You have to wear a belt *and* suspenders, you simply must pay attention, and that's the Zen part of it. You can't be anywhere else, you must be focused. You have to "be here now."

I found it to be a wonderful mental exercise, something that made me concentrate, made me memorize things, made me learn how to do things in a certain way, over and over again, skillfully, accurately. I think that people in their fifties and early sixties should look for something like that, that stretches you.

It also stretches the budget. I got to the point where the engines would run out. The FAA requires that after a certain amount of hours of operation, you have to either replace or rebuild the engines, and I didn't have the eighty or ninety thousand that it would have taken to do that. Since I couldn't afford the big hit for mandatory maintenance, I had to sell the Baron, which I regret to this day. Sigh. Some days you have to face reality, you can't have everything, and nowadays I have priorities.

Primary goal? Pay off my house. Second priority: make sure Django gets a great education. Third: make sure we continue to take care of ourselves and our health, and fourth is hanging on to the boat. I'm trying to downsize—I've already sold a plane, a horse, and a motorcycle—but if I can cover my principal goals, the next thing I'd do would be to get a Piper Cub. I'd do it in a heartbeat, just because it's such a blast, and there are a lot of guys flying planes who are older than I am. If you can afford them, you can't have too many toys.

I ran into a pilot friend of mine recently, and asked about going up in his Piper Cub. The smallest fifty horsepower tail dragger would be a thrill for me, and if I ever win the lottery, I'll get one. That way, Django and I can fly, a small light plane I can fly as a sport pilot, which doesn't require a FAA class three medical license, which means that Django and I could go putt-putt-putt up this canyon, down that canyon, between the trees, over the lake, and that's a blast! Low and slow is really the most fun part of flying. Except for the time I got to fly a really big bird.

CUT TO:

EXTERIOR — NEWARK AIRPORT — NIGHT
AIRCRAFT LANDING AND TAKING OFF, NEW YORK SKYLINE
IN THE BACKGROUND

Charter jets big enough for the band and key personnel are expensive, so we try and limit their use and stay on the buses, but the 2002 CSNY Tour was booked without a lot of lead time, so the jumps between shows didn't always permit us to travel by bus. What we use is usually a BBJ, a Boeing 737 in a noncommercial configuration. On the 2002 CSNY tour I was the only person aboard who was a pilot, besides the guys who were flying the plane, so I would always ride in the jump seat. Every night, every takeoff, every landing. I said to them: "Look, I won't say a word. I won't touch anything," but I learn a lot watching the big boys show me how it's really done. That was fine with them, they said that was my seat if I wanted it, so I flew a lot of flights and kept my mouth shut, which is quite an accomplishment for me.

At the end of the tour we landed in Teterboro, New Jersey, one of the closest executive terminals to Manhattan, near the big airport in New Jersey, Newark International. The command pilot says, "Why don't you hang around after everybody splits?" and I said, "Sure." He told me they had to reposition the plane over to Newark, so I let everyone leave for the hotel without me. They close the aircraft doors and button her up, and the pilot says, "Okay, get in the seat," I said, "You're kidding, right?" and he said, "No. Go ahead, taxi it out."

I'm in the copilot seat of an enormous jet—it's huge, ten times as big as anything I've flown; it weighs as much as our house—and I taxi it out. It's not all that difficult: the control systems are familiar, it feels reasonable, and the real pilot is handling the radios, talking to the tower, getting our runway assignment and clearance for takeoff. I get the plane to the runway, I'm stoked, and he says, "I'm going to run the throttles . . . at exactly this speed, rotate it no more than twelve degrees, it'll take off on its own." He advances the throttles and I fly this thing into the air. Then comes the fun part. Because Air Traffic Control doesn't want our 737 to pop up into the main traffic patterns, they hold us low. We're in a very congested airspace, three major commercial airfields, including one of the most heavily trafficked in North America, JFK International. Remember how I was raving about how going "low and slow" was so much fun? I got to do with a jet what no one ever gets to do with a jet, I flew a Boeing 737 jet at 3,500 feet over New Jersey, all the way to Newark, and landed it!

The pilot talked me through it, warned me about flaps, lowered the landing gear, told me as we're on the glide slope, on center line, coming to the inner marker, then the wheels touch down, and I'm still thirty feet in the air because that's how high off the ground the nose of this huge craft is. It was the wildest experience, man. I lucked out, perfectly, the pilot didn't touch the controls, just told me what I was doing, what to expect, and how to react. I'd done it on other airplanes, Gulfstreams, Learjets, pretty exciting airplanes, but never a 737. It's a cool thing, *and* very exciting.

In 1976, I was able to wangle a ride on the airship *Columbia*, the Goodyear Blimp, with Carl and his wife, Allison. He had a connection, a TV director who shot big sports events, and he hooked us up. It was stationed somewhere down off the 110 Freeway, and we all went aloft. It was a great experience because they let me fly the blimp! They were stunned that I could understand how long it took for the controls to take effect. The reason most people can't fly an airship, or Zeppelin, is because they've never sailed a big boat. On a big boat, you put in a direction or correction and wait for it to take effect, because its got masts and a rudder and mass and momentum, and it takes a while before steering takes effect. Same with the plane or the blimp. "Sloooowly, I turn." The Goodyear pilot said, "Most people can't fly this thing when they try.

They make the correction, nothing happens, so they turn the wheel back the other way, and they can't figure out why nothing happens." I said, "I sail a schooner all the time," and they said, "Ah." Me, too. I love flying.

But flying commercially has been reduced to a very unpleasant experience. Unless you're in first class, the seats are up to your knees and chin, and they don't even give you a meal; on a regular flight, you're lucky to have the opportunity to purchase a ten-day-old sandwich and a dried apple in a cardboard box. The airlines' principal concern is to sit on the lid of the garbage can they've put you in. I've been on a "first class" flight where they fed me a fucking cheeseburger that was mostly cardboard, probably made from the same boxes in which they sold crap to coach class.

Forty years of touring has given David more experience in private and commercial aviation than most passengers, and his involvement with piloting and technology provides him with more disturbing insights into the problems all of us face when we travel, as well as threats to our security at home. The apocalyptic world view that seemed far-fetched when he was a young man is a more realistic and threatening vision of the present time. We've witnessed the transformation of the Middle East, the radicalization of some large percentage of the world's Muslim population, sectarian violence from the Balkans to Indonesia and Africa, and environmental degradation on a planetary scale. Yesterday's science fiction has been prophetic to a degree that would have shocked the sensibilities of the writers who thought their work was simply speculative. We're doubly concerned, because the physical world we inhabit doesn't seem to have any parallel universe into which we can escape, and there don't seem to be any world leaders with the Dalai Lama's perspective and compassion.

Airport security is a tragic joke. I'll take off my shoes and open my laptop and leave my knives at home, but if you want me to get a knife or a gun on a plane, I can show you exactly how to do it. Not an issue.

Explosives? Gas? No problem. Anybody with half a brain can get any of those things onto any airplane they want. Metal detectors don't detect certain things. You can build a gun out of bronze, plastic, ceramics if you're just a moderately good gunsmith. How many gunsmiths are there in the United States?

While they're making some sixty-year-old woman take off her shoes, some guy whose identity might be a total mystery is cleaning the airplane—he can put anything he wants on it. They don't search him. They don't know who he is, they have no idea who his brother is. Nobody's going to try to take over an airplane these days, that movie's over. Passengers will never be passive again, not after Flight 93. Now, if terrorists want an airplane, they can simply buy one. They have enough money to buy a 747 anytime they want. Osama bin Laden had over three hundred million dollars when he started. As it stands right now, the Saudi government and the mullahs in Iran are giving him all the money he wants. The Saudi government gives him money just to stay away, because all the jihadists and fundamentalist Muslims want Mecca and Medina and, by the way, the oil too. They want the power, and they envision a time when they will rule the world. At the same time, somewhere in the dark and secret heart of Washington, other guys have been saying for a long time: "Somebody's gonna rule this world. I think it better be a white Christian American man," and that's what they're going to make damn sure happens. If they can. The Chinese might have a different view of it.

There is no version of "The end of civilization as we know it" that David hasn't seriously considered. The conclusions he reaches will convince anyone that he is not a sunny optimist. In two scenarios, he describes how we can end with a bang or a whimper. In the former, it's the detonation of a nuclear device. In the latter, it's deadly disease. Welcome to the dark side.

Let's start with the global map. There's Russia, formerly the Union of Soviet Socialist Republics, the good old USSR. Russia had twenty or thirty thousand nuclear warheads, we'll probably never know for sure. And they're broke. They can't even pay their soldiers. Due south, Central Asia and the Stans: Kazakhstan, Kyrgyzstan, Tajikistan, Uzbekistan, Turkmenistan, Pakistan, and Afghanistan; many like the Wild West, run by warlords without rules, a few with elected governments. Just underneath them, countries with massive amounts of money from oil, Iran and Iraq, who have good reason to hate us. Now, the last time I checked, we haven't repealed the law of supply and demand. To me, that adds up to weapons in the hands of people we don't want to have them. I'm not trying to side with George Bush here, because I think he can't find his ass with both hands, but the situation I just described to you is not only sensible, it's probable.

When it comes to warheads, all they have to do is shield one. Not hard to do, we've been doing it for years, which is why all the guys who serve on nuclear submarines don't glow in the dark. They've got shields. You shield a big nuke well enough, you put it in a container and ship it to any seaport on any coast. They can't look in all the containers. That's how dope's been getting into the country for years.

Years and years ago, some *jefe* of the cartels got tired of losing boats and planes, looked into the cargo container situation, and realized it depended on spot-checks. So some bad mustache goes to a port container facility, finds the right guys in the right office, and drops a suitcase on the desk with a million dollars in circulated nonsequential bills, and says to the guy, "You know that daughter of yours, the one in Dorm 6, Room 125 in Tallahassee? She's beautiful. She's a beautiful girl . . ." And the guy looks at the money, he's ready to say, "What do I have to do?" and they tell him: in the first half of each month you don't open up any containers that have this number in the combination, or have a blue mark on the corner, or any of a thousand ways of marking a container. They say, "Don't open that one. That's not the one you spot-check. You spot-check the next one, and your daughter will be growing up real pretty, no acid in her eyes, and you'll be a rich man. And next year, we'll come with another suitcase."

How hard is that? Tell me it's not logical, or it's not happening, and I'll tell you "Bullshit." It is happening, and that's how they get all the dope into the country. Remember, Afghanistan, where Osama's been hanging out for years, grows most of the opium in the world, and our guys control about a mile around the city and whatever little Green Zone they have, and the rest is warlords and bad guys who've been dodging troops since the days of the raj, and shooting down helicopters and tanks since we gave them the hardware to beat the Russians. Terrorists can go to the same people who get dope into our country to help them get this in. After that, it's horribly simple: container load goes on a truck, they drive the truck into the middle of Washington, Chicago, Los Angeles, pick a target, and say good-bye, and if the truckers are suicide guys, they can stay with the load and push the button that makes it go boom! I don't think I'm being paranoid or living in a fantasy, it's a logical train of events that's entirely possible.

If the doomsday boom is not to your liking, there's always the possibility of a modern plague, as David's fond of saying:

Basic biology and evolution: a radiological and chemical environment is what creates mutagens, which in turn cause mutation. In the past fifty years, we've changed the radiological environment of this planet drastically, depleted the ozone layer, multiplied greenhouse gases, and allowed solar radiation all across the spectrum to bombard us every day. We've changed the chemical environment of this planet, equally drastically. We've put all kinds of poisons and contaminants in the air, water, and soil, and in massive quantities.

TOM CAMPBELL:

If you throw your shit on the ground, it winds up in the ocean. And the plastic breaks down to the size of plankton and then the little fish eat the plankton and then the bigger fish, the birds eat them and the plastic don't do 'em much good. Plastic in the ocean is six times all the plankton. And if you lose the ocean, that protein source, then people like me that grow their own vegetables and have chickens, we're going to have to have a gun to keep you guys away.

Stay with me on this, or check with your local microbiologist: the very first things to mutate significantly are things that go through generations the fastest. That would be bacteria and viruses, so we have diseases that we never had before. Nasty, agile viruses like AIDS, and the one that's in me, hepatitis C. New shit, that evolved because we changed the radiological and chemical environment in which we live. If you can accept that, how the hell do you tell yourself that it's not going to happen at an accelerated rate? AIDS 3? Where is hepatitis D through F? If you think the United States government is going to save you from it, take a look at New Orleans.

The projections are imprecise, but it's entirely possible that we could lose some significant percentage of the world's population. Guy gets on a plane in Hong Kong, he's got avian flu 6, he flies to New York, has contact with a few hundred people in the next few days, some number of them were in the airport, they go flying off, sneezing and coughing on their neighbors, and the results are worldwide in a week. You don't have to wait for ships and rats to do the work.

That is what's been going on in my head all of my adult life, and made me positive that I need to be prepared for a change. That's the nicest way I can put it, because when change comes, it will be so drastic that only people who can accept change will survive it. People who cannot cope with change will die standing in line at the market, waiting for some of that meat that comes in plastic, because they've never seen meat on the hoof. I, on the other hand, will shoot something and eat it, and try to get through this thing alive.

Campbell and Crosby have parted company in recent years over personal issues, but having a gunfight over animal protein seems unlikely, especially since they live more than a hundred and fifty miles apart and will be deal-ing with separate starving, foraging hordes.

Michael Jensen is a publicist and has represented David for many years. His job is to say good things about his client, or repeat good things said by others, and minimize whatever bad press might come along. He is also a man who can be direct about a client who also happens to be his friend:

MIKE JENSEN:

David's always challenging. David is an amazing soul. He's like, what's the old line, "a riddle wrapped in a mystery inside an enigma"? That's David. He is really truly an American original and he can be Jekyll and Hyde. Some days he's good, some days he's bad, some days he's swearing at you, some days he's a sweetheart, at the end of the day you just either have to have faith in your relationship with him or you don't. Ultimately I don't know how to describe him other than a really complex bottle of red wine that gets better with age but takes a long time to mature.

I'm not a tremendously sophisticated person, nor a greatly learned per-son. In many ways, I'm simple, but if people can catch a glimpse of truth or some understanding of their life out of this book, more power to them and God bless them. If there's a chance of any good coming out of the narrative we've laid out, that makes it a worthy enterprise in my eyes. I don't feel I have the smarts or the knowledge to be a teacher or a preacher, I'm neither. When I have an insight, it usually becomes a lyric or set of notes for a song, that's about as much credit as I'd give myself. I think in-telligent people can watch a life like mine unfold, point to a sequence, and say, "Umm, look right there, that's where he went wrong, right there."

BONNIE RAITT:

We're all growing up together and I get great solace, inspiration, and comfort in knowing this community, this family that we're in . . . I don't take any of it for granted. Every day, every minute that David's still alive and that I'm still sober and we have our senses and we're able to have this incredible job, and be able to give back on top of it—none of us take it for granted, and that's why David is to be admired. He's really like the song he wrote, about the compass. He's a compass for so many people.

Twenty-three

"BE STILL MY HEART"

By the end of summer 2005, I had just finished the longest touring schedule I'd had in years. I had done a CPR tour, then went to Europe with Graham for a Crosby-Nash tour, just the two of us. Then we came back and did a tour for the money, a very long tour with Crosby, Stills, and Nash all over the United States, which really beat me into the ground.

By the time we got to the end of it I'd done well over a hundred gigs, and I was used up. Jannie and Django had left the tour before it was over, to come home for at least a short while before he started school. When I got home, I was as tired as I can remember ever being at the end of a touring season, which had me almost continually on the road for eight months. A lot of that time had been on a tight budget, which meant inexpensive hotels, more time on European buses, which lack the amenities of the high-end American coaches, and less down time between shows.

I had pain for a couple of years, and it got much worse during the tour. Every time I'd get home, I'd repeat to myself "Okay, the responsible thing to do here is to go find out what's wrong even though I don't really want to know."

Alan Hersh, an M.D. in family practice in the Santa Ynez Valley, met David soon after he and Jan moved in. His relationship with David is more than a simple patient-doctor connection: they share a common interest in speculative fiction, they are part of a close community, and he loves the music. Dr. Hersh sees more of David than many of his patients; David has a variety of ailments and conditions that are the natural consequences of his medical history. They include potentially dangerous infections, colds, and gastrointestinal complaints that would not be a problem to people with uncompromised immune systems.

DR. ALAN HERSH:

I've been pretty much coordinating his medical care here in the valley. [When I first saw him] he was going through a period of time when he'd had a lot of problems with intestinal stuff . . . Gary Gitnick was one of my professors when I was in medical school, not that we were real tight or anything like that, but periodically when new information comes in about David or if I have some concerns, I'll give Gary a call and every time, he says "Tell him he's got to lose the weight. Tell him he's got to lose the weight." That's all he ever talks about now. I'd lose it for him if I could.

David had just gotten back from Europe and called me and said, "I'm having this pain, especially when I've been walking up the hill over by Django's school," and I said, "Maybe you should get checked out," and right away he got into a cardiologist and had a treadmill test done. . . . That's got about a ten percent false positive rate, and about a ten percent false negative rate, so that ten percent at the time you're scaring somebody inappropriately and his was off. . . . Because of his deconditioning, it didn't go too far, but the idea of a treadmill test is to get him up to a peak heart rate and, frankly, even with David's

weight, deconditioning, and the orthopedic problems from his motorcycle accident, he was able to at least get what they thought was a
reasonable test, which looked okay.

*The cardiogram was taken on Friday, September 23, 2005. On Tuesday,
September 27, I was driving to meet David at his house for a scheduled
few days of work. I was speeding, trying to make up for time lost en route
on other personal business. I was anxious to return to work, when my cell
phone rang. It was Jan, saying, "I'm sorry if you're on the road, but don't
bother coming up, we're taking David to the hospital in Santa Barbara,
he's been in a lot of pain and we're very worried." I expressed concern, and
she was reassuring: "At least we know it's not his heart." "How do we
know?" I asked. "Because he just had a checkup and a stress cardiogram
and they said his heart was fine." I made a U-turn, and drove back to
LA. I'd call later to find out what the doctors said.*

I went to Santa Barbara for an endoscopy, an unpleasant procedure
during which they lower a camera down your throat and look at everything on the way and into your stomach. They find that there's a little
bit of irritation but not that much. I get done with the endoscopy and
I'm taken back to the room, where, as I'm getting up from the wheelchair
and getting into the bed, I feel it. I'm having a heart attack. It feels like
I'm being kicked in the chest. I was in a lot of pain and I asked for morphine, which they gave me. A doctor there didn't believe that I was having a heart attack and didn't believe any of my reasons for being there.
He thought I was there to get painkillers. It was obnoxious, but it's something you learn to live with—if you've been a junkie once, for the rest of
your life, people are going to look at you with that label attached.

JAN CROSBY:
It started the moment we crossed the threshold; a male nurse turned
around with a syringe in his hand after they had put the IV in David's

vein and said, "I just want you to know that I don't think I should give this to you because you have had a liver transplant . . . there's really no reason I should be giving you morphine. You obviously don't know how to treat your new organ. But I have to follow the orders, so I'm reluctantly going to give this to you." David was very grateful and very passive.

David slept through the night, while Jan waited. I called her cell phone several times when I got back from Los Angeles, into the evening, and got no response, which concerned me. I called the house, and got Django, who was alone. I asked how his dad was doing. "It's pretty bad," he said.

DJANGO:

I just kinda knew that he was going to make it. I had that feeling. I knew it wasn't time yet.

As soon as David was passive and relaxed from the morphine, he slept through the night. What followed was a series of escalating confrontations between Jan, desperately concerned for her husband's condition, and several physicians who had apparently formed an opinion that affected their diagnoses.

JAN CROSBY:

This doctor says, "There's nothing wrong with your husband," and I said, "Then why is he in so much pain? What do you think we should do?" and his reply is, "That's a good question . . . I'm going to send your husband home tonight." I said "Wait a minute, he's been here for over twenty-four hours, he's been heavily sedated with morphine and some other sedative to do this procedure, what happens if he wakes up from these drugs and he needs help?" His answer was something like, "Your husband's obviously here for drugs and needs some more morphine, just get the local guy, Alan Hersh, to give it to him, have him run over to your house and give him an injection."

Which was a crappy thing to say, completely uncalled for and totally shitty. That was one of the most irresponsible doctors I've ever found. I'm lucky that I have Alan Hersh there. He's never done anything like that in the entire time I've known him. This is a guy who really plays it kosher: he's come to me when I was so sick I couldn't get out of bed. When I was throwing up so bad that I could not get out of the bed, he made a house call, which is extremely rare for him; he's a really nice guy, and my close friend.

ALAN HERSH:

When I first met David, he was having some periods of being a pretty sick guy, in bed, vomiting. I was out there injecting him with antibiotics and antinausea medication. His plumbing isn't quite like it used to be, that's his real weak spot; he's on imunosuppresents, so anything that's coming through the community, it tends to hang on, and [he has] a school-age kid bringing exogenous germs home. He's always bitching about the stuff that he and Django are bouncing back and forth, and so we try to stay on top of it.

JAN CROSBY:

That's when I lost my temper, when the doctor pulled Alan Hersh into it, just because he had some kind of personal beef with David, and didn't understand what could be wrong with him, didn't find anything wrong with him, thought it couldn't be anything serious. Then he went to get the photograph to show me he'd gone down his esophagus, and I thought, "I've got to get David out of here or he's going to die." When he walked back in with the esophagus pictures I asked him to release my husband to me, because I wanted to move him to another hospital. I wanted to move David to UCLA and when I said that, he changed his posture from "Your husband has no problem, he's a drug addict and he's here for drugs." He conceded maybe something was wrong.

At that point, David's nurse comes in and says, "This patient is being too demanding, he's demanding he be fed immediately," and I said, "Excuse me, but my husband's been under sedation and if he's hungry when he wakes up, he's not demanding anything. He hasn't had any food for several days." I pissed them off, both of them, right there, and the nurse says, "I'm done with this guy, I'm not touching him again."

I couldn't get anybody to be on my side and I was a lone woman, in a devastating position without an advocate. Our previous experience was with wonderful care at UCLA, and I assumed it was like that in all hospitals. Well, it wasn't the case here. I bumped into what felt to me like genuine disinterest in helping him and it worried me. The next nurse to show up was giving him less pain medication than was on his orders, and I made her get the right dosage. While she was gone, David was in real pain. I know his face, and I can see this is a face I've never seen before and that's when I noticed his lip, I mean his mustache was starting to turn a funny color. I'd never seen that happen either. The nurse comes back with another syringe in her hand. Does she say anything to me? No. She just pushed it into his vein, and he's *bam,* out cold. I asked what she gave him, she said, "Ativan, it's a tranquilizer." I said, "Why did you tranquilize my husband while he's telling us where it hurt? How could you do that? He's giving us information." She said he was "very agitated."

At that point, Jan started to call outside for additional opinions, consultations, any help she could get from David's doctors in Los Angeles. Her independence and insistence were probably discomfiting to the medical fra-

ternity at Cottage Hospital in Santa Barbara. No one was responding to her satisfaction. Anyone who knows Jan and David is aware of their tenacious mutual support, especially in matters of vital interest and sheer survival. This was not a case of a rock star asking for a room with a view or his wife badgering the staff for extra pillows. Jan was obsessively pursuing a course of diagnosis and treatment that was at odds with their evaluations and assessments, regardless of the symptoms David was presenting.

DR. GARY GITNICK:

You may recall that when he first presented here in '93, he really came with right upper-quarter pain and he'd already had his gallbladder taken out. Now he's had abdominal pain ever since then. He had it before the transplant, during the period he was in the hospital and since, so abdominal discomfort is part of his life and it's reasonable to attribute anything, then, to gastrointestinal disease, but the pain that he described by phone that time was different. It was higher and had a different quality. It was not the same kind of discomfort that he'd been having for years . . .

They were obnoxious. The doctor still thinks I'm trying to get drugs. He has a confrontation or two with Jandy, she's fighting for me and defends me and is really pissed at this guy, who's being an absolute shit. Finally, two of the interns come to us and tell us that there's a simple test they can do, a scan or something. They do the procedure, and it shows quite clearly that I had a heart attack. No question about it. You're supposed to be able to see an entire circle and all you see is this obstructed fragment, not getting any blood flow. Heart attack.

At the same time, Jan and the doc are going round and round and Jan's trying to get someone from UCLA to talk to someone at Cottage Hospital, and finally gets some back-and-forth going. Meanwhile, I'm being dosed with less morphine than I need, and a lot of other drugs that were basically intended to keep me manageable: Ativan, and Versed, both of which are pretty stupefying medications in the dosage I was getting.

This goes on for days—Jan is without sleep and the lack of cooperation is driving her to distraction. Finally Gary Gitnick and the Santa Barbara doctors connect on the phone, but the local guys give him three different stories and that really upsets the shit out of him. Gary doesn't have a lot of tolerance for substandard medical care.

GARY GITNICK:

Yeah, I think that they, it's a matter of judgment, not so much of incompetence. I think they were competent. And they were sincere and cautious and you know you can talk to ten doctors and get twenty opinions, and they're all honest and good and you know, I think their original studies, from what they described by phone, it wasn't clear.

JAN:

They gave him more Ativan, made him a zombie, and we stayed in that room overnight. By nine o'clock the next morning they were wheeling him into nuclear medicine. I went with him and I asked a doctor, "If this was your family member, would you want to know what was going on?" He said, "Absolutely," so I told him what went down the day before as he was looking at the scan, and then I asked him what he would do if this was his family member. He said, "I'd get the hell out. You can't tell anybody I said that because it'll cost me my job, but if this was somebody in my family, I'd get the hell out of here." Then he showed me the photographs of the nuclear scan, at the same time describing that a healthy heart would look like a doughnut, but the picture wasn't a doughnut. There was a separation in it, and he explained that David's heart wasn't getting enough blood supply, that it was a dangerous condition, and it indicated he had a heart attack recently. Finally, someone who didn't want to go on the record told me that they saw what I saw.

The upshot of all this was that the medical fraternity agreed that David should have an extensive cardiology workup, including an angiogram, which is an invasive procedure requiring local or general anesthesia that may sometimes require major cardiothoracic surgery, if immediate danger is discovered. It was decided, at Jan and David's insistence, that they would do the procedure at UCLA, and David was discharged from Cottage Hospital. In typical Crosby fashion, he insisted on going home to sleep in his own bed. Considering the days of medicated semiconsciousness and Jan's worried confrontations and phone calls, the facts that he was short-tempered, snappish, and fearful make the request understandable. He went home to Santa Ynez.

I stayed home, recovering, and talked to a lot of people on the phone, everyone who Jan had talked to while I was in the hospital, and more. The consensus was clear; I needed an angiogram, right away, before anything else serious happened. Since we were going to UCLA, Jan and I agreed to go down Sunday night, stay in a hotel nearby, and be right there early Monday morning, when the procedure was scheduled. We drove down, checked into the Bel-Air, and decided to have dinner there with Jim Hart and Carl, who were anxious to see me, talk about business, this book, whatever would distract me while I was waiting to go back into my least favorite place in the world, another hospital. Even though it was going to be UCLA, where they'd saved my life and watched over me for the last ten years, I was apprehensive and, worse yet, experiencing severe chest pains.

David was not in good shape at dinner. We had planned to meet early and discuss this book, but I was unconscionably late, so all we had time for was a drink before dinner. He would grimace, or sigh, and admitted to experiencing pain as we spoke. I asked if he had a prescription for nitroglycerine for chest pain, and suggested it might be a good idea to take some. He did, and recovered enough to enjoy conversation with me and Jim Hart, and Django and Jan. We weren't exactly a merry table, but the five of us got through the meal. David ate very little, and took no pleasure in what he'd ordered. We shook hands all around, hugged, kissed, wished him a safe and quick procedure, and as Jim and I left, I couldn't help but notice David was moving slowly, practically shuffling, short of breath, and falling behind Jan and Django as they made their way back to their room.

GARY GITNICK:

I think most good doctors would rather be involved in a medical issue early in its course, [when] something can be done, than late in its course, when you may not be effective at all. I'd rather have David or anybody else call me on Saturday if something's happening than wait until the next Friday when I really can't be very good. I really can't help very much. On Saturday I may be able to prevent trouble. We talked by phone. I'm usually reachable. I carry phones and beepers and everything. I think we did it all by telephone and I put together the best, an excellent team. Same kind of people I'd put together for my own family. He clearly had obstructive disease.

I was not only feeling bad, I was scared out of my mind. I think I'm having another heart attack right then, because of the chest pains. I was taking the nitroglycerine and morphine tablets, and nothing could dull the pain. After the third nitro, when I called Gary Gitnick, he said "Mmmm, doesn't sound good, go to the emergency room." He's at a party forty-five minutes outside of Los Angeles. He calls the cardiologist, who I think was already asleep, but the guy gets up, gets dressed, and comes in, while Jan and Django drive me to the hospital.

DJANGO:

My parents woke me up and I thought it was really early in the morning, like six o'clock, because we were going to go to have his heart be checked out and fixed at six a.m the next day. Turns out it was eleven o'clock at night, and I didn't know. I thought I had had a whole night of sleep and it was the next day, and then I found out that we were going to the hospital because he was having a heart attack, or he was about to.

The team at UCLA emergency room conclude that luckily I'm not having a heart attack at that moment, but when the cardiologist arrives and looks the situation over, he decides that since he's there and I'm somewhat precarious, they might as well do the procedure right away. Miraculously, the cardiology team is available, most of them in bed, but they all get up and drive to UCLA, and about an hour later, they operate. Sent a miniature camera up a cardiac catheter in my femoral artery, found the blockage, pulled the camera, ran a stent to the blockage, opened it, installed the stent, and that was that. I was done.

DJANGO:
  Yeah, like two and a half hours after we got to the emergency room at UCLA, they fixed his heart. He was feeling ten times better, and his description of it is like a cement bag was being lifted off his chest. Felt like he had gone back ten years or twenty years. They showed us a picture of his heart and the vein was 95 percent collapsed. Five percent of the blood that the right-hand side of his heart needed to function, wasn't getting to it . . . It looked like there was a centimeter-long place where there was no vein, and they showed us that before, and after they did it, all the way through, it was nice and thick, flowing. They showed us before and they showed us after. Then we went back to the hotel and drove home in the morning.

This next bit is a verbatim transcript of two messages that were on my answering machine when I woke up, not much more than twelve hours after I left him panting and wincing at the hotel. David is speaking: "Carl, it's Croz. It started to get bad last night again so we left for the emergency room. They did me right then. I'm done. I feel a thousand percent better. We are checking out of the hotel. We are getting in the car to go home. We will be on our various cell phones, and we love you, Carl. It was a joy to see you last night and I love you and I will always love you . . . if you want us, we'll be in the car for the next couple of hours on our cell phones. Okay? Thanks, buddy." An hour later, another recorded message, obviously from a cell phone in a vehicle moving fast. David again: "Carl, Kim Garfunkel just gave me what I think might be the title for the book. She said the title should be Still Coming, *and I like that. No, she said the title should be* Keeps on Coming, *which I like a whole lot. It's a wonderful, wonderful title. I just thought I'd tell you that before I forgot it. Call me, we're on our cells . . ." I called, we discussed the title, and how a tiny tube of titanium mesh in a coronary artery could undo the pain and damage of years.*

The stunning thing is how you suddenly feel better. I'd had pain in my chest pretty much continuously for years, and all of a sudden, it wasn't there! It's like having somebody untie boots you've been wearing in your chest. Jan was the one who actually knew what was going on during that whole difficult episode, although I'm pretty sure I remember a lot of what went on while I was in Santa Barbara. Ultimately, I was the one flat on my back, and she was my defender and my advocate. Piece of advice? Don't ever go into the hospital without a defender and an advocate to watch your back, front, and sides. Life's tough enough.

Finale

"G'NIGHT EVERYBODY! YOU'VE BEEN GREAT!"

These have been stories of love, family, competition, adversity, thoughtless behavior, and political anger. A lot of it is just my sheer luck in life. I was tremendously lucky, surviving injury, illness, and stupidity. As for the music, I was blessed early and often, from the Byrds to Crosby, Stills, Nash, and Young, singing with Graham, meeting my son James and creating CPR, having the most astounding music come out of that, and just as I experience the wonderful exploratory forward motion of new music, here comes Neil, oops, out of left field, and he changes everything, as usual, and it'll change everything again when he splits, as he eventually will. It's practically Dickensian.

The crucial lessons are very clear. I wrote them down in the song "Time Is the Final Currency." No question about it. The time we have here is to do the things that are really important to us. We have to focus, define what matters, and spend your time accordingly. The lesson learned from coming close to death is that you have a limited lifespan, a finite amount of time that you have to spend wisely. Ultimately, what really matters is my family and the music. If I ever doubted that, the episode with my chest in 2005 was a grim reminder that I had been ignoring.

I like writing music. I like playing it for people. I also like to go sailing and fly airplanes. Yes, I love to go diving. Yes, I love to read a good book, I read constantly, and I trust we've written a book that will be read by others. I've learned not to obsess about people who've screwed me over—I won't even rent them any space in my head. They're working on their karma, and I'm working on mine. You can't do anything about other people, I can't change anyone except myself, and I can't even do that without major effort. My two biggest mistakes were to be mad and sad, and use those feelings as excuses to get loaded.

I'm a guy who was such a fuck-up that I was supposed to be dead years ago from drugs. I should have died in a gunfight or a deal gone bad or an overdose or died in prison, and to have somehow extricated myself from that, managed to quit doing hard drugs, dragged myself inch by inch back up to functioning, and then get to be at a level where I can do a completely successful performance in front of huge numbers of people and deeply affect them, is astounding. It's a reward for a long life of trying to pull this off in music. It makes all the road, all the money, all of the bad food, all of the crap that goes along with being in the music business, it makes all of that worthwhile when you play as we've been doing it. I'm so fucking grateful. I seem kind of corny about being grateful about it, but it's just that wonderful.

As with any film, there comes a time when the story's over. We leave the heroes and villains, the supporting players, and the images that have filled the frame during the time we've spent together. In a darkened theater, or on a screen at home, that moment declares itself. But one last scene . . .

EPILOGUE

Backstage is always rumbling or humming. The source of the sound is always equipment and people, and it's the same at an outdoor amphitheater, an indoor arena, a nightclub, or a television studio with an audience. It's an energy field that's sustained me and motivated me since I first discovered I could sing in public a half-century ago. On the wall of a large office building outside Paris, the words *La Musique, Toutes la Musique* are written large: "Music, All Music." That sums it up. Music has been humanity's celebration of itself since our primal ancestors danced around a campfire. They were having a party, and it's been the same ever since.

Think about it—what's the first thing people do when they want to celebrate or say, "Hey, this is fun," or, "Gosh, it's great you got married," or, "Whoopee for the new baby?" They have a party, and they sing or play. Music is what humans do when they're happy. They reach for music, and it's magic. It has a miraculous effect on people. What happens between us when we're playing or listening to music is one of the most civilizing and uplifting forces in human culture and civilization, ever, always, since the beginning. I'm a part of that, you're a part of that, it's our collective expression of joy at being alive.

On the sixth of July 2006, right after the long summer weekend that celebrates our country's birth, I put my hand in a circle backstage with three longtime partners and friends. Out front, twenty-two thousand people are waiting. Graham Nash, Neil Young, Stephen Stills, and I have been repeating this little ritual before every show since Crosby, Stills, Nash, and Young made our debut at the Auditorium Theater in Chicago on August 16, 1969. Our second gig was on a plywood stage in front of a half million people in the mud and rain—Woodstock.

As always, the tour manager calls the moment, the crew points the way, and the four of us make our way through a dark tangle of cable and equipment boxes, hundreds of glowing gauges shining from the lighting and sound equipment, and roadies' flashlights punching a safe path through the gloom. The warm glow from the stage is the preshow set lighting, the houselights are dimming, the crowd murmur turns into a throaty roar, and twenty-two thousand separate people become a single entity, an audience that's come to the opening night of the tour called "An Evening with Crosby, Stills, Nash, and Young: Freedom of Speech, '06.

We enter.

The stage lights hit us full on, there are few words, a count-off, and the concert begins. Out front, flashbulbs pop like electric pepper. The four of us are the front line, behind us are the other musicians, and surrounding them onstage is a crew of twenty men and women in the wings and more out in the auditorium. In the parking lot there are drivers and loaders for a dozen trucks and buses, a catering crew. Our families and friends and management are watching from offstage. There are people in the audience our age or older, there are enthusiastic adults who weren't born when we first toured, and some of them have brought their kids and grandkids. They will sing along with the words they know, hear new songs for the first time in their lives, and not all of them will know what it took to get us there, the history of the moment.

Neil Young, like most of us, has gotten more and more pissed about the war in Iraq. He's not foolish enough to think that mankind can evolve beyond fighting amongst ourselves any time soon, although we both believe that someday human beings will outgrow it. As it stands right now, this is not a just war, it's a war for profit, a war to put money into Bechtel and Halliburton and Exxon and Boeing and everybody else that profits from it. These people have thought for a long time that war is great way to regenerate an economy because it puts money into the military industrial complex.

Neil got very pissed about the war as it kept going on, because in wars, for every soldier that gets killed, ten, twenty, thirty civilians—men, women, and children—get killed, maimed, bombed, burned. That's the nature of war. It stinks. So he wrote his album *Living With War* and he knew we'd be the right ones to deliver the goods. Our songs make a context for his. We do Neil's songs in the middle of "Long Time Gone," and "For What It's Worth," and "Chicago," and "Teach Your Children," and they make sense. There's an obvious continuity from before and into the future. Neil said he wants to go on tour, and here we are.

On the floor is a giant groundcloth on which is reproduced the elegant calligraphy of the Constitution of the United States of America. A reviewer noted, "I saw these four icons standing on the Constitution and standing up for it."

I'm sure there are things people can say to criticize Neil Young, but not about music. Getting the chance to play with Neil, who is a wonderful musician and a terrific guy, was always a joy and it still is. He's always leaning forward into what's possible, musically. He's completely honest, completely driven about it, and he will do whatever it takes to make good music. It's what he lives for. He gets up in the morning, eats some music for breakfast, then runs a little music through his hair, then he washes with some music, then he does a little more music, and then he goes for a walk and thinks up some music.

To this day, Crosby, Stills, Nash, and Young pulls me at me because of Neil. We were as good as or better than we've ever been in 2006 and yet CSNY is an unstable element. It doesn't have a long half-life and it won't stabilize. We've always been like a wheel that's out of balance: it'll spin, but sooner or later, it's going to come off the axle.

I'm a guy who's been doing it for a long time, and in so many different ways. At this point in my life, it still astounds me that we're able to do a completely successful performance in front of huge numbers of people and affect them, deeply affect them. We can touch them places where it hurts or it feels joyful, or it feels triumphant, but we're touching them. It's a reward for a long life of trying and it makes it all worthwhile. It makes all the road, all the money and all the bad food, all of the crap that goes along with being in the music business, it makes all of that worthwhile when you play the way we did on that tour.

I like to think of myself as a stand-up guy, but it hasn't been easy to stay on my feet. Many hands and feet have knocked me down, picked me up, kicked my butt, set me straight, and eventually restored whatever equilibrium I enjoy at the moment. It's a moment that's part of melody that began before my birth, a tempo and a tune that stretches out ahead, an unbroken song I've been lucky to learn and sing and write.

AT THE EDGE

Our grasp is so fragile, the thread is so thin,
I wonder each day if I'm blowing away.
I know that I'm lucky, I wouldn't be here at all

EPILOGUE

if somebody's hand hadn't been where I stand
at the edge of a very great fall.

And like a lighthouse before you at the edge of the sea,
the woman whose grip holds when you slip,
but the darkness won't get you, your family won't go,
they will make your heart light to where you know what is right,
and you go where you know you should go.

And it's life and it's dying its beginnings and ends.
It's What did you do with the life they gave you?
It's Were you honest and did you make amends
to all the ones under your guns.
How have you treated your friends?

FADE TO BLACK

ROLL END CREDITS

ACKNOWLEDGMENTS

The authors wish to thank Dan Conaway, our editor at G. P. Putnam's Sons and the Penguin Group, for his vision and oversight, and his colleague Rachel Holtzman, for her efforts in the home stretch, and David Zimmer, who knows as much about CSNY as anyone, and did, in fact, "write the book."

Laurie Liss, our über agent at Sterling Lord Literistic, deserves the blame and the praise for her sale of the book to Mr. Conaway, and thanks for her continuing and unflagging support of her difficult but adorable clients. Likewise, continuing appreciation to Elliot Roberts and all his crew at Lookout Management.

Marcia Jacobs and Debbie Meister were superb assistants, and Ms. Jacobs and Morgan Ames transcribed hundreds of hours of recorded interviews, many of them made under difficult conditions with varying degrees of audibility and intelligibility. Kelli Maroney proofread the author's paper drafts, and Buzz Person, Dana Africa, Henry Diltz, Betty Crosby, and "the Italians" made superb contributions to the photo sections.

The Internet continues to be a valuable and irreplaceable resource for research, fact-checking, historical context, and gossip. Links to useful sites and web pages are cited in the endnotes, and we're particularly indebted to "The Italians" (half of whom are not): Francesco Lucarelli, Stefano Frollano, Herman Verbeke, and Lucien van Diggelen, who have privately published an exhaustive history called "Crosby, Stills, Nash, and Sometimes Young." Their discographies and details were extremely useful, as were the websites "4WaySite.com" and "Lee-shore@Yahoogroups.com."

David thanks his wife, Jan, and his son Django, and the rest of his extended family for their love and support. Carl thanks his cats and his friends for not intruding on him during the time required to collaborate on the text, and his partner and inspiration in this effort, David Crosby, The Croz Himself, his Crosnaciousness.

CAST

Dana Africa	Sailor/dive tour leader
Andy Allen	Founder of ADA, Alternative Distribution Alliance
Kirstie Alley	Actor
Herb Alpert	Cofounder of Atlantic Records/trumpet player
Mrs. Astor	Socialite wife of William/known only as Mrs. Astor
Joan Baez	Singer/activist
Bailey	Girl, daughter of Melissa Etheridge and Julie Cypher
John Perry Barlow	Former Grateful Dead lyricist
Drew Barrymore	Actor, producer
Beckett	Boy, son of Melissa Etheridge and Julie Cypher
Harry Belafonte	Singer/activist
Bob "Bobalou" Benavides	Biker/roadie, David's caretaker/friend
David Bender	Political journalist/commentator/theorist
Joel Bernstein	Photographer/archivist, musician
Ed Blue	Pseudonym for CPA who mismanaged David's money

Napoleon Bonaparte	Emperor of France, king of Italy
Joe Brandenberg	Parole officer
Jeff Bridges	Actor/childhood friend of David's/Santa Ynez neighbor
Susan Bridges	Wife of Jeff Bridges
Jackson Browne	Singer-songwriter
Jimmy Buffett	Singer-songwriter
George H.W. Bush	U.S. President
George W. Bush	U.S. President
Dr. Ronald Busuttil	David's doctor/director of organ transplantation at UCLA
Allison Caine	Coauthor's ex-wife
Rance Caldwell	Longtime touring associate
Tom Campbell	Backstage organizer for benefit concerts
Enrico Caruso	Singer
Charlie Chaplin	Actor/producer/director/songwriter
Dixie Chicks	Singing group
Gene Clark	Member of the Byrds
Michael Clarke	Member of the Byrds
Deanna Cohen	Jackson Browne's girlfriend, who visited David in the hospital
Marc Cohn	Singer-songwriter
Jill Collins	Friend who helped Jan during David's hospitalization
Phil Collins	Singer-songwriter, cowrote "Hero" with David
Shawn Colvin	Singer-songwriter
Alice Cooper	Singer
Aliph Crosby	David's mother
Betty Cormack Crosby	David's stepmother

Bing Crosby	Singer, no relation to David
Django Crosby	David's son
Donovan Anne Crosby	David's daughter
Ethan Crosby	David's brother
Floyd Crosby	David's father
Jan Dance Crosby	David's wife
Julie Cypher	Mother of Bailey and Beckett
Harper Dance	Jan's mother
Clive Davis	Record producer
Howard Dean	Former governor of Vermont
Mike Delich	Ran Gramophone Records
Ani DiFranco	Singer-songwriter, entrepreneur
Steve DiStanislao	"Stevie D," CPR drummer
Craig Doerge	Composer, musician
Raechel Donahue	Cofounder of radio station KMPX SF
Tom Donahue	Cofounder of radio station KMPX SF
Debbie Donovan	Mother of Donovan Anne Crosby
Tommy Dowd	Producer/engineer
Bob Dylan	Singer-songwriter/activist
Ahmet Ertegun	Legendary cofounder of Atlantic Records
Melissa Etheridge	Singer/mother of Bailey and Beckett
Don and Phil Everly	Singing duo
Jerry Falwell	Fundamentalist preacher
Mimi Fariña	Joan Baez's sister, singer, social activist
Russ Feingold	U.S. Senator
"Cindy" Ferguson	James Raymond's birth mother
Candy Finnigan	Interventionist
Mike Finnigan	Keyboard player

William Floyd	David's ancestor, signer of the Declaration of Independence
Andrew "Drew" Ford	CPR bass player
Aretha Franklin	Singer
Kinky Friedman	Writer/politician
Mahatma Gandhi	Activist/lawyer
Jerry Garcia	Grateful Dead leader
Art Garfunkel	Singer/actor
Bryan Garofalo	Cowriter, "The Loadout"
David Geffen	Founder of Asylum Records
Dan Gerber	Poet/former racecar driver/Santa Ynez activist
Terry Gilliam	Director of *The Fisher King*
Frank Gironda	Part of David's management team
Dr. Gary Gitnick	Gastroenterologist, UCLA
Whoopi Goldberg	Actor
Samuel Goldwyn	Pioneer film producer
John "Gonzo" Gonzales	Guitar tech, road manager
Berry Gordy	Record producer
Bill Graham	Legendary promoter in San Francisco
Arlo Guthrie	Singer-songwriter
Larry Hagman	Actor/recipient of liver transplant
John Hammond	Legendary record producer
Dr. Gene Harris	Orthopedic surgeon
Jake Hart	Jim and Judy's son
Jim Hart	Screenwriter of *Hook*/friend/fan
Judy Hart	Jim's wife/friend/fan
Julia Hart	Jim and Judy's daughter
William Randolph Hearst	Publishing mogul
Michael Hedges	Acoustic guitar player/composer

Wally Heider	Recording studio engineer/owner
Robert Heinlein	Science fiction writer, *Stranger in a Strange Land*
Don Henley	Singer-songwriter/Eagles drummer
Judy Henske	Lyricist, "Might as Well Have a Good Time," singer
Buddy Herzog	Litigator for David in Mikuni lawsuit
Chris Hillman	Member of the Byrds
Christine Hinton	David's girlfriend who died in car accident
Dustin Hoffman	Actor
Billie Holiday	Legendary jazz singer
Jackie Hyde	Erika Keller's birth mother, married to Arlo Guthrie
Joris Ivens	Dutch national progressive filmmaker
Janet Jackson	Singer
Mike Jensen	David's publicist
Steve Jobs	CEO, Apple Computer and Pixar Animation Studios
Glyn Johns	Record producer, *After the Storm*
Jack Johnson	Singer-songwriter
Lyndon Johnson	U.S. President
Al Jolson	Singer
Norah Jones	Singer-songwriter
Paul Kantner	Member, Jefferson Airplane
Alex Keller	Erika's husband
Alexa Keller	Erika's daughter, David's granddaughter
Erika Keller	David's daughter by Jackie Hyde
Jorge Keller	Erika's son, David's grandson
Roberta Keller	Erika's daughter, David's granddaughter
John Kerry	U.S. Senator
Val Kilmer	Actor

Carole King	Singer-songwriter
Dr. Martin Luther King, Jr.	Activist
Bill Kreutzmann	Grateful Dead drummer
Kris Kristofferson	Singer/activist/Farm Aid
Russ Kunkel	Rock and roll drummer
Jim Ladd	Legendary DJ
Carl Laemmle	Founder, Universal Studios
Richard LaGravenese	Screenwriter of *The Fisher King*
Dalai Lama	His Holiness the fourteenth Dalai Lama, Tenzin Gyatso
Barbara Langer	Car companion of Christine Hinton
Jesse Lasky	Pioneer film producer
Phil Lesh	Grateful Dead bass player
Goddard Lieberson	Record producer
Philip Livingston	David's ancestor, signer of Declaration of Independence
Pare Lorentz	Progressive filmmaker of the 1930s
Brin Luther	David's first cousin once removed
Charles Manson	Psycho serial killer
Mickey Mantle	Baseball player, recipient of liver due to celebrity
Dr. Richard Marrs	Jan's doctor/reproductive endocrinologist at UCLA
L. B. Mayer	Founder of MGM
John McCain	U.S. Senator
Judge Pat McDowall	Dallas court judge who sentenced David
Dan McGee	CPR tour manager
Roger McGuinn	Member of the Byrds
Marty Meehan	U.S. Congressman
Debbie Meister	Office manager at Bill Siddons/day-to-day liaison for CSNY
Terry Melcher	Record producer

Georgeanne Melvin	*Mayan* caretaker, Milan's wife
Milan Melvin	*Mayan* caretaker/certified divemaster
Tammy Lynn Michaels	Melissa Etheridge's current partner
Cree Miller	Manager/lawyer
Donald "Buddha" Miller	Manager/chef/motorcycle enthusiast
Mirais	South African folk singer and songwriter
Miranda	South African folk singer
Joni Mitchell	Singer-songwriter
Russell Mulcahy	Director of music videos
Graham Nash	Singer-songwriter, David's partner and best friend
Susan Nash	Graham's wife
Willie Nelson	Singer-songwriter/activist
Nickel Creek	Canadian singing group
Richard Nixon	U.S. President
Ted Nugent	Guitarist/ex-Amboy Dukes/conservative
Barak Obama	U.S. Senator
Sandra Day O'Connor	Former associate justice, Supreme Court
Jeff Palmer	Old school friend of David and Ethan's
Daniel Parker, Esq.	David's lawyer for New York bust (no relation to Fess)
Fess Parker	Actor/developer
Martha Parker	Fess Parker's wife
Jeff Parrish	*Mayan* skipper
Sean Penn	Actor/director
Buzz Person	Photographer/lawyer/fan
Jeff Pevar	CPR guitarist
John Phillips	Member, Mamas and Papas
Mary Pickford	Actor

Pink	Singer-songwriter
Elvis Presley	Singer
Bonnie Raitt	Singer-songwriter/activist
Grace Raymond	James and Stacia's daughter, David's granddaughter
James Raymond	David's son, CPR
John Raymond	James's adoptive father
Madeline Raymond	James's adoptive mother
Stacia Raymond	James's wife
Ronald Reagan	U.S. President
Frederick Remington	Artist/war correspondent
Elliot Roberts	David's manager since 1968
Pat Robertson	Fundamentalist
Spider Robinson	Science fiction writer
Rolling Stones	Singing group
Santana	Singing group
John Sebastian	Singer-songwriter
Pete Seeger	Singer-songwriter/activist
Mike "Coach" Sexton	Tour manager
Chris Shays	U.S. Congressman
Bill Siddons	David and Graham's manager
Steve Silberman	*Wired* magazine writer
Paul Simon	Singer-songwriter
Ashlee Simpson	Singer/actor
Jessica Simpson	Singer/actor
Grace Slick	Member Jefferson Airplane/visual artist
Smothers Brothers	Performers
Steven Spielberg	Director of *Hook, Jaws,* legendary filmmaker

Gloria Steinem	Activist, Voters for Choice
Martha Stewart	Billionaire whose trial took place during David's N.Y. bust
Stephen Stills	Singer-songwriter/longtime singing partner
Sting	Singer-songwriter/activist
Barbra Streisand	Singer/actor/director/producer
James Surowiecki	Writer of "Hello Cleveland" for *The New Yorker*
Charles Tacot	Pistolero
Henry David Thoreau	Writer
Tilley, Winans & Crosby	1948 camp trio with Ethan
Garry Tolman	Longtime manager Stills, Nash, CSN trio
Mark Twain	Writer
John Vanderslice	Tour manager, production manager
Josh Vanderslice	David's personal road manager, John's son
The Weavers	Singing group
Smokey Wendell	Stephen Stills's road manager/anti-drug bodyguard
Jerry Wexler	Record producer
Josh White	First folk blues singer/civil rights activist
Ron White	Comedian
Marsha Williams	Robin's wife
Robin Williams	Actor with David in *Hook*/old friend
Noah Wyle	Actor/Santa Ynez friend and neighbor
Neil Young	Singer-songwriter/longtime singing partner
Darryl Zanuck	Pioneer film producer
Fred Zinneman	Legendary director who worked with David's father during McCarthy era
Adolph Zukor	Founder of Paramount Pictures

NOTES

Chapter Thirteen . . . *her mother, Debbie, and stepfather, Steve Earle:* Steve and Debbie Donovan Earle are auto enthusiasts who organize vintage auto races throughout the United States, including the Monterey Historic Automobile Race and the Lime Rock Vintage Race. He is not the country music artist of the same name.

Chapter Fourteen *In her autobiography: "The Truth Is . . . My Life in Love and Music,"* by Melissa Etheridge with Laura Morton (New York: Villard Books, 2001).

. . . *Jackie Hyde married folk singer Arlo Guthrie:* For more information on the song-writer who created the folk classic "Alice's Restaurant," see http://risingson-records.com, and http://www.arlo.net, wherein can be found the details of Arlo and Jackie and their offspring. They tour, they record, and Arlo's a book unto himself, part of a folk dynasty that reaches back to the Great Depression and the IWW *Little Red Songbook* of almost a century ago.

Chapter Sixteen . . . *Camp Trinity on the Bar 717 Ranch:* Ethan and David's summer camp may be found on http://www.bar717.com. Hayfork, California, is a remote town, a dot on the map of the Trinity Wilderness.

Chapter Seventeen *Elliot Roberts . . . shook hands with David Geffen and started a company:* Within a few years of its inception, the Geffen-Roberts Company managed Crosby, Stills, Nash, and Young, as individuals and as a group, as well as Linda Ronstadt, the Eagles, America, Jackson Browne, Laura Nyro, the Cars, and Tracy Chapman. Apologies to other famous clients not named here.

Marc Cohn is a singer-songwriter: For a complete review of his remarkable career, see http://www.marccohn.net, or go to his original page, a decade-old pioneering music page, http://www.marccohn.org.

Russ Kunkel is one of rock's great drummers: For a complete overview and credits, see http://russellkunkel.com.

Ani DiFranco formed her own label: Her home page is a highly evolved example of Internet artist communication and definitely worth looking at if you have any interest in being an independent musician: http://www.righteousbabe.com/ani/index.asp. The full text of her open letter can be found at http://www.columbia.edu/~marg/ani/letter.html.

Alternative Distribution Alliance was begun in 1993: Want to sell your music on a national scale and get the benefits of a major marketing entity that loves indie labels? Go here: http://www.adamusic.com. But be warned: ADA is currently owned by Edgar Bronfman, Jr., the whiskey heir.

Tom Donahue came along: The noted DJ and innovator was already a big name (as well as a big man) in conventional Top 40 radio, having held key time slots in Philadelphia and on major AM rocker KYA in San Francisco. Raechel Donahue is still an active chronicler of those days, and has produced television and film documentaries like *Rock Jocks: The FM Revolution,* a definite must-see for those interested in the era.

Chapter Nineteen *Making* Stand and Be Counted *was an interesting ride: Stand and Be Counted,* television documentary distributed by the Learning Channel, 2000. *Stand and Be Counted: Making Music, Making History: The Dramatic Story of the Artists and Causes That Changed America,* by David Crosby and David Bender (Harper San Francisco, 2000).

Chapter Twenty . . . *in an unpublished short story called "The War Prayer":* Mark Twain's short story "The War Prayer" was rejected by his publisher, *Harper's* magazine, with whom he had an exclusive contract. It was finally printed in 1923. See http://www.wilsonsalmanac.com/mark_twain_war_prayer.html.

Chapter Twenty-one *This is what I said to the Committee on Indian Affairs:* On May 18, 2005, the committee concluded an oversight hearing to examine issues relating to the taking of land into trust by the Bureau of Indian Affairs (BIA) for federally recognized Indian tribes, focusing on land used for gaming purposes, after receiving testimony from George T. Skibine, Acting Deputy Assistant Secretary of the Interior for Policy and Economic Development, Office of Indian Affairs; David K. Sprague and John Shagonaby, both of the Gun Lake Tribe in Dorr, Michigan; James T. Martin, United South and Eastern Tribes, Inc., Nashville, Tennessee; Mike Jandernoa, 23 Is Enough, Grand Rapids, Michigan; and David Crosby, Santa Ynez, California.

Epilogue *La Musique, toutes la musique:* The building is the headquarters of SACEM (Société des Auteurs, Compositeurs et Éditeurs de Musique), the French collection society that oversees the collection and distribution of music royalties, much like ASCAP and BMI in the United States, only with more authority and a broader mandate for enforcement. We like all collection societies—they're how we get paid for our creations, our intellectual property.

MUSIC: SELECT DISCOGRAPHY

Excerpted in part from *Crosby, Stills, & Nash: The Authorized Biography* by Dave Zimmer (New York: St. Martin's Press, 1984; reissued Boulder, CO: Da Capo Press, 2003).

David Crosby, Early Recordings
Les Baxter's Balladeers: *Jack Linkletter Presents a Folk Festival* (Crescendo), 1963
Early L.A.: Archive Series Volume IV (Together), recorded 1964, released 1969

The Byrds
Preflyte, recorded 1964, released 1969 on Together, then on Columbia, 1973
Mr. Tambourine Man (Columbia), 1965
Turn! Turn! Turn! (Columbia), 1965
Fifth Dimension (Columbia), 1966
Younger Than Yesterday (Columbia), 1967
The Byrd's Greatest Hits (Columbia), 1967
The Notorious Byrd Brothers (Columbia), 1968
Byrds (Elektra/Asylum), 1973
The Byrds Box Set (Columbia), 1990
The Essential Byrds (Sony Legacy), 2003

Crosby, Stills & Nash
Crosby, Stills & Nash (Atlantic), 1969
CSN (Atlantic), 1977
Replay (Atlantic), 1980
Daylight Again (Atlantic), 1982

Allies (Atlantic), 1983
Live It Up (Atlantic), 1990
CSN (4-CD box set, Atlantic), 1991
After the Storm (Atlantic), 1994
Greatest Hits (Rhino), 2005

Crosby, Stills, Nash & Young
Déjà Vu (Atlantic), 1970
4 Way Street (Atlantic), 1971
So Far (Atlantic), 1974
American Dream (Atlantic), 1988
Looking Forward (Reprise), 1999

Crosby & Nash
Graham Nash/David Crosby (Atlantic), 1972
Wind on the Water (ABC), 1975
Whistling Down the Wire (ABC), 1976
Crosby-Nash Live (ABC), 1977
Crosby & Nash Greatest Hits (ABC), 1978
Another Stoney Evening (Grateful Dead Records), recorded 1971, released 1998
The Best of Crosby & Nash: The ABC Years (MCA), 2002
Crosby-Nash (Sanctuary), 2004

David Crosby
If I Could Only Remember My Name (Atlantic), 1971
Oh Yes I Can (A&M), 1989
Thousand Roads (Atlantic), 1993
It's All Coming Back to Me Now (Atlantic), 1995
King Biscuit Flower Hour Presents David Crosby (King Biscuit), recorded 1989, re-
    leased, 1996; repackaged as *Voyage,* a three-CD boxed set (Rhino), 2006
Greatest Hits Live (King Biscuit), 2003

CPR
CPR Live at Cuesta College (CPR), 1998
CPR (Samson Music/Gold Circle), 1998
Live at the Wiltern (CPR), 1999
Just Like Gravity (Gold Circle), 2001

PERMISSIONS

TAKE THE VOYAGE—HEAR THE STORY

DAVID CROSBY: VOYAGE

A Career-Spanning Three-CD Boxed Set

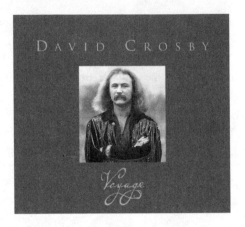

Two CDs of remastered essential tracks by The Byrds, Crosby, Stills & Nash,
CSNY, CPR, Crosby's solo material, and more

Plus one complete CD of previously unreleased demos, live cuts,
alternate mixes, and unissued studio recordings

Produced by Joel Bernstein and Graham Nash

In Stores Now